Realist of Distances

Lineberger Memorial

Library

Lutheran Theological Southern Seminary   Columbia, S. C.

Realist of Distances

Flannery O'Connor Revisited

Editors:
Karl-Heinz Westarp and Jan Nordby Gretlund

AARHUS UNIVERSITY PRESS

©Aarhus University Press, 1987
Set in Century Schoolbook and
printed in Denmark by Werks Offset, Aarhus
ISBN 87 7288 069 4

AARHUS UNIVERSITY PRESS
Aarhus University
DK-8000 Aarhus C, Denmark

Preface

Flannery O'Connor's main achievement is that she created a world unlike any in modern fiction. Shortly after her untimely death, however, Brainard Cheney noted regretfully that "there is as yet but limited understanding of this original, powerful, and prophetic writer." Today, some twenty years later, the full magnitude of Flannery O'Connor's genius is becoming apparent and is the subject of a growing body of criticism.

The publication of Flannery O'Connor's lectures and essays in *Mystery and Manners* (1969), *The Complete Stories* (1971), some of her letters in *The Habit of Being* (1979) and in *The Correspondence of Flannery O'Connor and the Brainard Cheneys* (1986), and her book reviews in *The Presence of Grace* (1983), plus numerous periodical publications have won a growing audience for her work. More and more frequently she is recognized as the writer of some of the finest American fiction of this century.

Realist of Distances: Flannery O'Connor Revisited contains critical essays celebrating Flannery O'Connor's unique vision of the convergence of the temporal and the eternal. Some essays point out that her fiction is grounded in the particularities of the South and in her awareness of her immediate world. Others emphasize her literary integrity and offer an evaluation of her literary impact. But all the essays deal with Flannery O'Connor the prophetic poet, the *realist of distances*, who tried to recall us to our largely forgotten relation to the world and to each other.

The title of this collection reflects her own definition of a prophet. It was chosen to indicate the focus of our differing interpretations of Flannery O'Connor's prophetic fiction. The list of contributors indicates that her vision is recognized beyond her native region. A range of O'Connor scholars from six countries offer their insight into her life and the literary and human qualities of her fiction. The present volume does not claim to be all-inclusive; there is much of her work we do not fully understand, but we trust that the most prominent approaches to her work and today's issues in O'Connor criticism are represented here.

We hope that new and experienced O'Connor readers will benefit from this presentation of O'Connor scholarship and that the essays will kindle new interest. We would be delighted if our readers would join us in our quest for a better appreciation of the distances Flannery O'Connor perceived.

Jan Nordby Gretlund
Karl-Heinz Westarp

Acknowledgements

We wish to express our gratitude to all who have encouraged us at various points in the planning and editing of this volume. We are especially indebted to Sally Fitzgerald and the other contributors for their assistance and patience. We thank Connie Relsted and Mona Andersen for their word-processing of the manuscript. We are also indebted to Tønnes Bekker-Nielsen, our publisher, for his sound advice.

We gratefully acknowledge the financial support from the Danish Research Council for the Humanities and from the Research Foundation of the University of Aarhus. We thank the English departments at the universities of Aarhus and Odense, Denmark, for their kind support.

We gratefully acknowledge the use in this volume of the Farrar, Straus & Giroux editions of Flannery O'Connor's works. Three of the essays have by now appeared in a slightly different form in other publications, and we thank Sheldon Currie and *Antigonish Review*, Robert Drake and *Modern Age*, and Marshall Bruce Gentry and the University Press of Mississippi, for permission to include their essays.

Contents

Degrees and Kinds: Introduction

Sally Fitzgerald

In the first week of August of 1984, a group of European and American scholars and critics met together in a country manor house known as Sandbjerg, outside Sønderborg, Denmark, fifty minutes flying time from Copenhagen: no easy place to reach for most of them. They had travelled the distance to discuss the literary works of a young American author, an unmarried Southern woman, semi-invalid, who had led a relatively reclusive life on a farm near Milledgeville, Georgia, and died there in 1964, at the age of thirty-nine. She left only a small body of work: two novels, two volumes of short stories, and a handful of deceptively simple essays which were then gathered and prepared for publication by friends five years after her death. Never a "popular" writer, she nevertheless enjoyed the immense respect of a coterie of perceptive admirers - among them many who were writers themselves - during her short lifetime, and this did not diminish at her death. She continued to be increasingly read and studied in universities, while monographs, articles and books on her work appeared in growing numbers. A collection of illuminating personal letters, published in 1979, not only extended public interest in her fiction but elicited considerable sympathy and warmth toward her as an extraordinary personality, correcting the bad guesses on the subject hazarded by readers acquainted only with her unsettling stories and novels. With the volume of letters, the number of books of her writings came to six. More recently, the scores of short book reviews she wrote as an act of cultural mercy for her diocesan newspaper were collected and published, raising her canon to seven volumes, none of which, except for the letters, reaches the length of three hundred pages. Of her fiction there are hardly more than a thousand pages in all.

Despite the embarrassment of critical riches accruing to this small account since her death, her own essays, published in 1969 under the title *Mystery and Manners*, have continued to serve as a kind of Rosetta stone in correctly deciphering what seemed to early readers, including critics, her somewhat hieroglyphic works; and in the course of time, her letters provided additional guidance and correction. Still, however strong the interest in the occasional prose, and in her correspondence, it is the fiction she left, four slim volumes, that provides the sturdy foundation on which rests one of the most secure reputations in twentieth-century American literature, a reputation which has already placed its owner among the writers produced by that country in this century whose books are regarded as most likely to become classics. It was primarily these remarkable works of imaginative art that the Symposium participants had come to reexamine and elucidate.

The members of the group represented half a dozen countries: France, Austria, Germany, Canada, Yugoslavia, and the United States, as well as Denmark itself, whence had come the initiative to organize such an international meeting devoted entirely to O'Connor and her work, the first of its kind on the continent. One of the savants present posed a question pertinent to the occasion itself: in effect, why were we there? Why does the "small oeuvre" of Flannery O'Connor still engage so many literary scholars "three decades and several literary fashions later?"

The author herself, who never lost sight of her own limitations, might have agreed - up to a point - in the general answer to the question, in which the critic reasoned that the myriad and often contradictory (to the point of becoming mutually exclusive) interpretations and analyses of her stories and novels had perhaps grown out of the weaknesses of her work rather than its strengths. The weaknesses that she discerned were not, however, the same as those he imputed to her. Still, she would have been the first to acknowledge that she sometimes failed, and she was willing enough to blame her own faults of execution for the lapses of understanding she so often had to face, even on the part of the trusted friends who served her as readers before she submitted a work to her editors for possible publication. *After* publication, she knew, misinterpretation would probably be general, and generally abysmal, for the most part because so many readers in her time and world had lost their familiarity with the metaphysical substructure of ideas and beliefs concerning human life that always underlay her fiction. The moral and spiritual views she subscribed to no longer prevailed, even in theory. Moreover, even the terms and the great Biblical *mythos* of the Western Judaeo-Christian tradition of which she strongly declared herself to be a part, once familiar to all, and upon which she drew for subliminal reinforcement of her stories, were no longer accepted, or in many cases even recognized in reference. What she saw as the grotesqueries, intellectual and moral, of much of present-day life and thought were regarded as the norm, while her characters were decried as too deformed in mind and soul for credibility. Or, at the least, too flat to be alive, and at worst to be perhaps symptomatic of some pathological condition, say cruelty, in her own mind, disposing her to a taste for "horror stories." "Usually," however, she once remarked, "they have hold of the wrong horror."

She was patient with misunderstanding. Moreover, she had always acknowledged that there might be other ways than her own in which a story could be read, even though she added an immediate *monitum*, "...but none other by which it could have been written." (MM p.109). This statement occurs in her introduction to a reading of her best-known short story, "A Good Man Is Hard to Find," but it is applicable to every piece of fiction, short or long, that she ever wrote. "Belief," she went on to state flatly, "in my own case, anyway, is the engine that makes the perception operate." The sort of perception to which she alludes here may be traced to a sentence she underlined in her copy of Stephen C. Pepper's book, *The Basis of Criticism in the Arts*: " The perception of a work of art is clearly the awareness of the quality of a situation." She regarded this observation as axiomatic, and to be as relevant to the artist in his making - and even to his "habit of art" - as to the critic in his explication.

As she well knew, she distinctly did not perceive her fictional situations as did most of her readers. More often than not, she was speaking what amounted to a different language, quite apart from the Southern rural accents and vocabulary. Even the terms in which her subject matter could be discussed, and some aspects of her work criticized and judged - grace, charity (or love), hope, redemption, damnation - meant to her something quite different from their modern popular usage. Certainly the word "tragic" did. In only one of her stories, "A View of the Woods," is a character unmistakably shown to choose (as she believed one must willfully choose) what she herself regarded as damnation, or hell, and that is the only one of her stories she herself would have called a tragedy, much as the word is bandied about in regard to her work as a whole. Fundamentally, she considered herself to be a comic writer, dealing in radical human grotesqueness - as well as in essential human dignity and potential hope for even the most spiritually deformed. In one of her letters, to a stranger, she tried to clarify this point:

I look on the grotesque as the normal human condition after the fall. We weren't totally corrupted but were made subject to incongruity (to put it mildly). I take the fictional grotesque to be that which brings this state to the fore and which (in my own case anyway) since it is a state connected so definitely with the *felix culpa*, does so with a certain relish.

Perhaps incomprehension was inevitable. A writer who thinks *sub specie aeternitatis* is almost certain to be misunderstood by a readership which limits its concerns to the temporal, demanding a temporal resolution, without mystery, and to whom the frequent deaths in O'Connor's stories represent the tragic annihilation of the characters, often amounting to their "damnation" in the reader's mind, rather than purely temporal deaths - passages almost always entailing, to the author's mind, a joyful, if painful, resolution, as in *Wise Blood*, "The River," and even "A Good Man Is Hard to Find."

Even readers who ostensibly shared her traditional Roman Catholic faith and convictions had grown accustomed to a sentimentalized and diluted sense of the divine reality they professed to acknowledge, and to an equally diminished sense of the nature and force of evil, including their own inner predispositions. This comfortable dimness was especially true with regard to what a majority perceived as acceptably "edifying" literature. A kind of mock daintiness had set in, corrupting popular taste and ill preparing religiously oriented readers for the powerful vicarious encounters and experiences (with either the demonic or the divine, or both) to which O'Connor subjected them, or even for her strong comedy. No more than others could they recognize everyday familiar absurdities, and evils, in her exaggerated fictional versions of characters and events, or the necessity for the violence that in her fiction so often preceded or followed what Joyce termed "a vertical epiphany."

After something of her intentions and her methods were better grasped, however, Catholic criticism burgeoned, challenged only by other kinds of doctrinally founded interpretation, which sometimes pugnaciously pronounced her to be in fact obviously Protestant, despite her own claims. Others, even while taking account of her religious point of view, simply judged her to be a "failed artist" who had not succeeded in conveying her Christian vision (by which they often meant their own conception of that vision). A kind of critical Reformation period ensued. Religious criticism threatened to engulf the purely literary.

She would have been amused by all this scholastic uproar, and perhaps regarded it as proof of her Catholic catholicity. Primarily secular critics were not amused: they were bored by the theological and doctrinal arguments, most holding that such discussion had no place in literary criticism. Although few attempted to deny that a religious dimension characterized her work, they ascribed less importance to it than she herself did. There were too many other observations to make.

The work was approached, as the essays in this volume exemplify, from numerous points of view and areas of particular interest: philosophy, psychology, aesthetics, regionalism, sociology, humor, literary source study, et al. Some of the putative insights set forth she would have rejected; others she would have found both valid and instructive,

14

discoveries she might have failed to make in her own work, but which were nonetheless recognizably pertinent.

It amuses me to speculate as to how she might have reacted to the Sandbjerg meeting, had she sat there, invisible, among us. Certainly she would have been pleased by some of the features of the bucolic setting, which included "the lowing herd and other details" she had described at her own country home, Andalusia. A long deep "moo-o" would occasionally float through the bright windows of the conference room, as though by way of comment, and the clucking and quacking and crowing of nearby barnyard fowl punctuated the discourse. She would have liked that. Her own work had been done within earshot of farm life, and I suspect that she would have thought it well that such intensive critical activity should be pursued in a place that would keep a sense of the natural world alive, perhaps saving the occasion from a descent into deconstructionism.

But she would have found much more to interest her. The papers offered a range of interpretation, although strongly contentious disagreement was not of the essence, and the tenor of the meeting was far from hostile or dismissive. For the most part, the participants were there to call the attention of their colleagues to new facets they had found, to hear discussion of those uncovered by others, and to meet and talk informally with each other on the subject of such great interest to them all. In short, they had come to praise, and not to bury, O'Connor. The most exceptional position was taken by the aforementioned demurrer who marveled at the attention still being paid to an author whose writing seemed to him far from deserving the acclaim accorded it. As I have said, she might not have disagreed with this judgement, but his overall conclusion - that her work was essentially private, and her "own terrain" that of "tongue-in-cheek outrage at God's injustice in daily operation, of which she was, after all, a life-long victim" - might have occasioned a small ghostly sigh at the sheer sweep of misapprehension of her far from private stories of deracinated Southerners (who yet comprise a modern Everyman). Living, unlike herself, in a state of anomie, contingency and homelessness, or wandering in a wasteland not entirely of their own construction, her characters nevertheless seem determined to perpetuate - or worsen - their condition, until they are pulled up short, and by no means unjustly, by a God whose very "mercy burns," as one of her prophets warns. She knew, of course, that the intentions of a writer have to be found in the work itself and not in his declarations of intent, and it was in the effort to convey her meanings that she felt she had sometimes fallen short, but she never doubted the immediacy of her subject or the reality of what she saw in the distances to which so many of us are purblind.

The following papers, whatever the approach of the essayist, are for the most part quite specific in their examination of a variety of features and aspects of the works, and the inferences and conclusions drawn are too numerous for special mention of each one in a short introduction. All are enriching to our understanding of the writer and her art, and all testify to the attraction she holds for very diverse critical minds, and to the close attention these scholars, and many others like them all over the world, feel is owing to so considerable an artist. In the larger critical arena, contention will no doubt continue. Indeed, it has grown more heated in her own country since the Danish symposium. Evidently she cannot be dismissed in silence. Even those who take a strongly contrary or reductive view appear to feel that she must be engaged. The unsettling questions she raises apparently cannot be ignored; she seems to act on her readers as what an old term from the American West calls "a burr under the saddle." Whatever the final consensus of opinion, if there is one (and there may never be), it is not likely to counter effectively a comment, quoted from George Santayana, which she underlined in one of her books and was perhaps sometimes reassured by: "Nothing has less to do with the real merit of a work of the imagination than the capacity of all men to appreciate it; the true test is the degree and kind of satisfaction it can give to him who appreciates it most."

Developing
Artist

Flannery O'Connor: A Literary Memoir

Ashley Brown

My friendship with Flannery O'Connor began in the American way, through correspondence, in 1952. The early correspondence, long since lost, had to do with *Wise Blood*, the novel with which she made a small reputation in the spring of that year. It was reviewed in *Time* and *Newsweek* and the New York *Times* - no mean feat for a first novel. I, like some others, had read and remembered three disconnected episodes published back in the late 1940s in the *Sewanee Review* and the *Partisan Review*, and in those days I tended to set my literary standards by the writers who were admitted to their pages. Now the novel was out, and the fragments took their place within a design. *Wise Blood*, I thought and still think, is somewhat episodic, and when I talked to Flannery about it the following year she altogether agreed. The very format of the first edition, with its spacing between the chapters, suggests this. But what made me buy the book immediately was a statement on the jacket by Caroline Gordon, a writer for whom I had the utmost respect. She said there, "I was more impressed by *Wise Blood* than any novel I have read for a long time. Her picture of the modern world is literally terrifying. Kafka is almost the only one of our contemporaries who has achieved such effects." Caroline Gordon had already assisted Faulkner in his comeback with an important review of the *Portable Faulkner* in the New York *Times* in 1946, and she was doing as much as anyone to revive Ford Madox Ford during the early 1950s. Now she was recommending another genius. And to put this young writer beside Kafka, who was a special literary hero of that period! How percipient she was. In retrospect the comparison seems just; the scale of Flannery O'Connor's work is much the same as Kafka's; their thematic concerns are indeed similar.

In 1952 I was living in Virginia as an instructor at Washington and Lee University, where I had helped to found and edit a small literary quarterly called *Shenandoah*. It was great fun thinking up projects for writers we admired, some of them not at all famous at that time. I decided that we must run a longish review of *Wise Blood*, something more substantial than the notices in *Time* and *Newsweek*. So I turned to the Tennessee novelist Brainard Cheney, who I knew was a close friend of Caroline Gordon and Allen Tate. He responded with a splendid review that we published in our Autumn 1952 issue, immediately following Faulkner's little review of *The Old Man and the Sea*. The five pages of Mr. Cheney's piece are too long to summarize here, but I like especially the way in which he brings together *Wise Blood*, Erskine Caldwell's *Tobacco Road*, and Faulkner's *As I Lay Dying*, three novels which "present the same sort of people in the same passage of history." Caldwell he dismisses as "no artist and only a dull pornographer" who refuses to allow his characters a religious dimension in which to fulfill their wretched existence. Faulkner, on the other hand, "knows that death is not merely phenomenal and he remembers that there is a more persistent hunger than physical hunger. The Bundrens are not absorbed in their precarious economy....Faulkner, one of the great visionaries of our time, showed religious perspective here, but he had not then been granted the grace of vision." *Wise Blood*, says Mr. Cheney, "is about man's inescapable need of his fearful, if blind, search for salvation. Miss O'Connor has not been confused by the symptoms." Then he makes this interesting observation:

I would agree, however, that Miss O'Connor could not have done what she has done twenty years ago. We have here essentially the same people and the same essential motivation, but the Lesters and the Bundrens could not have been made to force the issue of the Church Without Christ. The technique Miss O'Connor employs had not ripened then, and if it had been so employed perhaps could not have been generally understood. In contrast to Caldwell's reportorial naturalism and Faulkner's poetic expressionism, she uses, under the face of naturalism, a theologically weighted symbolism.

This, I submit, was the best review that *Wise Blood* had at its first appearance. Rather curiously, neither the *Sewanee Review* nor the *Partisan Review*, which had originally published those episodes, bothered to review the completed novel at any time.

Flannery was very pleased with Brainard Cheney's piece. Before long she was writing to him, and her first letter, which dates from February, 1953, marks the beginning of another friendship. As for *Shenandoah*, we were quite poor and always apologized to our contributors for not paying them anything, but I went ahead and asked Flannery if she had a story we could use. No, she had nothing new that wasn't already spoken for, but she wanted to retrieve an old story and have it reprinted. That is how we happened to publish "A Stroke of Good Fortune," which had originally appeared in a magazine called *Tomorrow* in 1949. It came out in our issue for Spring 1953. It was in fact the earliest written of the stories that were eventually collected in *A Good Man Is Hard to Find*, but by 1954 Flannery had second thoughts about using it in a collection at all; it was "too much of a farce," she wrote to the Fitzgeralds. It is clearly not one of her best things, but I have found that university students rather enjoy it as an example of literary craft. They love the way in which the author deploys the various ages of mankind through a limited cast of characters within a highly restricted setting and time scheme. And they like the raucous treatment of the Fountain of Youth theme. It may be the work of a superior creative writing student, but one is always glad to have it in the *Complete Stories*.

I finally met Flannery in July of that year, 1953. The Brainard Cheneys had stopped by Andalusia Farm that spring during one of their trips to south Georgia and invited her to a house party at their place in Tennessee. I had known them since my student days at Vanderbilt and was of course delighted to be included. The Cheneys, I gathered, had recently become Roman Catholics through the influence of Caroline Gordon and had a special interest in Flannery at this moment. She had in person that same wonderful combination of caustic wit and friendly assurance that she had conveyed in her letters. The Cheneys had mentioned something about a disability that imposed certain restrictions on her, but at this time she wasn't on crutches and she never referred to her illness. I was indeed very ignorant of lupus then; I had simply never heard of it. A photograph made on this occasion depicts Flannery sitting on the steps of an abandoned smokehouse at the Cheneys' place; the steps are rotting away, the vines are gradually taking over. She is quite ladylike in a dark blue dress with white trim and the only earrings that I ever saw her wear; perhaps they were suggested by her mother. She looks relaxed though she is unsmiling. There is nothing to arouse her sense of humor, not even the slight incongruity of the setting. I prefer this photograph to one that appeared in *Harper's Bazaar* two years later. This time she is sitting on the front steps of Andalusia - I can tell by the pattern of the bricks - dressed in a work shirt, as though she had just stepped out from her typewriter. But the camera shot is done in a kind of soft focus; she is looking away with a strangely evasive glance; the effect, though "glamorous" as they used to say, isn't at all natural. The photograph is almost belied by Flannery's accompanying comment: "A lady in Macon told me she read me under the dryer. I was gratified." (HB p. 78).

The Cheneys' house in those days was called Cold Chimneys; later, after central heating was installed, it became Idler's Retreat. A large brick house in the Greek Revival manner, not quite antebellum, it stands outside Smyrna, a little town perhaps twenty miles from Nashville. The Cheneys gradually moved themselves out there from the city after the Second World War, but they were very busy people and could not at first find the endless time that it takes to keep up such a place. Brainard or "Lon" Cheney, as he has been known to hundreds of people for decades, has been a journalist often involved with politics during a long career; now and then he has managed to buy the time to write his four novels and his literary and theological essays. Frances or Fannie is an eminent librarian, at one time president of the American Library Association. The Cheneys attended Vanderbilt during Fugitive days, and their friendships with the Nashville literati go back more than half a century. Cold Chimneys has always been a center of hospitality, for the young and unknown as well as the famous. Here, in the 1950s, one might meet Allen Tate and Caroline Gordon, or "Red" Warren, or on one occasion Katherine Anne Porter. A frequent guest was Andrew Lytle who had known Flannery longer than any of us, because he had been one of her teachers at Iowa. Young writers from Nashville were always bringing out their first novels or books of poems, and they soon took their place at the Cheneys' table.

Cleanth Brooks and others have suggested that there are some similarities between the literary renaissance in Ireland and that in the Southern United States. In retrospect it seems to me that Cold Chimneys was something like Coole Park in County Galway, Lady Gregory's house, where for thirty years William Butler Yeats and his friends gathered. Nothing at Coole Park remains except the ruins of the foundations, the tree on which the visiting writers carved their names, and of course the famous swans. Yeats celebrated the house and what it stood for in a memorable poem which will outlast everything else. Nobody, I believe, has celebrated Cold Chimneys except a former student of mine, a brilliant youth named Tom Carter from Virginia; he spent one year of his short life as a graduate student at Vanderbilt. Upon leaving Tennessee for Virginia in 1956, never to return, he wrote something entitled "Stray Stanzas from an Occasional Poem for Some Friends." I quote one of his eight quatrains, this about our host and hostess:

> Convivial Lon, Odysseus wise,
> oves God and politics and plays.
> Sweet Fannie graced to civilize
> articulates Smyrna soirées.

Since I have retrieved the poem, I can't resist quoting another quatrain, because Flannery wrote an amusing prose account of the same occasion in a letter dated 20 October 1955 (HB p. 112); the subject is Russell Kirk, the philosopher of conservatism who was also a house guest at Cold Chimneys:

> The procrastinator Kirk, hambone in hand,
> speaks joyfully of his barren land;
> then having been most amply dined,
> expounds the simple, conservative mind.

In July, 1953, when she first visited Cold Chimneys, Flannery had just published three stories: "A Good Man Is Hard to Find," "The Life You Save May Be Your Own," and "The River." "A Stroke of Good Fortune" had been reprinted in *Shenandoah* and "A Late Encounter with the Enemy" was about to come out in *Harper's Bazaar*. During the next two years she would bring out five more stories. All of these were collected in *A Good Man Is Hard to Find* in 1955. This seems to me her great creative moment; after that, as we know, she wrote another ten stories, perhaps one a year, and in 1959 she managed to finish a short novel, *The Violent Bear It Away*, on which she had been working for seven years. In 1953, when these stories were being published so quickly, they weren't always easy to take account of. I remember very well Flannery's first reading of "A Good Man Is Hard To Find" in the great library at Cold Chimneys. A few people came out from Nashville to meet her, but hardly anyone had read this new story. She started out in her Georgia drawl that was so perfect for rendering those awful selfish children, John Wesley and June Star, and their grandmother; it was comedy in a Southern tradition that goes back to Longstreet's *Georgia Scenes,* written, as Allen Tate once said, "by an accomplished gentleman for other accomplished gentlemen." (*Essays of Four Decades*, 1968, p. 591). Flannery's modern Georgia scene is much funnier than Longstreet's; the social details are more sharply observed, her ear for the vernacular is better. We all succumbed to laughter by the time we reached Red Sammy's barbecue place along the highway. The author had us in her hands. Then, at a certain point after Pitty Sing the cat sprang onto Bailey's shoulder, thus causing the accident, something sinister came into the narrative. Our reactions began to be crossed, and by the time that the grandmother found herself alone with The Misfit we were stunned into silence. It was a masterful performance. Flannery was not a trained reader. Once she got out into public she felt she should try other stories, but nothing ever seemed to work as well as this one, which eventually she called her "reading story." I grew to know her version of it well, as one knows a favorite musical composition that never fails to delight no matter how often one hears it.

Incidentally, I think that the note of the sinister comes with a very short sentence at the end of the paragraph describing The Misfit's two companions: "Neither spoke." (CS p. 126). The little world of the story is an oral culture; everybody talks at one level or another; to withhold comment is to be inhuman.

In July, 1953, I was just about to visit Ireland for the first time. This would be the first stage in a kind of *Wanderjahr*, and I was already looking forward to my descent on Coole Park and Joyce's Martello tower and Bowen's Court. It was to be a literary pilgrimage all the way. I was astonished when Flannery brought me up short by saying, "Whatever do you want to go *there* for?" She had in fact a rather developed prejudice against Ireland which I, not Irish at all, could never understand. She was right to make fun of the sham Irishness that takes in so many people, and her caustic remark about Baloney Castle is worthy of Joyce himself. All the same, I thought this was a curious attitude on her part. She gave me the address of one of her favorite writers, J.F. Powers, who was then living in County Wicklow. Powers of course is Irish-American. His first book of stories, *Prince of Darkness*, had been published in 1947 to considerable acclaim, and I was impressed by the esteem in which he was held by other short-story writers of my acquaintance, Flannery and Peter Taylor and Robie Macauley. In 1953 he was writing some of the stories that he would collect in a volume called *The Presence of Grace* (1956), and later he extended his career with a fine novel, *Morte D'Urban* (1962), and another collection of stories, *Look How the Fish Live* (1975). He isn't a very fashionable writer now; I haven't seen one of his stories in an anthology for at least a decade. He really deserves a better reputation than many others. This is all apart from the fact that he was the first Catholic writer of the highest quality in the United States. His fictional world of priests and parish houses in the Midwest might seem to promise no more than Flannery's; his tone is light even when his issues are serious; but his work is a remarkable achievement. I suspect that he was a kind of model for Flannery when she was still trying herself out as a writer at the State University of Iowa, and her first story, "The Geranium," was published in *Accent*, the little magazine at the University of Illinois that was chiefly responsible for sponsoring Powers' work. It is no accident that she listed him first among American Catholic writers in a letter written to Father John McCown in March, 1964. (HB p. 570).

Another Catholic writer of a quite different sort whom we argued about in the 1950s was François Mauriac. After he won the Nobel Prize in 1952 many of his earlier books were translated and published, usually by

Farrar, Straus and Cudahy, who were to be Flannery's publishers. Some of our friends had misgivings about his Jansenist tendencies, especially Caroline Gordon. Indeed her strictures about him were in an essay called "Some Readings and Misreadings," which came out in the *Sewanee Review*, Summer 1953; it was lying at hand in the library at Cold Chimneys during Flannery's first visit. This issue was rather prominently displayed, because it also contained Flannery's story "The River" as well as essays by Warren and Lytle. Caroline's general argument against the most eminent living Catholic novelist (as he was then) is that he denies the natural order, unlike Yeats and Faulkner, whose "patient, passionate portrayal of natural objects" is at least "Christian in hope":

Mauriac's loftiest edifices, lacking such a solid foundation, seem always on the verge of toppling. The lurid flames that light up his scenes make them appear less rather than more substantial. He has said that he regrets that he does not find human nature more admirable but that he must portray it as he sees it. One wonders if he would not be a better novelist if he found it *natural?*

This is a long and very subtle essay which Flannery, like the rest of us, pondered at the time. I am sure that it influenced her thinking about the art of fiction. Her admiration for Mauriac, however, continued to the end. She owned at least fifteen of his books and I used to think that her work resembled his in certain respects. But she seems to have had some misgivings about him, and in January, 1956, she said, in a letter to Father John McCown:

The Catholic fiction writer has very little high-powered "Catholic" fiction to influence him except that written by these three, Bloy, Bernanos, and Mauriac, and Greene. But at some point reading them reaches the place of diminishing returns and you get more benefit reading someone like Hemingway, where there is apparently a hunger for a Catholic completeness in life, or Joyce who can't get rid of it no matter what he does. It may be a matter of recognizing the Holy Ghost in fiction by the way He chooses to conceal himself. (HB p. 130).

In her essay on "Some Readings and Misreadings" Caroline Gordon has some things to say about Evelyn Waugh. She has distinct reservations about his earlier novels, simply because he "does not explore the consciousness of any one of his characters..." But then she takes up *Brideshead Revisited* and finds that he has a new subject, "which arouses not moral indignation but awe, a rendering of the mystery of human existence." She finally attributes to this novel a "love of the natural order" which she doesn't find in Mauriac, Bernanos, or Graham Greene. Flannery had enjoyed Waugh's earlier novels, especially *A Handful of Dust* and *Vile Bodies*, but she had no particular enthusiasm for *Brideshead Revisited*. Waugh in his turn read *Wise Blood*, and on the jacket of the first British edition, published in 1955, he stated: "If this is really the unaided work of a young lady, it is a remarkable product." The jacket, by the way, is dominated by a ghastly picture of Hazel Motes, presumably in the act of prayer, his eyes lifted up, his mouth open, the figure posed against a pink background. I bought the book in London many years ago just for the jacket. On the back, beneath the same photograph of Flannery that appears on the first American edition, is the information that she "is at present completing her second novel, *Whom the Plague Beckons*, to be published by us in the autumn." Well, as we know, the novel took another four years to finish and eventually it had another title. Back to Evelyn Waugh. I was very fond of his military trilogy, *The Sword of Honour*, which had started appearing in 1952, and I sent Flannery a paperback of the first two parts in 1961. But it was the third part, called *Unconditional Surrender* in the British edition, that aroused her full enthusiasm. I had the idea that Waugh had modelled his trilogy on the first three parts of Ford Madox Ford's *Parade's End*, which is a tetralogy. Waugh, I think, got this notion by way of Graham Greene, who had been a great friend of Ford. But Flannery, it turned out, simply couldn't read *Parade's End*. I see now that it was a question of fictional method. Waugh, even in his trilogy, had a style of great economy and precision, not unlike Flannery's, whereas Ford is expansive with his endless time-shifts. Flannery certainly heard about Ford at Cold Chimneys, because his name was held in great regard in that house. He had never set foot there during his visits to Tennessee in the 1930s, but Fannie Cheney had been acquainted with him and was about the only person around who had a coherent account of the famous banquet given for John Crowe Ransom's departure in 1937, at which occasion Ford was the master of ceremonies. He was a real literary hero in that part of Tennessee.

My former student, Tom Carter, didn't meet Flannery till July, 1955, at Cold Chimneys, but they had frequently corresponded and seemed to understand each other immediately. Tom had been the editor of *Shenandoah* at Washington and Lee, and this post led to all kinds of literary relationships. Unlike most of his contemporaries, he never travelled much, and I suppose he was content to know people at a distance. Among his correspondents were Ezra Pound and Wyndham Lewis. He met Pound just once, in St. Elizabeth's hospital in Washington when I happened to be along. After that I believe they wrote each other every day. Pound was always looking for disciples. Wyndham Lewis was a very remote figure then, living out his last years at Notting Hill Gate in London where few people saw him. This famous survivor of the 1914 Vortex was almost blind; he could no longer paint or draw, but he had an extraordinary burst of literary creativity near the end. "Milton had his daughters," he used to say. "but I have my dictaphone." Tom Carter edited a special issue of *Shenandoah* in honor of Lewis in 1953; several writers contributed, including T.S. Eliot, Marshall McLuhan, and Lewis himself, who wrote a story especially for this issue. In September, 1953, I called on him twice, the first time bearing an advance copy of Tom's magazine. Tom communicated his interest in Lewis to a number of friends, especially Flannery, and I suppose she read at least ten of his books, from the early Vorticist novel *Tarr* to a late one called *Self Condemned*. I think there are some real affinities between his work and hers; she refers to him quite a few times in her letters. But as she said in a letter to "A" in November, 1956, "I'm more interested in the way Lewis writes than what he has to say." (HB p. 179). Tom also sent Flannery a copy of Marshall McLuhan's early book, *The Mechanical Bride*, an outrageous but funny satire on modern advertising. McLuhan wasn't famous at that time, around 1954, but he, a Canadian Catholic, had for some years been interested in the South, and one of his essays, "The Southern Quality" (1947), made a great impression on Flannery. She was fascinated to learn that he was the original for one of the characters in *Self Condemned*.

I used to be very amused when I listened to Flannery and Tom; they were likely to say anything. They decided one day that most books, epecially novels, were too long and that 250 pages should be the limit. This was what they called The Test. I think Flannery was at least half serious about this. Perhaps she was rationalizing her own tendencies, because she seemed almost inevitably a short-story writer. In her lecture on "The Grotesque in Southern Literature," she says:

Instead of reflecting a balance from the world around him, the novelist now has to achieve one from a felt balance inside himself....The direction of many of us will be towards concentration and the distortion that is necessary to get our vision across; it will be toward poetry rather than the traditional novel. The problem for such a novelist will be to know how far he can distort without destroying.... (Cp. MM p. 50).

The "concentration" that she speaks of was deliberate and almost precluded novels as they are generally written. Flannery, after all, had been brought up on the short story; it was an American tradition that went back to Poe and Hawthorne, her first masters. In February, 1956, she wrote to the Cheneys, "I have just got through writing a story about a lady who gets gored by a bull. I get so sick of my novel that I have to have a diversion." Nearly all of the modern American fiction that she liked best came in the short form: the early stories of Peter Taylor and J.F. Powers, Bernard Malamud's *The Magic Barrel*, some of Caroline's stories in *The Forest of the South*, some of Katherine Anne Porter's. What of Faulkner? Flannery had read some of the great early novels when they were reissued in the 1940s, but she took no interest in the work of his long decline - *Requiem for a Nun, The Town, A Fable*, and the others. The story of Faulkner's that she always described as "the work of a master" was "Spotted Horses."

One novel that we all read in the 1950s was Caroline Gordon's *The Malefactors*. From the day it came out in 1956 it was a kind of *cause célèbre* for us. Everybody knew that she had based some of her characters on Dorothy Day (to whom the novel was originally dedicated), Hart Crane, and others, living or dead; the general assumption was that Caroline was using Allen Tate as the central figure, a poet whom she calls Tom Claiborne. It seemed to Flannery, as to me, a remarkable portrayal of the dilemma of a modern poet whose creativity has dwindled away and who is eventually brought to the edge of a religious conversion. I think that Caroline did not simply use Allen for her model; her poet is much more like Allen's friend John Peale Bishop. We thought the novel was a splendid technical achievement, a tribute to Henry James, whom Caroline adored. Allen Tate, by the way, always liked the novel, and towards the end of his life he included it in a short list of neglected books of the 20th Century. What Flannery objected to was not Caroline's human figures but a prize bull who figures in the first part of the novel. The scene is a kind of harvest festival given on the estate owned by the poet's rich wife, and her bull is a major symbol of the action at this point. Nearby is an exhibit sponsored by a society for breeding cattle through artificial insemination. Caroline here introduces an old Dunkard farmer who heartily disapproves of this practice, and clearly the author has him as her spokesman. This is the situation that caused Flannery to remark in a letter to "A" in May, 1956: "I agree with you about the bulls. Nothing wrong with artificial insemination as long as it's animals and bringing those Hookers or Shakers or whatever they were and their disapproval to bear just confused the moral point, if any. But I suspect that she just wasn't able to resist doing that inseminator, as she had him down." Flannery felt that the bull episode threw the novel off balance.

This wasn't quite the end of the story. In October,1959, I drove Caroline to Andalusia for her first visit. Andalusia was a real farm which Regina O'Connor operated with the practical instincts that she had developed there; she was never sentimental about it. Anyway, I didn't know this at the time but it seems that the matter of artificial insemination was discussed by Regina and Caroline, who considered the practice a crime against the natural order. Now that Caroline has departed from this life, I can't resist quoting part of a letter that Flannery wrote to me upon my return to South Carolina:

My own nerves were jangled when it was over - the job of trying to keep the two ladies' personalities from meeting head-on. While you were opening gates, there was a little altercation about artificial breeding. All those cows sitting there, I guess it was inevitable. I am afraid Caroline forthwith consigned us to hell. She does not seem to make the necessary distinction between man and animal...She was at her best doctoring my prose.

Although I don't think that the issue ever came up between them, Flannery and Caroline would certainly have disagreed about another novelist who was becoming famous. In the summer of 1956 Donald Davie, the English poet-critic then living in Dublin, sent me a copy of the original edition of Nabokov's *Lolita*, I can't remember why. Nabokov, I gathered, had been unable to get his novel published in the United States, and so he turned to the Olympia Press in Paris. The Olympia Press published writers like Henry Miller, but most of their product was hardly more than pornography. So *Lolita* arrived unexpectedly one day, two little paperback volumes bound in a horrid shade of green. I was dissertation-writing at the time and stoutly refused to be tempted by this diversion from abroad. It went first to a friend in Nashville, who happened to be the mother of a young daughter; she returned it indignantly the next day. Then off it went to Flannery, and a week or so later she returned it with a note stating flatly that *Lolita* was the funniest novel she had ever read. She was one of the first people in the United States to have seen a copy. Actually Nabokov had been a favorite writer of hers for some time. I don't think she had yet read his first novel in English, *The Real Life of Sebastian Knight*, but she certainly admired his second, *Bend Sinister*, a satire on totalitarianism. She mentions it in a letter to John Hawkes in July 1959. (HB pp. 343/344). *Bend Sinister* was published in 1947; Allen Tate, who was then associated with a publishing house in New York, had something to do with this, and Caroline was very disapproving; she could never accept any of Nabokov's books. Flannery's favorite among his works may have been his little book on Gogol, simply because of her great admiration for *Dead Souls*, which she read at Iowa. Our friend Robie Macauley, then a young writer of the most cosmopolitan sort who was a great partisan of Gogol, insisted that *Dead Souls* was a necessary part of one's literary equipment. In Flannery's case his enthusiasm took hold.

Flannery O'Connor's stories take their place in the great American tradition of short fiction, and one can already see her as the heir to Hawthorne, Poe, Stephen Crane, and a dozen others. Indeed, twenty years after her death, she is the last American writer to have attained this kind of classic status. Although she certainly belongs to the mode of American romance, as it has been described by Richard Chase and other critics, I am inclined to place her, in matters of style, closer to a tradition of modern British fiction, as represented by the early Wyndham Lewis, Anthony Powell, Evelyn Waugh, and Muriel Spark. These are the writers who have resisted the descent into introspection represented by Joyce, Virginia Woolf, Lawrence, and Ford. They are usually comic writers, unillusioned, witty, astringent at times; the surfaces of their work have a bright clarity of definition; their dialogue is spare. To some Americans they seem cruel. But then we have never had such novelists, with the possible exception of Nathanael West. Flannery liked writers of this kind; she never wanted to imitate them, but they had achieved a distant kind of perfection that was an ideal for a young American woman who deplored the "general mess of imprecision of feeling" in many of her contemporaries. (The phrase is T.S. Eliot's in *East Coker*.) There is much more to be said about her as a writer; these are merely notes on part of her literary experience during the period when I first knew her.

"The Lady *Frum* Somewhere": Flannery O'Connor Then and Now

Robert Drake

I can recall the first time I ever read a word by Flannery O'Connor. I had seen *A Good Man Is Hard to Find* reviewed, I think, in *Time* magazine - and characterized there as another example of Southern Gothic. But I thought I had about done my time with that sort of thing for a while; so I would just put her on the back burner - perhaps indefinitely. But a couple of years later, when I was teaching at the University of Michigan, I came upon her almost by accident and not, at first, with any particular enthusiasm. It was a cold gray afternoon in the fall of 1957, I was wandering through the main library and came across a copy of *A Good Man Is Hard to Find* on the shelf of "new" books and thought, well here was yet another Southern author I hadn't read and I'd look her over. (And I had come to Southern fiction late in the day anyhow - had hardly read Faulkner or Eudora Welty till I was out of graduate school.) So I checked the book out and took it home and that very afternoon began reading. And what happened then was something that had never happened to me before in my life. I read a book of stories straight through, just like a novel. And I've never been the same since. If reading Eudora Welty was something of a Damascus Road experience in my life (for one thing, the story, "Why I Live at the P.O.", made me realize something of the dramatic and artistic possibilities of the language I'd been hearing and speaking all my life), making the acquaintance of Miss O'Connor's work was something akin to the Wedding Guest's meeting with the Ancient Mariner!

I'd never read anything in my life like the title story itself, and it was by no means all downhill after that either. I had already had some taste of the Southern Gothic - and didn't think very much of it either - particularly in authors like Tennessee Williams and Truman Capote, to say nothing of Erskine Caldwell. Not on any squeamish grounds, I should hasten to add: it just didn't seem to go anywhere, quite often it didn't seem to *work*. Not so Faulkner, of course. The humor-horror conjunction which constitutes the grotesque, the black comedy in his work was nothing if not functional

- for instance, the countryman's remark about the nearly decapitated body of Miss Joanna Burden in *Light in August* to the effect that, with her head so nearly off that it seemed to be looking behind her, if she'd just looked that way when she was alive, she might not be looking that way now! There's a whole world view implicit in that observation, I think. And of course I've always thought Huck Finn's observation about the wooden leg he and Jim find on the "house of death" one of the funniest - and most apt - things in American literature: he said they looked all over for the other one but never could find it! I can wake up in the night and laugh about that. I myself knew of a very high-tempered woman - out in Texas - who got so angry at her husband one day that she burnt up all his clothes and his wooden leg too and then had to go buy him some more clothes and another leg!

I should just observe here that I come from a family, particularly on my father's side, which finds wooden legs and glass eyes and physical deformities amusing; indeed, we have often been accused, especially by those who have married into the family, of having a perverse sense of humor. And it's almost useless to try to explain to people who don't share this predilection that we aren't making fun of those poor unfortunates but, rather, laughing at some sort of divine joke the Universe has played on them - and presumably on us. Who did they think they were anyhow, who do we think we are - to escape the Universe's or God's or Whoever's, Whatever's calling the shots here having the last word? What a genuinely Divine Comedy it all is, seen from far enough away, maybe even as the Deity (assuming He exists) sees it! And no matter how high a man sits, according to Montaigne, he still sits on his own bottom! I might just digress here and note that it has often seemed to me that this sense of humor seems endemic - and no wonder - in the American South, in the Bible Belt, where lots of folks still believe, along with Robert Penn Warren's Willie Stark, that man is conceived in sin and born in corruption and passeth from the stink of the didie to the stench of the shroud: they still believe in Original Sin. And you are quite literally a *damned fool* if you think anything else. (Miss O'Connor herself once observed that perhaps Southerners were the only people left who knew a freak when they saw it.)

But back to my first reading of the story, "A Good Man Is Hard to Find." Here was a whole family - father, mother, children, tiny baby, and grandmother - all murdered in cold blood, in broad open daylight, out in the middle of rural Georgia. At the center of the whole story was a genuine theological argument between the psychopathic killer who calls himself The Misfit and the grandmother about, of all things, the identity of Jesus

Christ! And it was as serious as can be - and also very funny, with the grandmother's real religion of Southern Ladyhood ("anyone seeing her dead on the highway would know at once that she was a lady") (CS p. 118) colliding with The Misfit's thoroughly businesslike attempt to settle what I have called the Jesus Question once and for all - who was he, what was he? ("Jesus was the only One that ever raised the dead ... and He shouldn't have done it.") (CS p. 132). And Miss O'Connor then proceeded to do it again and again, in the same volume - humor and horror over and over, the serious and the comic, the outrageous and the dead earnest mixed and mingled, with never a thought of suggesting you couldn't be both at once.

And this went on through the entire volume, with silly-sad, proud-foolish old Joy-Hulga Hopewell in "Good Country People", with her wooden leg *and* her Ph.D. in philosophy; with "Temple One" and "Temple Two" in "A Temple of the Holy Ghost" and their ignorant response to the hermaphrodite at the fair, all seen through the eyes of the smart-aleck child; with sanctimonious - and one-armed - Mr. Shiftlet (another of Miss O'Connor's symbolic or allegorical names) in "The Life You Save May Be Your Own" and his out-conning old Mrs. Crater, who wants him as a husband for her deaf-mute "innocent" daughter, while all he wants is to resurrect and possess himself of her defunct old automobile, which he then proceeds to do, driving it out of the shed with "an expression of serious modesty on his face as if he had just raised the dead." (CS p. 151). On and on it went too till we got to the biggest and most villainous fool of all - Mrs. McIntyre, in what I think may be Miss O'Connor's finest story, "The Displaced Person." And she thinks that Jesus Christ is just another D.P.! And never once did I recoil in horror or find myself nauseated with disgust. But how I laughed!

So what? Perhaps in the greatest moments in the arts, tears and laughter keep mighty close company, as they can in life - the Divine Comedy again. King Lear is not only a wicked old man; he's also a very foolish one, as his own Fool points out. And the sublime trio and duet at the close of *Der Rosenkavalier* point up the follies, as well as the pathos of ageing. Look at Shakespeare's last plays too and some of Katherine Mansfield's stories. And always, of course, there is Chekhov. Whatever the case, life goes on and *it will be served*, as outrageous as it can sometimes appear - witness the concluding speech from a novel Miss O'Connor very much admired - *As I Lay Dying*, which I defy anybody with the root of the matter in him to read without bursting into laughter. And this after the very real horrors the book has conjured up along the way. "Meet Mrs. Bundren," says Anse, the old son of a bitch who, having milked all his children of their savings and their substance to get in to town, ostensibly to bury his dead wife but also to get himself some new teeth, now introduces to them his new wife, whom he just met scarcely minutes before when he went to borrow a shovel from her to dig his first wife's grave! There's nothing for it, finally, but to marvel at it - such effrontery, such impudence, as we do at life itself and finally at man himself - the glory,jest, and riddle of the world. Indeed, isn't there perhaps something *impudent* about a glass eye or a wooden leg? And we almost have to laugh: the "victim" may be down but he's certainly not out! As Huck Finn might say, it's almost "too various" for us - the life force in its naked form.

But of course it's not all fun and games with Miss O'Connor. And if you think the good life is synonymous with consumer goods and hardware, with air-conditioning and indoor plumbing, you may be in for a surprise. All I can say is, has she got news for you! We kick against the pricks, of course. Indeed, when Mr. Shiftlet officiously tells old Mrs. Crater, by way of reminding her that creature comforts may not be the be-all and end-all of our existence here, that the monks of old slept in their coffins, she smugly replies, "They wasn't as advanced as we are." (CS p. 149). And Mrs. Hopewell, mother of "the big spectacled Joy-Hulga," (CS p. 275) feels frustrated because she can't tell people her daughter is a philosopher, even with a Ph.D.; after all, "that was something that had ended with the Greeks and Romans." (CS p. 276). But when Hazel Motes' landlady in *Wise Blood*, horrified by his attempt at mortifying the flesh - wearing the equivalent of a hair shirt and such like, protests that people have quit *doing* such things, Hazel sternly replies that they haven't quit doing it as long as he's doing it. The Old Adam is still hairy and still sweaty, and we are fools to think otherwise. (Is some such perception implicit in the novel in Enoch Emery's donning the gorilla suit and thereby achieving an identity he had been denied in the big city?)

Such, at any rate, I take to be one of Miss O'Connor's principal themes, along with her scorn for the attempted deodorization of life by modern secular humanism. Miss O'Connor believes in ugliness, in nastiness, at the heart of life, in the vitals of man; and it's real and you don't blink it away. And sometimes you do have to laugh to keep from crying; sometimes, indeed, you may have to do both. Perhaps that's at the very center of the perception of *outrage*, which may be her most nearly central vision, maybe even her most important theme: the world is an outrage, man is an outrage, but perhaps the most outrageous thing of all is the grace of God in Jesus Christ, which is a scandal and doesn't make any *sense* at all, as the world goes. As Mrs. McIntyre cries out in a dream, ostensibly of the D.P. but really of Jesus Christ, "He's extra and he's upset the balance around here." (CS p. 231).

I don't think it was any accident, by the way, that Miss O'Connor was a great admirer of the work of Nathanael West, particularly *Miss Lonelyhearts*. And furthermore, I don't think it's any accident that Nathanael West was the brother-in-law of S.J. Perelman, who, in turn, often wrote material for those great artists of the outrageous, the Marx Brothers! I'm also happy to report that, in her pubished letters, we even discover that Miss O'Connor was once known to postpone work to catch a W.C. Fields movie on television. Surely homage to yet another artist of the outrageous, the Archetypal Con Man himself, could, in her case, go no further! All this is not to yoke personalities as well as images by violence together but to suggest that the fundamental principles of comedy abide, shared as they may often be by what appear to be highly dissimilar talents.

Yes, the world, one way considered, is a joke but not the kind held to be the case by Harry-Bevel's parents in "The River." Instead, at the heart of Miss O'Connor's joke world is something or perhaps Someone deadly in earnest about the whole thing. Otherwise, indeed, it wouldn't even be funny. With the Ashfields, Harry-Bevel's parents, *everything* is a joke; but Miss O'Connor would seem to side with G.K. Chesterton, who observed that where everything is funny, nothing is funny. And if, in the strictest sense, you can't see the joke in it all, if you really don't have a sense of humor (which of course doesn't mean laughing indiscriminately, all the time), there may be no place for you here, whether in this world or in Miss O'Connor's works. (Her worst critics have always been the humorless ones.) It's been suggested, I believe, that the one thing the Devil can't stand is to be laughed at; I'm sure he never laughs himself. In any case, I myself have always been afraid of people who don't laugh. (Miss O'Connor's villains hardly ever laugh.) On the other hand, I should certainly be afraid of anybody who laughed all the time.

I have digressed from my first encounter with Miss O'Connor's work in my eagerness here to explain why she impressed me so favorably when I first read her. Clearly, as I believe the Quakers say, she spoke to my condition. Indeed, in quite another context, I might have said, indeed did say later on, that she was preaching to the converted, though I never for one moment envisaged Miss O'Connor as a writer in any kind of doctrinaire or programmatic role. Obviously, as a Southerner and as a Christian, I share many of what appeared to be her preoccupations; but that would not have made me blind to whatever faults I might have felt she had as a writer of fiction. Because, when you come right down to it, what any writer, anywhere is doing is just that: reporting not on the news of the day, the fashions of the hour, or even the book of the month but just the doings and the devilment of *folks*. And his religious beliefs, his philosophical positions are just like anything else about him - like his skin, his place, his time. They are not *confiners* but *definers*, conditioning the way he looks at life and the world but not determining his vision, I think, certainly not in the sense of a "message" to be marketed. In any case there was a lot *to* Miss O'Connor, I was convinced; and I wanted to know her work better, read everything she'd ever written, maybe even some day meet the lady herself.

I began, of course, by reading *Wise Blood*, which I liked very much; but I felt then - as I still feel today - that it is as short story writer that Miss O'Connor excels. Perhaps the *cartoon* form (and she began as a cartoonist), the *tale* genre in which she said she worked doesn't lend itself to extension over a longer terrain. (Was this part of the trouble with John Huston's admirable attempt at filming the novel?) As a short story writer myself, I don't think one has to try anything longer in order to have his credentials as a fiction writer validated. And there was no doubt in my mind that Miss O'Connor's work was all of a piece, story and novel alike, and that it was all the product of a very sharp intelligence and a formidable artistic commitment.

In due course, I began to press her work on my friends. Some of them were less than enthusiastic, and I suspected that they had long ago begun believing everything they read in the newspapers or heard "come out over the radio," as we say down home. On the other hand, there were some very favorable responses indeed, one of the most ardent being that of a close friend who was a Baptist from Georgia. Certainly, she knew the flora and the fauna of Miss O'Connor's world; it was her world too. But her appreciation went much further than that. She thought wooden legs were funny; and she loved the female Greek chorus figures - the lower-class-white Mrs. Pritchards and Mrs. Shortleys - who comment on and evaluate the predicaments and dilemmas of their strong-willed "lady" employers. She'd been there too. But again, it wasn't just that Georgia and flagrant Christianity was the scenery she knew: it was her *home* , where she *belonged*, however much she might wander in later life. It was where she was *from*, and it didn't matter what she knew or didn't know then or later.

And this brings me to my main topic and a side of Miss O'Connor that I think needs further investigation, certainly deeper appreciation: her home, where she was from. Or as Sally Poker Sash of "A Late Encounter With the Enemy" might have said, "what all was behind her" and *not* behind the ignorant upstarts of the modern world - those of whom Mrs.

Shortley might have said (though she was speaking of the D.P.'s) that they ain't where they belonged to be at. And it's grounded in a remark Miss O'Connor made to me during the memorable day I spent with her in August of 1963 - almost a year to the day before her untimely death. Ever since first reading her work, I had longed to meet her. Then in 1960, I was asked to review her second novel, *The Violent Bear It Away*, for one of the journals. And after my review appeared, I made bold to send her a copy, by way of introducing myself to her and making sure she knew, right from the beginning, of my great admiration for her work. She replied almost at once to say that she had already seen the review: her publishers had sent her a copy. And she went on to say that she had decided it was about the best one she had gotten and I was a reviewer who seemed to share her prejudices! The book, she concluded, had been reviewed by Raybers (the novel's villain) "all over the country" and she had no idea there were " *that* many of them"! And yes, she would be glad to see me when I was in the neighborhood and they lived four miles north of Milledgeville on Highway 441.

So a few years later I did indeed arrive there on the day I mentioned, met her mother also, enjoyed some mighty good frozen daiquiris, and took Flannery to lunch in town at the Sanford House - then a very good restaurant in a restored antebellum house and, I believe, the place where the O'Connors, mother and daughter, lunched nearly every day. Later, we adjourned back to Andalusia Farm and resumed our seats in the high-backed rockers on the front porch. Most of the conversation will stay with me as long as I live, I think; in particular one exchange I've never tired of quoting and pondering. Flannery spoke of having been taken to a literary soirée in New York by one of her old writer friends - Robert Lowell. And the hostess was none other than Mary McCarthy, "back when she was Mrs. Broadwater," Flannery said. (I didn't learn until much later, after Flannery's death, that this was the memorable evening when the exchange between hostess and guest about the nature of the Eucharist took place. Miss McCarthy remarked that the Eucharist *was* a good symbol, whereupon Flannery replied that if it was just a symbol, then she'd say the Hell with it!) (HB p. 125). She observed to me that nobody there took any notice of her from the time she got there till the time she left and they didn't sit down to eat till midnight: before that, it was just all drinking. But then, fixing me with her good solid glare (the glare of outrage?), she asked, "You know what's the matter with all that kind of folks?" And I said, well, I'd had some ideas but what did she think? And she replied, "They ain't *frum* anywhere!"

Our modern world suffers from what I've called a great rage against context: just filter off all the differentiae like sex, race, creed, color, and God knows what else - to say nothing of that disturbing consideration of *place*, and you'll get truth or anyhow something good and universal and absolutely uniform and all will be well. And nobody can ever accuse you of bigotry or prejudice or favoritism or, I should add, sense: you'll be so open-minded your brains will all fall out! Well, this is as tiresome as can be - and as false as Hell for the would-be writer. Because if the arts feed on anything, are grounded in anything, it's a respect for the particularities and peculiarities of time and place - history and geography - and folks and all that goes with these prickly considerations. I don't think the arts are concerned with *ideas* - at least not in the sense of merely providing envelopes. One might object here that Miss O'Connor's fiction raises all sorts of theologial questions, so what about the ideas then? Well, I think theology is more concerned with *persons* than ideas; and that's quite another thing.

But anyhow here was yet another Southern writer who had a respect for her homeland - where she was *frum*. And of course that didn't mean that she had necessarily to *like* it - or dislike it either, for that matter; but she did take it for what it was because it was her source of supply. Robert Coles, the Harvard psychiatrist, in what I thought was a very silly book about Miss O'Connor several years ago, was scandalized that Flannery once refused to meet James Baldwin in Georgia because, she said, she couldn't thereby compromise her standing with the home folks: they - and Georgia - were what she fed on, as she put it. (She said she would have been glad to meet Baldwin elsewhere.) But one doesn't necessarily thereby convict Miss O'Connor of racism: white and black and all the rest come in under that greatest of all demoracies - Original Sin. And nobody has a corner on that market, as you might say.

But to go back to what Miss O'Connor said about the guests at the soirée, I think you have to take her observation for exactly what it purported to be: the statement of a writer who was convinced that whatever might be the case with others, she herself had a home, not just in a geographical or temporal sense but somewhere where she *belonged* and thus something other and larger than herself to write about. Just as Miss O'Connor once observed that if she went to Japan and lived for twenty years and then tried to write a story about the Japanese, the characters would all talk like Herman Talmadge, she also remarked, "I'm interested in the Old Adam. He just talks Southern because I do." But this all is what was *behind* Miss O'Connor; this was where she was *frum* . And it has nothing to do with local color or any such, which is all but another form of writing up the news - and for export too. In any case, she never seemed to have any doubts about it - what her subject was, what her story was. Sure, as a Roman Catholic - and a "cradle" one at that, she didn't have many of her own persuasion living right down the road in Georgia to write about. But since her story wasn't sectarian (*pace* , some of her good Roman brethren - and sistren), that was no problem; it was just orthodox Christian revelation that informed her vision, as I see it. But she wasn't "selling" that either except insofar as every writer is "selling" his perception of the world in whatever he does. Miss O'Connor's work is amazingly consistent too: a seamless garment. And nobody else in the world could have written it, I think. That's one of the signs always of a real original. But that should come as no surprise either when we stop to reflect on the commitment - the *home* - from which it sprang.

But again, what was the nature of this commitment, what did it give Miss O'Connor which nourished her art, which she might not have found elsewhere? Well, like many writers from the American South, she got at least three things: history and geography and community. Southerners, for one thing, have had some of this forced on them: they - or their ancestors - lost a war; they - or their ancestors - saw their homeland occupied and, in many cases, devastated by the enemy - a "typical," European experience not many Americans have undergone, according to C. Vann Woodward. And most Southerners have grown up around older people with long memories (my own grandfather, whom I remember quite well, was a Confederate veteran who had been at Appomattox), people who respect the differences of time and place because they have a respect for and not a rage against differences. Ohio *is* different from Mississippi; Massachusetts, from Tennessee; and the country and the city have not always been one, in the homogeneity one of my friends ruefully observes has been brought on by the "malling of America" - into one gigantic suburban shopping center! And behind most of them has been the traditional agrarian rural or small-town community - a something that existed before them and, *mutatis mutandis*, may endure afterwards, a something which by its very presence more or less cuts them down to size. Furthermore, it's a something where everyone has a place, where his origins are known, where the individual can stand out from the group, but where his very individuality, to say nothing of his independence, even rebellion, is conditioned by what Cleanth Brooks has called the culture in being, against which he is seen. And thus the loners, the outcasts, the exiles so prominent in much modern literature have been noticeably lacking in the literature of the modern South or else, in such cases as that of Faulkner's Joe Christmas, seen as all the more "outstanding" because of the ordered and stable background against which they are discerned.

It's an interconnected world Southern authors have inherited to write about, with a before and after and a here and a there - not just a series of discrete experiments. And perhaps their greatest literary theme, understandably, has been the conflict between past and present, traditionalism and modernism, in one form or another.

Certainly, this conflict looms large in Miss O'Connor's world, with the modern, forward-lookers - always the children of this world - as the villains and the old-fashioned traditionalists, whether in religion or elsewhere, constituting something of a saving remnant. (Of course, it's not a rigged conflict as "A Late Encounter With the Enemy" ought to show: *old* isn't necessarily better.) And sometimes they are a pretty unpalatable remnant too: there's nothing deodorized about them. Indeed, Miss O'Connor refers at least once to "the bleeding, stinking, mad shadow of Jesus" as the Lord they serve - and not always easily or gladly either. And the villains are often the very people we've been taught in our modern world to admire: do-gooders, enlightened folks, intellectuals, social workers, all the rest. Accordingly, we find ourselves shocked, at least momentarily, when the rug gets pulled out from under them and we are confronted instead with the defective and the deformed as instruments of grace. Even the language of grace itself may be insulting if not scandalous: "Go back to hell where you came from, you old wart hog," (CS p. 500) which is what the berserk Wellesley College student mutters to Mrs. Turpin in "Revelation." And tiresome old Asbury Fox, all set to die a memorable and vengeful death in "The Enduring Chill," learns from Dr. Block that he's not going to die at all: he's just got undulant fever, which is "the same as Bang's in a cow." (CS p. 381). Or what about The Misfit's saying of the grandmother, whom he has just killed, "She would of been a good woman if it had been somebody there to shoot her every minute of her life"? (CS p. 133). It *is* a fearful thing to fall into the hands of the living God. And as *The Violent Bear It Away* concludes, mercy itself moves with a "terrible speed."

Well, a lot of this is unpalatable to modern tastes, this turning of things upside down (as the Christian religion itself does, with the first, last and the last, first). And what about its commitment to *mystery,* not the occult, which our own time finds singularly - and rather pathetically - alluring? What about the mystery of the hermaphrodite in "A Temple of the Holy Ghost," whose very existence seems to call God's love and goodness into question, who nevertheless blesses his Creator and his own creation? What about the mystery of the "artificial nigger " in the story of that title (one of Miss O'Connor's finest, I think)? Surely, this is not a story about race or prejudice or any such consideration but about man's inability to know it all, as foolish, proud old Mr. Head (another significant name) thinks he does. There are some things Miss O'Connor isn't about to offer any answers for; she just presents us with the mysteries of their being. Can we or anybody else sort them out; or do we simply have to draw back as the old Negro woman on the O'Connor place did when one of Flannery's peacocks suddenly spread his tail for her one day and exclaim, "Amen! Amen!"? Again, we notice out of the corner of our eyes the slender beauty of a sentence like "the trees were full of silver-white sunlight and the meanest of them sparkled," (CS p. 119) as the obnoxious family begins what will turn out to be literally their last ride together in the title story of Miss O'Connor's first volume. And this in a story which many people would call an unrelieved descent into the Inferno, the only one of her stories, incidentally, she confessed to me, she could read in public without laughing! Perhaps that's what all Miss O'Connor's work finally comes down to: to mystery and such sight as we now have mediated through a glass darkly, to a great wonder and a great silence, and not even the Pope himself knows for sure who is saved. And all this despite the fairly obvious theological configurations and designs in the work itself - to mystery and grace, in which only and by which only we are saved. There is much ugliness in the stories, to be sure, also a glorious apprehension of the vulgar - both of them sometimes, paradoxically, chosen vessels. But there is beauty and life and health - and at the core of it all, finally, order and peace.

Well, I've never recovered from that first and only meeting, the day I spent with Flannery in August, 1963. When I told her I sometimes wrote stories myself, she generously suggested I send some of them to Elizabeth McKee, her agent in New York - and this before she had read a single one of them. Later on, I did send her some of the published ones; and she told me she liked them, not without a demurrer, though: "Dear Robt.," she would begin a letter, "you write real well but ..."And then would follow the strictures - usually ones I had halfway come to see by intuition. Experience has always taught me to listen to that kind of criticism. Not many weeks later, she wrote that she was writing Elizabeth McKee about my work herself. To my amusement, I found that, when her letters were published, in *The Habit of Being*, the letter to Miss McKee duly appeared there; and I was able to see for myself what she had said about my stories: " ...I thought they might make a book," she wrote, "that would have some kind of limited popular appeal." (HB p. 560). In due course it turned out just that way - my first book, *Amazing Grace*. And I'll be forever in her debt. But unfortunately, she didn't live to see that or my subsequent books.

I may have said it elsewhere but it may be worth repeating here that whereas Eudora Welty had taught me to listen, Flannery taught me to see - to know what I had been looking at all my life but maybe didn't understand, particularly the grotesque, the vulgar, the deformed, along with their "doubleness," which is to say their significance as outward and visible signs of an inward and spiritual *dis-grace*. But along with this perception came an understanding of them as quite often possible ministers of grace - and always overwhelmingly, even terrifyingly *alive*. And the question would then arise as to who or what was the real grotesque. Just as the world might say it was Jesus Christ, the ultimate D.P., the children of light might come to see that it was, in truth, the Mrs. McIntyres, the Mrs. Copes, the Mrs. Mays, the Asburys, the Julians, and all the rest who seek to straighten out (or is it deaden?) the universe - in any case, re-write the script they've been given to play. By the same token, I even enjoy reflecting from time to time on the anger of the truck driver who gives Tarwater a lift near the end of *The Violent Bear It Away*. He's so incensed by Tarwater's obsession with matters of the spirit that he finally tells him he belongs in the "booby hatch." "You ride through these states and you see they all belong in it," he says. "I won't see nobody sane again until I get back to Detroit." (VBIA p. 213). Again, though, as in most such diagnoses, I should just say consider the source!

That Christmas of 1963 I had an amusing exchange of season's greetings with Flannery. She wrote that Ernest, her burro, whom she described as having a "bad though friendly character," was taking part in the annual Christmas pageant at the local Methodist Church and added that it all might bring about the end of the ecumenical movement in Milledgeville. When I later pressed her for details, she replied that on the night of the dress rehearsal, Ernest paraded all over the church, good as gold, with the little girl portraying the Virgin Mary riding safely on his back but, when the night of the performance came, Ernest, whether actuated by sectarianism she couldn't say, wouldn't "put a hoof over the threshold." Meanwhile, I had been busy helping to arrange for her to come to speak at the University of Texas, where I was then teaching; and she graciously accepted our invitation. When I wrote her that I was planning a party in her honor and was already making out a list of all those whom I wasn't going to invite, she wrote back that, by the time she got there, I might have "struck out as unfit" all but her and me and that would be all right too!

Alas, only a short time later she wrote to cancel the engagement, saying she had been ordered into the hospital for a totally unexpected operation and she wouldn't be able to write me but that I should keep on writing her because, as she characteristically put it, "I intend to survive this." I had little news as the months went on, but I didn't think any of it sounded good; and early in the summer, when I saw Elizabeth McKee, who had now become my agent, in New York, she told me that she feared Flannery was dying. So the news of her death, which I received in London (appropriately enough, from Cleanth Brooks, who was then serving as cultural attaché at our embassy there), was not unexpected. I immediately wrote a brief "tribute" for the London *Sunday Times* and shortly thereafter something longer for *The Christian Century* in Chicago.

The next year, in 1965, I was asked by the publishing firm of Eerdmans in Grand Rapids to write the study of Flannery's work they wanted to publish, to help inaugurate their new series, "Contemporary Writers in Christian Perspective." And my work appeared in 1966, after which time I spent several years in what I suppose you might now call the O'Connor Industry. I supervised graduate work on Flannery's fiction, including a doctoral dissertation which reviewed all the O'Connor scholarship and criticism published before 1972 - already then a staggering amount. I reviewed her posthumous books and some of the early studies by our scholars and critics, even wrote a few more essays on her myself. But I've written little on Flannery's work for some years now - not because of any lack of interest, certainly not because of any waning enthusiasm. Indeed, my admiration for Flannery and her work has increased as time has gone on. When one of her closest associates remarked to me shortly after her death that she believed Flannery's work would endure, I replied that I had not a shadow of a doubt about it. And I think now I understand why better than I did then. But on the whole, I've felt that I had said my say about her; and by and large, I don't take any of it back - what I wrote and said earlier. I haven't changed my mind.

Certain convictions, certain impressions have grown with the years. For one thing, I think it's a mistake to overpraise Flannery's work. She's a major-minor writer if there is such a term; and there are vast areas of human experience that she simply does not speak about or speak to. And granting that the world of most any writer has got to be somewhat narrow, his one story or stories somewhat of a muchness, I have sometimes felt that Flannery's one story (which, in some ways, of course, is the biggest one there is) isn't, after all, the whole story. And her work does often have the intensity and the urgency of prophetic utterance; and there's a limit to how much of that sort of thing we can take at one time. We miss the quietness, the returning and rest in which we are saved; and I think we miss the joy - albeit all these things make themselves manifest offstage in her work. I don't find much genuine love between human beings there either. And sex is a bad business there too. Miss O'Connor's female villains, particularly those self-reliant, humorless widows and divorcées, seem to view it as something they can easily do without - something like the other "foolishness" they want to root out of the universe. As Sarah Ruth Parker in "Parker's Back" remarked of her husband's tattoos, they might say that they don't have any use for it! And besides sex, others of God's gifts - the material pleasures of this life - seem to be there ignored or else easily dismissed.

This is not the place for theological argument, of course; but I seem to recall Miss O'Connor's saying somewhere that the role of the Christian in this life is to prepare his death in Christ. Well, I'm a Christian, but I don't know that I altogether believe that. I know that the Kingdom of God cometh not with observation and every day is Judgment Day. But I think the dead should bury the dead, and life has got to be lived and one shouldn't be afraid to be happy in a world which God made, found good, and is determined to keep that way - though man has done - and continues to do - his literal damnedest to pervert and defile His glorious handiwork. (I think Hopkins' sonnet, "God's Grandeur," perfectly expresses Miss O'Connor's views on *that*). Neverthelesss, we must grant Miss O'Connor her donnée, as Henry James said we must do with any writer. Her experience of life and her work are narrow, however deep we may feel they go; and we simply cannot ignore that. But then so were Jane Austen's life and works and Emily Dickinson's, for that matter. And it hasn't held their reputations back any, certainly hasn't vitiated the power and authority of their work.

The O'Connor criticism that I have read in recent years - I think Dr. Coles' is but an *exemplum horribile* - seems often wrong-headed if not downright ignorant and of course utterly humorless. I think there are just as many readers as ever who "can't take all that theology," as they put it, and use their distaste for *that* as an excuse to dismiss her whole work. On the other hand, I think also there are still many readers who would like to turn Miss O'Connor into the house-Christian-writer or something of the sort. And that's no service to her or the Christian religion or anything else I can think of. I fear there are also those (and they seem to be increasing in number) who look back on the times in which Miss O'Connor wrote and wish she had spent more time reporting the news of the day. On her testimony to me, the only time, for example, that she ever consciously wrote about the racial situation in the South was in the story, "Everything That Rises Must Converge," which doesn't seem to be very flattering to either side. And we're right back in what is still the hottest news story going: Original Sin and God's provision in Christ therefor.

This seems to have been the only *news* Miss O'Connor ever cared to write about: the Good News itself. She certainly, as I hope I've already made clear, wasn't falling a prey to that other writer's seduction - the itch to preach and convert. That's where her fellow Christians have not always served her well - in their desire to read her as a preacher rather than as a prophet.

A further word about Flannery's villains: they have discomfited some modern readers because, at least on the surface, they seem to embody admirable modern virtues: they're often teachers and intellectuals and social workers or lone women trying to make their way in the world. They often seem to be motivated by good, altruistic impulses; they want to help other people. But that's not always the way it works out. Too often it's the same old thing: pride, the bold and impious self-will that is determined to foist itself not only on other individuals but also onto the fabric of the big wide world itself. Remember what Flannery said, in her introduction to *A Memoir of Mary Ann*, about the "tenderness" which has often supplanted faith in the modern world? "When tenderness is detached from the source of tenderness, its logical outcome is terror," she wrote. "It ends in forced-labor camps and in the fumes of the gas chamber." (MM p. 227). It's not that the do-gooders are not "good" (which may be irrelevant), they "ain't *right*," (CS p. 454) as Rufus Florida Johnson might have objected - the club-footed delinquent of "The Lame Shall Enter First." It was Rufus who protested to "that big tin Jesus," Sheppard, the social worker trying to "understand" him, "I lie and steal because I'm good at it! My foot don't have a thing to do with it!" (CS p. 480). There are no cop-cuts allowed in Miss O'Connor's world.

The lone women may call for some further comment, as I suggested earlier. Indeed, I've never been quite sure the female villain (who is more often than not one such) in Flannery's work has been adequately dealt with. Is there a double standard at work here? When woman, the traditional conserver of cultural values, repudiates her historic role, does she become more hideous than sea-monster man? Perhaps it doesn't matter. In any case, what can one say about such women except that their determination to make it on their own, without the aid of a husband or any other man, while in some ways admirable in itself, may be nothing but the same old thing all over again: pride and self-will? And neither sex has a monopoly on that. Most of these women do seem to look on men (and sex) as some sort of imperfection, some sort of "foolishness" in the universe - the same way they do their poor-white employees or the Negro workers on their farms or the nut grass or whatever interferes with the cows' breeding schedule or even Jesus Christ Himself! Of Mrs. McIntyre, for example, we are told that "Christ in the conversation embarrassed her the way sex had her mother." (CS p. 226). Presumably, for them, sex and Jesus are just a couple more things that "upset the balance around here." But I'm not sure one can say more. In Flannery's work, devilment seems pretty evenly divided between the sexes.

This is all Flannery's world - where she was *frum*. And I'm sure you could find the counterparts or "reasonably accurate facsimiles" of her characters and their stories right on the scene if you took the time and trouble to journey down to Milledgeville. And I can speak from some personal experience here. Most of my own family and friends in West Tennessee are still convinced, after all these years, that I'm writing them up in my stories. It's no good my telling them that even if I wanted to do such a thing, which I really don't, it wouldn't be the *they* that a biographer or historian would write about that would interest me but, rather, what *they* had turned into in my head. We don't read Miss O'Connor as writing the news of the day; we do read her as writing the news which never grows old - in her case, what I've elsewhere called her harrowing evangel. She neither asked nor gave any quarter herself. It was her story; and sometimes she throws it down almost like a gauntlet, as though she is well aware just how disturbing it may be to many of her readers. By the same token, I've never known anyone who was *indifferent* to her work: most of her readers either applaud heartily (and often laugh loudly) or else they draw in their lips in genteel disapproval, not to say outrage. One of my undergraduate students did tell me one time - and I never knew whether he was bragging or complaining - that reading the story, "A Good Man Is Hard to Find," was the first time he had ever been *shocked* by a story! In any case, her body of work, her story was all part of where she was *frum*; and she never went back on it, never denied it and what it required of her. And verily, she has her reward.

I'm not in the least worried about her work's being around for a long time to come. I've always thought that if you told the truth about one part of the universe - the part you know in a way nobody ever quite has before, you've told it about the whole business. In plane geometry, you learn to reconstruct a whole circle from just a fragment, or arc, however small. It's the same thing here, I think. And Flannery's work speaks - and will continue to speak - to all those who believe that this world we live in always has been and still is in what is literally one Hell of a fix but that relief is on the way, indeed has already arrived if we but have the literal grace to see it! And it's the greatest, most mysterious story there ever has been or ever will be. And maybe also it's one of the most outrageous - and one of the funniest!

45

Flannery O'Connor's Development: An Analysis of the Judgement-Day Material

Karl-Heinz Westarp

The Judgement-Day material is unique in Flannery O'Connor's *oeuvre* . She used it in her very first published story, "The Geranium" (1946); in 1954 she rewrote it and considered it for publication as "An Exile in the East" in *A Good Man Is Hard to Find* (1955).[1] However, in her characteristically self-critical way, she commented on it in her letters to McKee:

The carbon of "An Exile in the East" is enclosed, but I don't know if you realize or not that this is a rewritten version of "The Geranium" originally printed in *Accent*. *Accent* didn't pay me for it and it is rather much changed, but I enclose both stories so [the editor] can see what she's doing. I don't want to go to the penitentiary for selling a story twice (but if I do I would like to get a good price for the story). (HB pp. 74-75).

Also you have a copy of a story called "An Exile in the East" that they didn't put in the collection.[2] Please send this back to me and in my spare time I may give it a shot of ACTH[3] and send it back in some better shape. (HB p. 88).

She started on those revisions in the last months of 1963,[4] but as late as June 17 she wrote to her friend and literary adviser C. Carver that she was "not satisfied" (HB p. 585) with it, and on June 28 she "completed" it, but wanted "to keep it a few weeks longer and think about it". (HB p. 589). In the very last week of her life she polished it off for publication.[5] The result was a much better version than the one we now have in *The Complete Stories*, as I have tried to prove elsewhere. When she started the 1964 revisions O'Connor called the story "Getting Home",[6] an important title on which I shall comment later. One might be tempted to discard the many revisions of the same material as a lack of imagination, but I suggest that we consider them as an indication of the central position this material holds in O'Connor's universe. In the following I shall try to prove that the material is indicative of Flannery O'Connor's development as artist and thinker.

First I want to look at the manuscripts that are in the O'Connor Collection in Milledgeville. There is only one full-length manuscript of "The Geranium" (Dunn 12 d), a working draft (Dunn 12 c) and two three-page fragments (Dunn 12 a, b). In Dunn 12 b and c, O'Connor makes Old Dudley jump out of the window to pick up the geranium. This version would have clearly underlined the parallel of uprootedness between Old Dudley and the geranium. There is no hint why O'Connor scrapped this version in favor of the much less conclusive ending of the published story with the owner's threat "'I only tell people once'" (CS p. 14) hovering in the air.

The collection has only one 16-page manuscript of "An Exile in the East." (Dunn 193). The final version of the material is represented with no less than twenty-one manuscripts,[7] four entitled "Getting Home,"[8] which shows how seriously she worked to get the final version right. There are no less than ten different versions of the end of the story. What are the major variants in style, structure and message in the manuscripts?

In "An Exile in the East" the protagonist has acquired a new name, Old Tanner, which he will retain in "Judgement Day" after his early manuscript identity of "Franklyn Turner Fairlee."[9] In keeping with the two parts of the title "An Exile in the East" the East is dramatized in greater - negative - detail. The son-in-law comes alive with "his nasel (sic) yankee whisper" calling Tanner "the cotton bale."[10] The characteristic O'Connor tone has found its way into the story: "His daughter wouldn't let him wear his hat inside except when he sat like this in front of the window. He told her it was necessary to keep the light out of his eyes; which it was not: the light here was as weak as everything else." (Dunn 193 p. 2).There is a rather noisy introduction to the next-door neighbor whom Tanner hears rent the flat. "Outside a woman shrieked something unintelligible and a garbage can fell on one of the fire escapes and banged to the concrete. Then inside, the door to the next apartment slammed and he heard a sharp distinct footstep clip down the hall."[11]Tanner hates him from the beginning although the Negro is drawn even more sympathetically than in "The Geranium". Tanner is lacking physical strength much more than in "The Geranium". Therefore the entire New York outing (CS p. 7) with his daughter is cut to her asking him to go for a stroll. "A stroll. He could barely manage to stay upright on his feet and she used the word *stroll* " (Dunn 193 p. 3). Similarly, when Tanner is asked to go down to Mrs Smith, he "moved off, watching his feet under him as if they were two small children he was encouraging to get out of his way." (Dunn 193 p. 12). We learn more about the Tanner family background: "He had raised up five boys and this girl with sawmilling and farming...(Dunn

193 p. 4). Tanner hates his daughter's dutifulness even more: "...she was hog-wild. She was thirsting for some duty to do,... She had shivered all over with duty." (Dunn 193 p. 4). A postcard from Coleman, who in this version replaces Rabie et al. and one from Tanner to Coleman underline Tanner's forty-year acquaintance with Coleman, as does Tanner's first meeting with Coleman, who is much more fully drawn here than in the later "Judgement Day" text. Accordingly Tanner's longing for the South grows stronger: "He would probably be dead by the time he got halfway there but it would be better to be dead halfway home than to be living here." (Dunn 193 p. 11). Tanner makes several plans to escape from his exile. In one of them "he had imagined than he would pretend he was dead and have his body shipped back and when he arrived he would knock on the inside of the box and they would let him out. Coleman would stand there with his red eyeballs starting out and think he had rose from the dead." (Dunn 193 p. 13).Here we have the first indication that the South means more than simply getting home.

To sum up: "The Geranium" is a third-person narrative, set in New York, with little dialogue. Old Dudley feels out of place here as does the flower he sees in the window across the street. With some ease we move in and out of Dudley's mind, but there are only two short dramatized memories of Dudley's past in the South, i.e. his fishing and hunting with Rabie. (CS pp. 5; 11-12). But there is no vision of the future. Old Dudley feels "his throat knotting up" and he weeps. He is frightened and isolated in a hostile environment, but he does nothing about his situation, despite the fact that he is not as near death as he is in the later versions. Old Dudley romanticizes his past in the South as opposed to his present in New York where "people boiled out of trains." There is next to no distancing irony, and at the end the reader is left with the morbid impression that Old Dudley might end up as his displaced friend, the geranium, "roots in the air", also in the concrete sense.

"An Exile in the East" is also a third-person narrative, but whenever we leave the narrator's mind - and we do so with greater ease than in "The Geranium" - we encounter episodes with dialogue from Tanner's past, present and future. The dreaming about the South is replaced by dramatized narrative. The style with its detached irony is much more O'Connor's trademark. Thanks to the dramatizations also the minor characters come alive. Tanner feels his isolation and humiliation much more, and though weaker, he is making plans for a journey home. In this connection I see the addition of the story about Tanner's imagined death as an essentially new venture. Home is no longer an idealized South, it is the safe haven to be reached after death. Similarly, the "here" or New

48

York of the story also symbolizes man's ambience before death.However, the story ends in almost the same way as "The Geranium", and this may have induced O'Connor to further re-writings.

The "Getting Home" version shows many signs of stylistic polishing, and O'Connor reaches here some of the happy formulations that she kept in the final version. There is Old Fairlee's confession: "He would have been a nigger's white nigger any day."[12] It is in this version that O'Connor lets the daughter live in "a pigeon-hutch of a building."[13] But Flannery O'Connor does not seem to have been sure about the ending. In Dunn 194 b, which is a full-length manuscript of this version but to which she added a hand-written note saying "Not for publication,"[14] she ends the story with a discussion between daughter and husband, in which the daughter convinces him that the old man must be buried in the South. This is crossed out in Dunn 194 d and replaced by the version we know from "Judgement Day" (CS p. 550), but the last subordinate clause runs, "which at her time of life is essential." (Dunn 194 d p. 27). O'Connor must have noticed the unfortunate transition from the third-person point-of-view in "Now she rests well at night" to the authorial comment "which at her time of life is essential." It needed many revisions before the perfect formulation with the obligatory O'Connor irony was reached in "and her good looks have mostly returned."

In this version the next-door Negro is identified further. He becomes the "nigger-actor" (Dunn 194 b p. 16), and the sympathetic character traits O'Connor had given him in "An Exile in the East" are dropped; thus it is more convincing that he slams Old Fairlee against the wall and finally kills him. Now it is Old Fairlee who desperately tries to get in contact with him. In the dramatization of Old Fairlee's journey to the South we read, "'Judgment (sic) Day!'" he cried, sitting up in the box and catching hold of Coleman's coat." (Dunn 194 b p. 26). This is the first occurrence of the later title in the entire manuscript material. Not surprisingly so, since one of the two distinctive additions in Dunn 194 b to the material as we know it up to "An Exile in the East" is the mentioning of biblical references. This may also have induced O'Connor to change the title "Getting Home" to the final "Judgement Day." Jesus is mentioned early in this version,[15] later Old Fairlee asks for the daughter's Bible,[16] and there is a long passage[17] where father and daughter talk about death and hell in the course of which the old man asks "'What did Jesus do?'" (Dunn 194 b p. 23). His daughter explains that he was crucified but rose from the dead; but that she does not believe in any of it. O'Connor must have found that these references made the story much less ambivalent. Consequently she crossed out those pages in Dunn 194 d, a carbon copy of 194 b. The only reminiscences of these direct references to the Bible that found their way into the published version are the actor's remarks: "'And I'm not no preacher! I'm not even no Christian. I don't believe in that crap. There ain't no Jesus and there ain't no God.'" (CS p. 545). The other essential addition in the "Getting Home" version is the figure of Dr. Foley.[18] "He was only part black. The rest was white and Indian." (Dunn 194 b p. 7). In Dunn 194 d O'Connor made him "part Jew" but already in Dunn 195 c, p. 6 this was erased in favor of the final "The rest was Indian and white." (CS p. 535). Old Fairlee's meeting with Foley is here as in the "Judgement Day" versions the frame around the flashback about Old Fairlee's first meeting with Coleman, whom he had on his hands "for thirty years" (Dunn 194 b, p. 12), not forty as in the "An Exile in the East" version. (Dunn 193 p. 6). One other change is important: whereas the story so far was set in the summer: "They set it out and let the hot sun bake it all day" (CS p. 3) we read in "The Geranium". New York is now snow-clad: "The window ledge across the street was covered with snow".[19] With this change O'Connor brought the setting in line with the heavy emphasis on death in the final version. Old Fairlee's resolution to get home is firm in spite of the weather.

Also, in the last "Getting Home" manuscript O'Connor changed Old Fairlee's name to Tanner, though not consistently.[20] The Dunn 195 fragments prove that O'Connor was uncertain about keeping or striking the references to the Bible;[21] she decided against them in the end. The most interesting feature of these freagments are the new endings. Here the daughter keeps her promise and sees to it that Tanner is buried in the South.[22] All along there are small stylistic improvements which bring the manuscripts closer to the published version, which pulls together most of the earlier strings. Unfortunately O'Connor's last improvements didn't reach Giroux's desk. They made a fine story even more perfect, as I have shown in the article mentioned above.[23] Therefore I will restrict myself here to some remarks about the published version of "Judgement Day".

The Economy of the first paragraph is perfect: In spite of his weakness[24] Tanner is entirely in charge; he *will* make his trip home, trusting only in himself for the first part of the trip and in the Almighty for the rest. "He had allowed his daughter to dress him." (CS p. 531). "Today" he will escape from a New York, which is even less charming than in the earlier versions "an alley full of New York air, the kind fit for cats and garbage." (CS p. 531). He will escape in spite of the snow and the growing cold "the snow was beginning to stick and freeze to the outside pane." (CS p. 547). The narrated time comprises only a few hours and the story is told as a third-person narrative, restricted almost entirely to Tanner's point of view. Seamlessly we move with him from his present to flashbacks and flashforwards. This point-of-view technique leads O'Connor to the externalization of the daughter's interior duologue, interspersed with Tanner's comments. "Her voice rose from the kitchen. 'As bad as having a child. He wanted to come and now he's here, he don't like it.' He had not wanted to come. 'Pretended he didn't but I could tell'." (CS pp. 533-534). The story starts in the present with Tanner's eavesdropping on his daughter's talking to herself and to her husband. After a short tête-à-tête with his daughter about her promise to bury him in the South, we move into the past. "She had put her face in the door of the shack and had stared, expressionless, for a second." (CS p. 534). This flashback leads to the Dr. Foley flashback, only a few hours less remote in the past. "He had found out in time to go back with her. If he had found out a day later, he might still be there, squatting on the doctor's land. When he saw the brown porpoise-shaped figure striding across the field that afternoon, he had known at once what had happened." (CS p. 535). This again glides brilliantly over into the distant past and Tanner's first meeting with Coleman. "He had had Coleman on his back for thirty years. Tanner had first seen Coleman when he was working six of them." (CS p. 536). From this account we move smoothly back into the Foley story (CS p. 539) from which we are led back into Tanner's New York present with his daughter (CS p. 540), who tries to cheer him up and make him "quit thinking about morbid stuff, death and hell and judgement." (CS p. 541). With a fine touch of tragic irony O'Connor lets Tanner answer, "'The Judgement[25] is coming.'" (CS p. 541). Here Tanner is thinking of Judgement Day in general, but is not aware of his own personal judgement, with which he will be faced that same day. After Tanner's musing about Coleman's imagined visit to New York we are in the immediate past and Tanner's confrontation with the actor, which shows Tanner utterly out of touch with the reality of his situation. Disillusioned more than ever, we hear him tell his daughter about his plans to leave. Once she has promised him that "she would ship him back," (CS p. 546) he can sleep peacefully and in this sleep he experiences his flashforward about his trip to the South in the box. "He could feel the cold early morning air of home coming in through the cracks of the pine box." (CS p. 546). Back in the present for a final meeting with his daughter, Tanner is on his way. The last movements between present and future and back to the present are almost unnoticeable. O'Connor is technically at her best here: "He landed upside down in the middle of the flight.He felt presently the tilt of the box as they took it off the train....'Coleman?' he murmured. The negro bending over him had a large surly mouth and sullen eyes. 'Ain't any coal man, either,'

51

he said." (CS pp. 548-549). When Tanner realizes that he has muddled up the future and the present, he asks the actor "'Hep me up, Preacher. I'm on my way home!'" (CS p. 549). And the actor sends him home in many a sense of that word.

To sum up: after many revisions "Judgement Day" is not only perfect in style and structure, also the characters are fully drawn: Tanner shows concern for Coleman and for his daughter and vice versa. And the message has reached new dimensions: the longing for the South of "The Geranium" has been activized and spiritualized. Tanner is no longer nostalgically longing for his home in the South, which wasn't so perfect, after all; he really makes an effort to get home, but home not only means safety, warmth and understanding, it is the final goal of life to which death is the door. His journey is life's journey. Tanner is prepared for that journey, he has reached self-recognition, he has shown concern for others, and he has given himself over into the hands of the Almighty. However, the moment of judgement reaches him unawares, as it does many of his fellow O'Connor characters and from an entirely unexpected source. The different stages in the development of the "Judgement-Day" material have shown Flannery O'Connor on her way home artistically. The early versions show simple story telling, as do her other stories up to the publication of *Wise Blood* (1952). She worked hard for greater precision, more liveliness through dialogized passages and greater complexity through handling of point of view and double-edged language. We saw this in the "An Exile in the East" version and it is true of most of her stories in *A Good Man Is Hard to Find* (1955). Also structurally her stories grow more complex, especially through her handling of time, where transitions flow seamlessly. With the final polishings of "Judgement Day" she reached the peak of her artistic achievement, as we also know it from such stories as "Revelation" and "Parker's Back." She accomplished a way of telling stories, which is unmistakably her own.

Her development as a thinker was paced in a similar way. Her stories of the forties contain messages which they share with us on the surface. With *A Good Man Is Hard to Find* the messages can only be found on a deeper level. Though her characters are concrete, they become "everyman," their particular experiences gain universal validity. The "Getting Home" version clearly shows the lines along which O'Connor was thinking: she wanted the story to be more clearly Christian with an unmistakable message about the metaphysical dimension of man's life. True enough, she cut those passages again in the final version, where direct references are minimized, but they are there at the core of "Judgement Day" as they are in the other stories, though disguised under grotesque appearances. With examples taken from her own experience in the South O'Connor shows man's situation in life, almost always against his wish "on his way home," that is on the way back to his maker, as the author was when she finished the final version of the "Judgement-Day" story. This material epitomizes the different phases in O'Connor's development from first promises in "The Geranium" to final perfection in "Judgement Day," both as artist and as thinker; it "marks the distance she has traveled." (HB p. 559).

Notes

1 It was published posthumously in *The South Carolina Review* vol. 11, Nov. 1978 pp. 12-21 and in *The Best American Short Stories 1979* , ed. Joyce Carol Oates pp. 28-38.
2 I.e. *A Good Man Is Hard to Find*.
3 The medicine she used against her disease.
4 Cp. her letter to C. Carver of June 17, 1964, where she says: "I've got one [Judgement Day] that I'm not satisfied with that I finished about the same time as 'Revelation'" (HB p. 585), which must have been towards the end of November 1963, since she wrote to M. Lee on November 29, "I have writ a story [Revelation] with which I am, for the time anyway, pleased pleased pleased." (HB p. 551). On May 21, 1964 she wrote to her publisher Giroux. "There is a story [Judgement Day] that I have been working on off and on for several years that I may be able to finish in time to include." I.e. in *Everything That Rises Must Converge*. (HB pp. 579-580).
5 Cp. my article "'Judgement Day': The Published Text Versus Flannery O'Connor's Final Version" in *The Flannery O'Connor Bulletin*, vol 11 (1982) 108-122.
6 Cp. the Flannery O'Connor collection manuscripts Dunn 194 a,b,c. In 194 d, which is a carbon copy of 194 b, O'Connor crossed out "Getting Home" and replaced it by "Judgement Day".
7 Dunn 194 a,b,c,d; 195 a,b,c,d,e,f,g,h; 196 a,b,c,d,e,f,g; and 197 a,b. 197 a, called "Judgment (*sic*) Day" is the 25 page manuscript of the published version. 197 b is a carbon copy of 197 a, which C. Carver had returned with comments to O'Connor by July 15, 1964 (HB p. 593) and which O'Connor used for last minute corrections. Cp. my line-to-line comparison in the article mentioned in note no. 5.
8 Dunn 194 a,b,c,d. Except for p 1, 194 c is a carbon copy of 194 b. So is 194 d, where O'Connor replaced "Getting Home" by "Judgement Day".
9 Dunn 194 b; 195 g,h; 196 b,c,d,e,f,g; 197 a.
10 Dunn 193 p. 1. Later in the story Tanner thinks of himself in the same way: "There were two trickles of water running over his tight cheeks and he leaned farther forward and let them fall on the steps as if his head were a pitcher he was emptying. Then he began to move on up the steps, like a cotton bale with short legs and a black hat." p. 15.

11 Ibid. p. 9. A comparison with the passage in the published version (CS pp. 7-8) shows how much more concrete the "Exile" version is.

12 Dunn 194 b p. 13. Cp. CS p. 540.

13 Dunn 194 d p. 15. Cp. CS p. 541.

14 Dunn 194 b, p. 1.

15 Dunn 194 a, p. 5, 194 b, p. 5.

16 Dunn 194 b, p. 14; also 195 e, p. 14; 195 f, p. 21.

17 Dunn 194 b, pp. 21, 23, 24.

18 Dunn 194 b, pp. 7, 12.

19 Dunn 194 a, p 4; and it is snowing outside 194 b, p. 23.

20 Dunn 194 d, p. 4; see also my article l.c. p. 109 and note no. 9.

21 In Dunn 195 e, p. 14 the Bible discussion is kept; in 195 f, p. 20 Tanner's thoughts about death are crossed out, but on p. 21 the Bible references are kept.

22 Dunn 195 h, p. 26; 196 f, p. 26; 196 g, pp. 26-7.

23 My conclusion there was that Dunn 197 b "is technically an even more satisfactory story and...its characters have more depth in their relations with each other." L.c. p. 120.

24 Now also his vision is failing and he is paralyzed by a stroke. "He controlled one hand by holding the other on top of it." "All he had to do was push one foot in front of the other." CS pp. 531-532.

25 Notice the capital J against the daughter's small j.

Pilgrims of the Absolute: Léon Bloy and Flannery O'Connor

Linda Schlafer

Among the least discussed of the influences on Flannery O'Connor's thought and work are the writings of a number of French authors of the nineteenth and early twentieth centuries. The lack of scholarly attention to these writers is the more remarkable inasmuch as O'Connor herself was insistent upon their importance in her religious and artistic formation. When a Frenchman named Pierre Brodin wrote to ask O'Connor what influence, if any, French literature had had on her fiction, she answered: "You ask about any possible French influence on my writing. When I first began to write fiction (around 1945) I read everything I could of the French Catholic novelists, Bloy, Bernanos, and Mauriac. My point of view was Catholic and I naturally looked for the best writers I could find who shared it; they were French."[1] O'Connor also mentioned these French writers, and many others, repeatedly and emphatically in her letters.

By tracing O'Connor's French reading chronologically, I find a discernible correlation between O'Connor's handling of aesthetic distance in her fiction and the tenor of the French writers whom she was reading at different stages in her work. In her early writing we find almost perfect examples of the aesthetic of the grotesque, one aspect of which is a carefully controlled distance between reader and narrator, on the one hand, and the materials of the fiction on the other. In the "middle period" of her work, during which time she was reading such French writers as Marcel, Weil, and Malraux, O'Connor began to narrow this distance, and to draw the reader more closely into the lives and events of her characters. In her last stories (including, I think, her unfinished and unpublished third novel) she also moved the crisis points of her stories back from their closing scenes into their interiors, so that she committed herself to working out not only the advent of gracious catastrophes into the lives of her protagonists, but also some of the consequences which they entailed. Within this larger context, it is my purpose here to examine in brief the part played by Léon Bloy in the early stages of O'Connor's artistic development. I will first consider some of the ways in which Bloy's work reinforced O'Connor's use of the grotesque as an art form, then discuss the related but separable issues of the violent and the prophetic.

O'Connor first read Bloy's work, along with that of a score of other writers, during the period of her graduate work at Iowa. She must have read Bloy at very nearly the same time as she read Maritain, and may, indeed, have heard of Bloy by way of the Maritains, who were converted and received into the Roman Catholic Church under Bloy's tutelage. The book by Léon Bloy which remains in O'Connor's library is *Pilgrim of the Absolute,* a collection of excerpts from various of Bloy's works selected by Raissa Maritain and introduced by Jacques Maritain. This translation by John Coleman and Harry Lorin Binsse was published in 1947 and inscribed by O'Connor in the same year. She also had the biography by Albert Béguin called *Léon Bloy: A Study in Impatience* (also of 1947), which she annotated.[2]

Léon Bloy, who lived from 1846 to 1917, is less well known in the United States than are either Bernanos or Mauriac. Much less of his work is available in translation, and he was such an extremist in thought and manner as to discourage many people from reading his books, even in his own country. Bloy's work, however, is very interesting to read as an early source for O'Connor, particularly in conjunction with Maritain's *Art and Scholasticism* which was so foundational to O'Connor's aesthetic method. Whereas Maritain's work is a carefully reasoned explanation as to the *manner* in which artistic work should be pursued, Bloy, both temperamentally and topically, bears a significant relationship to the *matter* of O'Connor's fiction. This is perhaps similar to the distinction made by the Danish poet Johannes Jørgensen, when he said, "Ernest Hello taught me to *think* as a Catholic ... Léon Bloy taught me to *feel* as a Catholic."[3] (My italics).

In *Flannery O'Connor: The Imagination of Extremity,*[4] Frederick Asals focuses on O'Connor's attraction to polarities in both form and content as a key to understanding the powerful effect of her fiction. For one acquainted with O'Connor's "imagination of extremity," the first salient impression upon reading Léon Bloy's work is of a person who thought, felt, lived, and wrote only in extremes, and often apparently contradictory extremes. Asals notes of O'Connor's writing that "... while the antipodal perspectives introduced are played with and explored, characteristically they are not resolved. Rather than merging, blending, informing one another, they are sustained in a set of vibrant tensions that seem to open ever wider, to strain furiously toward a breaking point."[5] Bloy also held seeming opposites in paradoxical tension, beginning in his own experience and extending to his writing. "I was born sad, profoundly, horribly sad," he wrote in 1889 to his fiancee, "and if I am possessed with the most violent longing for joy, it is because of the mysterious law which attracts opposites."[6]

Along with the control of aesthetic distance, the delicate and carefully contrived *balance* between sets of seemingly contradictory aspects of experience is essential to the grotesque as a literary art form. As Carl Hartman says: "...that which is merely distorted or merely horrible or merely funny is not grotesque; that which *is* grotesque, must, to exist as such, remain always on a very fine line somewhere in between the divergent forces which comprise and orient its grotesqueness."[7] Much of what Léon Bloy did and said seems, in retrospect, merely distorted, horrible, or funny. He had, for example, a violent antipathy for the "respectable middle class," particularly in feminine form, and when a fire raged one day through a charity bazaar, his only regret was that so few of the participants perished. "Only the small number of victims limited my joy," he said. "Many rich ladies gathered to do good!"[8] On the other hand, he cherished a romantic view of prostitutes whom he saw as among the sublime poor who alone were worthy of salvation. Bloy wanted desperately to save those unfortunate women of his acquaintance and embarked upon several ardent, if not very successful, crusades to redeem them. Unfortunately, his love was not always on an ideal plane but was mingled with a violent physical passion which resulted in his living with at least two of his proposed converts.[9] In countless ways, Bloy's life and his writings provided O'Connor with the absurdities and the extremities of which the grotesque is compounded. Unlike Bloy, however, who saw himself as a prophet but despised any notion of "art," O'Connor was able to exercise the aesthetic control which added the authority of art to the force of violent extremes.

Another essential aspect of the aesthetic of the grotesque is the comic treatment of potentially horrible material, and, according to Gilbert Muller, the major comic technique employed in the grotesque is that of exaggeration.[10] Léon Bloy seems to have been virtually devoid of humor in his outlook, but he had a lot to say about exaggeration. "One sees this world's evil accurately only by exaggerating it," he said.

To say something worthwhile, as well as to give an impression of the Beautiful, it is essential to seem to exaggerate, that is, to carry one's scrutiny beyond the object, and then one arrives at exactness itself devoid of exaggeration, something which can be verified in the Prophets, who were all accused of exaggerating. (PA p. 121).

Bloy, like O'Connor, had read Edgar Allan Poe, whom he caricatured as "a mouth with a moustache of snakes over it,"[11] and he "certainly shared the Romantics' predilection for the bizarre and the occult."[12] As with O'Connor, however, these effects in Bloy are never intended as ends in themselves but for the purpose of making people *see*. Speaking of the grotesque in her work O'Connor said: "Distortion in this case is an instrument ; exaggeration has a purpose and the whole structure of the story or novel has been made what it is because of belief. This is not the kind of distortion that destroys; it is the kind that reveals...." (MM p. 162). Asals has mentioned Carl Jung's suggestion that "Catholicism seems to nourish extremes."[13] For both Bloy and O'Connor, this was true partly because they felt that their existence was anchored to Absolutes and partly because they believed that they had to use extreme measures to get the attention of and to communicate with an apostate audience. O'Connor's analogies in justification of this process are well known - that "to the hard of hearing you shout, for the almost-blind you draw large and startling figures." (MM p. 34). The stylization or abstraction of character is a special instance of the kind of comic distortion which aids the grotesque. O'Connor had a model for this in Bloy also as he habitually reduced particular people and specific circumstances to "specifications" of spiritual principles.[14]

Exaggeration also functions, in grotesque literature, in the form of melodramatic action, in the stock comic devices of suddenness, surprise, and shock which are integral to such a plot. This trait, in conjunction with the sets of tensions which, in Asals' words, "strain furiously toward a breaking point" makes violence an implicit aspect of grotesque form and makes such a form very congenial to an exploration of violence as fictional subject matter. The word "violent" is among the more frequently invoked adjectives in O'Connor criticism. O'Connor's preoccupation with violence as a subject always went hand in hand with her attempts to render vital aspects of her faith in fictional form. "I keep thinking more and more about the presentation of love and charity," she wrote in a letter to Andrew Lytle, "or better call it grace, as love suggests tenderness, whereas grace can be violent or would have to be to compete with the kind of evil I can make concrete." (HB p.373). O'Connor made an explicit connection between the violence explored in her second novel and her reading of Bloy. I quote again from her letter to Brodin: "I was considerably fascinated by the violence with which [Bloy] held his faith, a violence which both revolts and attracts me. I think that the character of Old Tarwater in *The Violent Bear It Away* owes something to Léon Bloy, however far removed from him I may be in regard to culture." Bloy was a violent man by temperament, and he justified the use of violence in his religious endeavors (which included his writing), even to insisting that it was part of his God-given mission to voice his incessant indignation. In one of his novels, the character who represents Bloy says: "...as long as no one kills me, I shall be the trustee of Vengeance and the very obedient manservant of an *alien* Fury who will command me to speak.... I suffer from an infinite violence, and the fits of anger that come forth from me are but echoes, singularly weakened echoes of a higher Imprecation I have the astounding misfortune to reverberate." (PA p.93). Bloy loathed the soft and the sentimental and was always grateful that, as he said, "a thorny-handed Providence watched over me and spared me from becoming a charming young man by slashing me with its caresses." (PA p.93). From Bloy, (and later as amplified by Fuller's *Man in Modern Fiction*),[15] O'Connor may have learned her distrust of the "compassion" invoked by her contemporaries. Bloy called the public version of this attribute a "cheerful crocodile" and believed that it was a great disservice to teach only the tender side of religious reality. "You've been told," he wrote, "that my violent writings offend Charity."

Justice and Mercy are identical and consubstantial in their absolutes. Here is what neither the sentimentalist nor the fanatic is willing to understand. A teaching that proposes the Love of God as its supreme end above all needs to be virile, under the pain of allowing all the illusions of self-love or of carnal love. It is all too easy to emasculate souls by teaching them nothing by the precept of loving one's brothers, to the hurt of all other precepts which you seek to hide from them. What one gets in this way is a flabby and sticky religion, more fearful in its effects than even Nihilism itself. (PA pp.100-101).

It is Bloy's identification of justice with mercy that we find in the religious outlook of the Tarwaters. O'Connor referred several times to old Tarwater as a "Protestant prophet" and said that "the modern reader will identify himself with the schoolteacher, but it is the old man who speaks for me." (HB p.350). The Tarwaters are violent and bizarre but their religion is neither flabby nor sticky and they are strongly contrasted with the nihilist Rayber. Concerning readers who were depressed by the ending of *The Violent Bear It Away* O'Connor said, "They forget that the old man has taught [young Tarwater] the truth and that now he's doing what is right, however crazy." (HB p.536).

Violence as a constructive force is used in O'Connor's stories to reveal what is most essential in a character, for, as she said, "the man in the violent situation reveals those qualities least dispensable in his personality, those qualities which are all he will have to take into eternity with him." (MM p.114). Violence, O'Connor said, "is strangely capable of returning my characters to reality" and reality is "...something to which we must be returned at considerable cost...." (MM p.112). Shocking events prepare a character to accept or reject his "moment of grace." O'Connor was not surprised that so many of her readers were puzzled by these violent moments in her fiction, because, as she put it, "Our age not only does not have a very sharp eye for the almost imperceptible intrusions of grace, it no longer has much feeling for the nature of the violences which precede and follow them." (MM p.112).

Most essentially, Léon Bloy and Flannery O'Connor shared an anagogical vision, "the kind of vision that is able to see different levels of reality in one image or one situation." (MM p.72). Fiction, for both, was an outgrowth of "a way that you habitually look at things." (MM p.92). "The novelist," O'Connor said, "writes about what he sees on the surface, but his angle of vision is such that he begins to see before he gets to the surface and he continues to see after he has gone past it. He begins to see in the depths of himself." (MM pp. 131-132). Béguin makes much the same point concerning Bloy, whom he contrasts with these "whose vision is reduced to a single plane, one which neither perceives nor admits what lies beneath the surface."[16] Maurice Maeterlinck called Bloy's first novel: "the only work of the present day in which there are evident marks of genius, if by genius we understand certain flashes in the depth which link what is seen to what is not seen, and what is not yet understood to what will be understood one day."[17] These "flashes in the depths" lead the artist's eye from surface reality into mystery. It then becomes the artist's task to recreate the visible world in such a way that it reflects these flashes for the reader who is equipped to see them. According to Béguin, Bloy's

need for verbal invention matches his need to detect the presence of mystery, not in order to say what it is but to say where it dwells - which is everywhere.... Looking below the surface, he set out to discover what each thing typified and what place it occupied in the plan of God; to fit it into the endless succession of analogies which forms the secret fabric of the created world and extends mysteriously into the invisible.[18]

For both Bloy and O'Connor, the role of the prophet was not prediction or pre-vision but rather the accurate present vision of reality. Given O'Connor's own prophetic vision and her preoccupation with the role of the prophet in her stories, we see once again how apt was her choice of the grotesque as an aesthetic form to the peculiar quality of her imagination. Muller, who has traced the contemporary use of the grotesque from its sources in medieval graphic art, maintains that the grotesque in literature is always a "method of investigating certain metaphysical problems through fictive constructions."[19] Grotesque art has the capacity for functioning anagogically because "a connection can be established between existential dislocation, which is at the core of the grotesque, and spiritual dissociation."[20] Unlike Gothic, surreal, and absurdist literature, however, grotesque art does not employ horror, dislocation, or deformity as ends in themselves which ultimately dead-end in meaninglessness. The art of the grotesque functions, like absurdist literature, between the two poles of the comic and the terrible, but whereas tragicomedy is ultimately comprised of "neither...nor," the grotesque leads toward the ultimate synthesis of "both...and." It points to the possibility of "new-making," as Marcel called it, through the "acceptance and ultimate reconciliation of contradictory possibilities"[21] which characterized medieval High Gothic art, and which, of course, was compatible with O'Connor's Catholic eschatological understanding.

The list of correspondences between Bloy and O'Connor could be extended considerably. They had remarkably similar views, for example, on place and country, time and eternity, limitations and excesses, personal and vocational identity, and the "poor." Although it is usually impossible to know whether such correspondences are causal or coincidental, these parallels are all to be found between O'Connor's work and material of Bloy's which we know that she read. I would like briefly to point out that striking resemblances also exist between O'Connor and material of Bloy's which she said that she had *not* read. O'Connor told Brodin that she had "never read any of Bloy's fiction" (which she didn't think she would have liked) "only some essays." I will mention, however, four instances from *The Woman Who Was Poor*,[22] three of them brief images, and one a more extended metaphor, which at least suggest O'Connor's acquaintance with it. First, when Clotilde is speaking of having struck her "stepfather," she says, "I felt as if I had an oak-tree growing from my heart."[23] This image is echoed in O'Connor's remarks about "A Good Man Is Hard to Find": "I prefer to think that...the old lady's gesture, like the mustard-seed, will grow to be a great crow-filled tree in The Misfit's heart." (MM pp.112-113). Second, Marchenoir in describing Leopold's illuminations says that "in those letters amorous elaboration of the text was replaced by a network tracery of arabesques."[24] It is the "perfect arabesque of colors," of course, that Parker aspires to in his endless acquisition of tatoos, but he only achieves this result at the moment of *his* illumination at sunrise when he feels the light pouring through him and his spider web soul is transformed. (CS p.528). Again, after Clotilde had undergone her own conversion, "when she slept, she beheld a loaf of bread which she shared out among the poor. That bread, instead of casting any shadow, cast a *light*...."[25] This quotation is suggestive of the bread/hunger imagery associated with young Tarwater throughout *The Violent Bear It Away*, and particularly of the closing scene in which the rising tide of his hunger converges with the line of prophets and culminates in the vision of the red-gold tree of fire. Finally, there is in *The Woman Who Was Poor* the lengthy and significant section in which Gacougnal and Clotilde make a trip to the zoo to study the lions and meet Cain Marchenoir. This threesome even goes to a cafe near the zoo and orders drinks. This episode may only coincidentally resemble that of Hazel's and Enoch's antics at the zoo in *Wise Blood*, including their stop at the Frosty Bottle, just as the images paralleled above may be coincidental. There is enough material like this, however, to warrant asking whether by 1963, when O'Connor wrote to Pierre Brodin, she had forgotten having read *The Woman Who Was Poor*. Or perhaps it should simply make us cautious in pressing the causality of *any* literary predecessor on the grounds of material resemblance.

It also, of course, is always difficult to assess influences because it is precisely in the nature of the creative act to transform the aggregate of data, ideas, feelings, and experiences accumulated in the creative subconscious and to make of them something new. "I have one of those food-chopper brains," O'Connor said, "that nothing comes out of the way it went in." (HB p.68). The "food-chopper" metaphor is entirely appropriate to the creative process and an awareness of its function must restrain us from an over-zealous seeking of one-to-one correspondences between O'Connor's sources and her work. Nonetheless, an acquaintance with the work of Léon Bloy helps us to grasp significant ways in which O'Connor's work is not only unique, but also continuous with a literary tradition. It makes up a small but important part of a complex context which enables us more accurately to understand, and thus to enjoy and appreciate, the fictional work of Flannery O'Connor.

Notes

1   Pierre Brodin, *Presences contemporaines: ecrivains americains d'aujourd'hui,* Paris 1964, pp.206-207.
2   Trans. Edith M.Riley, New York. *Pilgrims of the Absolute* will hereafter be designated PA.
3   From E.T. DuBois, *Portrait of Léon Bloy,* London and New York 1951, pp.110-111.
4   Athens, Georgia, 1982.

5 Asals p.2

6 Quoted by Emmanuela Polimeni in *Léon Bloy: The Pauper Prophet, 1846-1917*, New York, 1951, p.10.

7 "Jesus Without Christ," *Western Review*, 17 (1952), 76.

8 DuBois, p.21.

9 Cp.DuBois, pp.34-37.

10 *Nightmares and Visions: Flannery O'Connor and the Catholic Grotesque* Athens, Georgia, 1972, pp.8-10.

11 Bloy's penchant for verbal caricature makes an interesting parallel to O'Connor's early cartooning, an art form which relies heavily on caricature, and which feeds directly into the abstracted exaggerations of grotesque art.

12 Polimeni p.30.

13 Asals p.3.

14 Cp.introduction to PA p.11.

15 Edmund Fuller, *Man in Modern Fiction: Some Minority Opinions on Contemporary American Fiction*, New York, 1958.

16 Béguin p.101.

17 DuBois, p.107.

18 Béguin, p.10.

19 Muller, p.5.

20 Muller, p.17.

21 Hartmann p.77.

22 Trans. I.J. Collins, New York, 1939.

23 Bloy, *The Woman Who Was Poor*, p.70.

24 Bloy, op.cit. p.153.

25 Bloy, op.cit. p.330.

Narrator

"Mine is a Comic Art..." Flannery O'Connor

Kathleen Feeley, S.S.N.D.

In an early press interview,[1] Flannery O'Connor stated: "Mine is a comic art, but that does not detract from its seriousness." This is a typical example of her wry understatement. O'Connor's readers know that the comic tone of her works, and the art that produces that tone, adds greatly to the seriousness of her stories. Her comic art is the working out of a vision of reality which measures what is and what could be, and laughs at the infinite distance between them. This laugh is not one of disdain or despondency or superiority, but rather one of deep understanding. Within the limits of her vision, Flannery O'Connor "knew what was in man," and that knowledge made her hopeful that her stories would both amuse her readers and move their hearts.

When O'Connor was a relatively unknown writer, Caroline Gordon had a party for her to which she invited various writers. Malcolm Cowley requested her to read one of her stories; she read "A Good Man Is Hard to Find." Caroline Gordon told me that for the first half of her story the audience laughed continuously. Then, at the midpoint of the story when The Misfit enters, a strained silence gripped the group. This story illustrates O'Connor's ability to change the tone of a story. Yet, a careful reader will see that elements of O'Connor's humor remain in the stylization of the murders with which the story closes. O'Connor herself explained the shift in the story to an English professor who wrote to her to ask if the last half of the story is a product of Bailey's imagination. Confessing herself to be in a state of shock at the question, O'Connor responded: "There is a change of tension from the first part of the story to the second where the Misfit enters, but this is no lessening of reality. This story is, of course, not meant to be realistic in the sense that it portrays the everyday doings of people in Georgia. It is stylized and its conventions are comic even though its meaning is serious." (HB p. 437).

The comic conventions, the stylization - actually an inheritance from Poe down through W.C. Fields - are expressions of O'Connor's spirit of comedy which echoes through her letters and informs her fiction. She admitted that she had a hard time reading her fiction aloud, because she couldn't control her laughter. She practiced reading a few stories with deliberate self-control, so that she could read these on public occasions. Her readers have attested that it is not unusual to laugh aloud while reading an O'Connor story to oneself. The roots of O'Connor's humor lie in her view of reality. In a lecture in which she discussed her talent and her faith, she said, "...it is well to realize that the maximum amount of seriousness admits the maximum amount of comedy. Only if we are secure in our beliefs can we see the comical side of the universe." (MM p. 167). O'Connor's secure faith enabled her to portray the foolishness of others in a way which makes the reader smile and recognize himself.

O'Connor's literary style is intrinsically related to her early career as a cartoonist. As a small child, she had a penchant for making little booklets of words and pictures, similar to a comic strip. When I was visiting her home, I saw one with the title, "Ladies and Gents, Meet the Three Mister Noseys." Under the appropriate faces were the titles, "Mr. Long Nose; Mr. Sharp Nose; Mr. Snut Nose." I also found a small booklet with several typed pages entitled, "My Relitives." In it were short satiric descriptions of uncles, cousins, etc. The best example of her youthful cartooning I found in a folder in her library. A cartoon showed mother, father, and child walking down a street. Out of the mother's mouth came a balloon saying, "Hold your head up, Mary Flannery, and you are just as bad, Ed." Out of the child's mouth came the words, "I was readin where someone died of holding up their head." The cartoon had "age 9" written at the bottom of it. In a local newspaper on June 13, 1943, an article headlined "Mary O'Connor Shows Talent as Cartoonist" featured college freshman O'Connor, who "is fast making a name for herself as an up-and-coming cartoonist." According to the article, Flannery "doesn't remember the day when she wasn't writing and illustrating humorous verse." During her days at Peabody High School, as well as in college, her cartoons - linoleum block cuts - appeared in the school paper. Each carried her signature - a bird fashioned from her initials, M.F.O. The article closes with the following paragraph: "Miss O'Connor frankly states that her literary ambition is to be able to write prose satire. She plans to work hard and hopes some day to find a place where her satiric essays and cartoons will fit to good advantage."[2]

In studying her cartoons, one can see signs of things to come. The cartoonist has two tools: a drawing, usually quite simple in design and uncomplicated in detail, and a trenchant line of comment or dialogue. Together, the drawing and the commentary make a point. For example, one O'Connor cartoon depicts a student looking at a stern librarian with the question: "Do you have any books the faculty doesn't particularly recommend?" These cartoons done for the *Colonnade*, her college newspaper, show a blend of visual and verbal art. They also show a comic mindset toward "role reversal" which is evident in her fiction. For instance, in the newspaper of October 5, 1943, a cartoon showed two students, one of whom carried a big load of books, with the caption: "Do you think teachers are necessary?" On May 23, 1944, there appeared a cartoon showing two students in an evident bad humor. It bore the tagline: "This place will never amount to anything until they get a Student Committee on Faculty Relations."

As feature editor of *Spectrum*, the college yearbook, in 1945, O'Connor drew satiric cartoons for the endpieces of various sections. Here her cartooning method changes to rounder lines and less detail. She seems to rely more on suggestion than explicit rendering. That same year, O'Connor was editor of the *Corinthian*, the college magazine, and art editor of the *Colonnade*. Her writing in those periodicals is pale and flat compared to her art. She evidently realized that herself. She said later that when she arrived at the University of Iowa to begin a writing career, she "didn't know a short story from an ad in the newspaper."[3] It is very possible that she did not realize what a good preparation her cartooning was for the fiction that lay ahead. At the University of Iowa, O'Connor seemed to put cartooning behind her. Actually she turned her talent for pictorial representation into verbal art. One watches with delight her increasing ability to draw pictures with words. A study of her stories in the order of their composition shows how adroit she became in the verbal creation of people and situations which the reader can "see" as clearly as one of her cartoons.

Before I visited Flannery O'Connor's home, I had a correspondence with Leo Zuber, the editor for whom O'Connor wrote many book reviews. In one of his letters to me, Zuber wrote, "Once when we were visiting her, she dropped the comment that one could get some good pictorial leads by reading the ads in the *Market Bulletin.*" Zuber sent me several copies of the *Bulletin* and I saw for myself how those looking for employment, or seeking hired hands, unwittingly drew satiric pictures of themselves. This native material was grist for O'Connor's imagination. In the same letter, Zuber added these ideas about O'Connor's sources:

I have to add that even though your interests may be in what she read, there were other sources for her material. Kitchen or parlor gossip or conversation. She could not get around very well on foot but would sit in the car while her Mother shopped or did other business in town; one can observe a very great deal just sitting in a car on the square in a Southern town; the whole local universe passes by.... Have you ever attended a tent revival? Flannery's characters may seem to be grotesque or ludicrous; they may be, to the degree that she may have blended two or three real ones into one fictional one but she didn't have to go very far to find them. Now what she did with them is quite another matter.[4]

However, before she could "do" anything with them, she had to learn to make them real to her readers. An unpublished letter from O'Connor to Zuber (a copy of which he sent to me) illustrates how she continually thought in pictures. On August 3, 1960, O'Connor wrote to Zuber, newly appointed to replace a Mrs. Hall as editor of the book section of *The Bulletin*. She requested a specific book to review and then added: "I have often wondered why Mrs. Hall didn't have the publishers send the book directly to the person who wanted to review it. I have had a mental picture of her spending her life on the way to and from the post office."[5]

One way to instruct oneself about O'Connor's comic art is to compare versions of her early stories. "A Circle in the Fire," published in the *Kenyon Review* in Spring, 1954, was included in her first collection, *A Good Man Is Hard to Find*. Comparing the two published versions shows stylistic improvements which aid the comic tone. One of these is the use of indirect discourse instead of direct quotation. For example, when Mrs. Pritchard and Mrs. Cope are discussing the unwanted visitors, this dialogue ensued in the first version:"'They only played with what we gave them to eat,' Mrs. Cope said in a hurt voice. 'Maybe they don't like *soft* drinks,' Mrs. Pritchard muttered. 'They certainly looked hungry,' Mrs. Cope said." In the final version, Mrs. Pritchard's direct quotation is changed to "Mrs. Pritchard suggested that they might not like *soft* drinks." (CS p. 183). Somehow the tone of her remark comes through more comically in the indirect discourse. One finds that O'Connor used this technique to great advantage as she developed her art.

The same story illustrates O'Connor's developing understanding that specifics are more comic than summaries. When Mrs. Cope is trying to make conversation with the boys, the *Kenyon* version says only, "They answered in short explosive sentences, pushing each other's shoulders and doubling up with laughter, as if the questions had meanings she didn't know about." While one can picture these boys openly ridiculing their unwilling hostess, the whole scene becomes clear and funnier with the next two lines, which were added before the story was published in the collection: "'And do you have men teachers or lady teachers at your school?,' she asked. 'Some of both and some you couldn't tell which,' the big boy hooted." (CS p. 184).The same careful adding and subtracting to increase the comic tone can be found in two versions of "A Late Encounter with the Enemy." Originally published in *Harper's Bazaar* in September, 1953, it also appeared in her first collection. To heighten the character of the General, O'Connor made such minor changes as "innerduced" for "introduced" in his dialogue, and described him as frail as a "dried spider" instead of a "dried leaf." When the General is having his heart attack, the original version reads, "He saw the faces of his children and of his wife and of his Mother." O'Connor changed this to the following: "He saw his wife's narrow face looking at him critically through her round gold-rimmed glasses; he saw one of his squinting bald-headed sons; and his mother ran toward him with an anxious look." (CS p. 143) Such specificity is an example of visual art being translated into verbal art.

A comic device that O'Connor uses frequently is the juxtaposition of two contrary ideas. For example, in "Parker's Back," after Sarah Ruth has knocked Parker out of the car during their first date, one reads: "He made up his mind then and there to have nothing further to do with her." (CS p. 518). The next paragraph begins, "They were married in the County Ordinary's Office." This buildup of expectation followed by the intrusion of the unexpected is a striking O'Connor device to produce humor. O'Connor's letters reveal that this was a characteristic habit. In a group of unpublished letters to Paul Curry Steele, which I saw in her study, she writes: "Tell anybody as asts you that you have it from me personally. I have been influenced only by Poe, Cardinal Newman, and the Book of Daniel. You might add Ella Wheeler Wilcox or somebody, if you see fit."[6]

Just as the cartoonist takes the obvious and renders it remarkable by distortion, so O'Connor takes a worn-out phrase - a cliché - and gives it new meaning. In such stories as "Parker's Back," this device is used for the kind of comedy that has symbolic reverberations. "It's your funeral," (CS p. 522) the tattoo artist says as he begins to emblazon the Byzantine Christ on Parker's back. And so, metaphorically, it was."If you know who you are, you can go anywhere," (CS p. 407) Julian's mother repeats in "Everything That Rises Must Converge." She goes to her death by being, innately, "who she is" in a changing society.

One of the books which I found in Flannery O'Connor's library was a small monograph by Henry James, entitled "Daumier, Caricaturist." (This essay is now collected in *The Painter's Eye: Notes and Essays on the Pictorial Arts*.) In James' discussion of Daumier, I see a strong parallel to O'Connor's art. To explain the reason why Daumier's drawings belong to the very highest art, James says:

I think this reason is that, on the whole, he is so peculiarly serious. This may seem an odd ground of praise for a jocose draughtsman, and of course what I mean is that his comic force is serious - a very different thing from the absence of comedy.... Daumier's figures are almost always either foolish, fatuous politicians or frightened mystified bourgeois; yet they help him to give us a strong sense of the nature of man.... We feel that Daumier reproduces admirably the particular life that he sees, because it is the very medium in which he moves. He has no wide horizon; the absolute bourgeois hems him in, and he is a bourgeois himself, without poetic ironies, to whom a big cracked mirror has been given.[7]

O'Connor's horizons were not wide; her figures reflect the life she saw. And her comic force is serious.

A key to O'Connor's comedy is her quality of detachment. This can be illustrated by her reaction to two noted comedians: Charlie Chaplin and W.C. Fields. One of her friends wrote that she "adored W.C. Fields... and did not like Chaplin."[8] Devotees of those two film comedians will remember that Chaplin seemed to be genuinely affected by all the zany things that happened to him. Fields seemed to be innately above the comic foibles which ensnared him. He gave the impression of having the situation in hand, even while he was ostensibly a victim of it. This attitude informs the fiction of Flannery O'Connor and makes it truly comic. It combines the metaphysical attitude of Dante as he looked down from his place near the Fixed Stars at "the little earth that made us passionate," the biblical assurance that God would be faithful to his covenant, and the theological view of St. Paul, that "the visible things are but for a time, whereas the invisible are eternal." O'Connor lets the reader share her perspective as she looks with compassion, salted with wry amusement, at the plight of man. This detached, elevated viewpoint carries the comic tone in stories which probe the great mystery of Redemption.

From a clever caricaturist - who carved local comedy into linoleum blocks - to a realistic writer - who probed the infinite in well-crafted fiction: this is the artistic progression of Flannery O'Connor. She did not *choose* her talent, her milieu, her penchant for large and startling figures. She chose only to accept and work with the "givens" in her life. It was a choice which has enriched us all.

Notes

1 Betsy Lochridge, "An Afternoon With Flannery O'Connor," *Atlanta Journal and Constitution*, 1 November 1959, pp. 38-40.
2 "Mary O'Connor Shows Talent as Cartoonist," *Macon Telegraph and News*, 13 June 1943, p. 6.

3 Flannery O'Connor in "An Interview With Flannery O'Connor," *Censer* [College of St. Teresa, Winona, Minnesota], (Fall, 1960), p. 30.
4 Unpublished letter from Leo Zuber to Sister Kathleen Feeley, 22 June 1969.
5 Unpublished letter from Flannery O'Connor to Leo Zuber, 3 August 1960.
6 Unpublished letter, 10 February 1956.
7 Henry James, *The Painter's Eye* (Cambridge: Harvard University Press, 1956), p. 240.
8 James O. Tate, "An O'Connor Remembrance," unpublished manuscript in the library of Georgia State College, Milledgeville, Georgia.

Throwing the Big Book: The Narrator Voice in Flannery O'Connor's Stories

Jack Dillard Ashley

"all of a sudden WHAM! She throws this big book she was reading at me . . . ."
("Revelation," CS p. 504)

"For we mean to employ for our souls' health the rougher and severer poet or storyteller, . . ." Plato[1]

"Let James help your structure but not your style" Flannery O'Connor advised "A" in 1959 (HB p. 317), advice which had been liberally given her by her Jamesian mentor Caroline Gordon. But this Jacobitish counsel had proved inadequate for her own artistic purposes in the short stories. If structure means the way the story is told, composed, arranged and by whom - in a phrase point of view - then James did not help her own structure. This essay undertakes to define O'Connor's point of view, identify the narrator's voice, and determine the effects of that voice on the theme and tone of her stories. The author was keenly aware of the gravity of point of view. In 1956 she wrote "A" " Point of view drives me nuts. If you violate the point of view, you destroy the sense of reality and louse yourself up generally.... It's more complicated than I make it out to be. Anyway you just can't sit down and write a novel. You have to know who's seeing what and all that kind of stuff." (HB p. 157). Later (August 1957) she wrote to Cecil Dawkins: "Point of view runs me crazy when I think about it but I believe that when you are writing well, you don't think about it. I seldom think about it when I am writing a short story but on [*sic*] the novel it gets to be a considerable worry...I seem to stay in a snarl with mine." (HB p. 239).

Leon Edel claims the most important innovation of Henry James to be freeing fiction of the "traditionally ubiquitous and often garrulous narrator who used to interpose his own personality and preachments between the story and the reader."[2] This honor may be overstated, however; Aristotle, recalling Plato's distinction between imitative, dramatic, and mixed modes[3] maintains that "it is necessary for the poet himself to speak in his own person in the poem as little as possible...."[4]

James, O'Connor wrote, "started this business of telling a story through what he called a central intelligence - like he did with Strether in *The Ambassadors*. (HB p. 157). The teller is situated within the story and has a limited and finite but profound view which, according to O'Connor, "gives the thing a dramatic unity that's hard to get otherwise." (HB p. 157). But she got it otherwise: her own point of view is ominiscient, unlimited, and within the microcosm of the story, infinite.

Omniscient point of view for her seems foregone, virtually a donnée of her craft. Three times in the letters she worries about matters of tone in omniscient narration. In March 1954: "the omniscient narrator is not properly supposed to use colloquial expressions...Caroline Gordon...is always writing me that I mustn't say such things, that the om.nar. never speaks like anyone but Dr. Johnson. Of course, it is a great strain for me to speak like Dr. Johnson." (HB p. 69). In August 1955: "In any fiction where the omniscient narrator uses the same language as the characters, there is a loss of tension and a lowering of tone." (HB p. 95). In September 1958: "...the omniscient narrator NEVER speaks colloquially. This is something it has taken me a long time to learn myself." (HB p. 295). Her most intriguing comment on omniscient point of view is a curt dismissal, near kin to Dr. Johnson's own treatment of free will, "Sir, we *know* our will is free, and there's an end on't."[5] In 1961 O'Connor wrote of "A Good Man Is Hard to Find": "...point of view never entered my head when I wrote that story. I just wrote it. It's all seen from the eye of the omniscient narrator and that's that. I never gave it a thought." (HB p. 426).

Point of view of all her stories could be dismissed with the same "that's that." All are told by a traditional all-knowing narrator, "that blend of bard, *histor*, and maker which characterizes the narrative voice in *War and Peace* and the similar voices of *Middlemarch*, *The Red and the Black*, *Vanity Fair* and *Tom Jones*."[6] This narrator is multifarious seeing from a variety of separable perspectives but resolving them into a single authoritative vision. Traditionally he can interpret and explain, delving into both head and heart of his characters; he can correct statements of fact, sometimes mockingly; knowing the future as well as the past and present, he can foreshadow and anticipate. O'Connor's narrators freely indulge these three privileges. First, instances of commentary on head and heart abound as when the narrator comments of Lucynell Crater: "She was ravenous for a son-in-law." (CS p. 150). Of Mrs. May: "She was a good Christian woman with a large respect for religion, though she did not, of course, believe any of it was true." (CS p. 316). Of Ruby Turpin: "There was no doubt in her mind that the girl did know her, knew her in some intense and personal way." (CS p. 500). Next, as for correcting statements of fact, if a character lies the narrator knowing like God the heart of man often reveals it, as when the grandmother tells of the secret panel "craftily, not telling the truth but wishing that she were." (CS p. 123). Of Mrs. Hopewell's alleged Bible by her bedside: "This was not the truth. It was in the attic somewhere." (CS p. 278). In such correcting the narrator often mocks the idiom of the speaker thus falling into the colloquial as when Manley Pointer says "his father had been crushed under a tree when he himself was eight year old.... He was now nineteen year old." (CS p. 280). In one case the narrator makes a pungent grammatical error precisely indicative of the speaker: "Above she and Claud were people with a lot of money." (CS p. 491). Finally, comically but grimly foreshadowing the future the narrator describes the grandmother's get-up: "In case of an accident, anyone seeing her dead on the highway would know at once that she was a lady." (CS p. 118).

So much then for the conventional privileges of a narrator who sees in all places at all times and who risks intrusiveness by authoritative commentary, brusque interposition, ironic foreshadowing. All this is merely technique and of this "merely" Wayne Booth comments: "It is a choice of the moral, not merely the technical, angle of vision from which the story is to be told."[7] Could there be even other choices, the metaphysical? It is the thesis of this essay that the striking and singular tonal effects of O'Connor's stories proceed from profounder implications and possibilities of ominiscient point of view which for the sake of order will now be set forth on three levels of meaning: the literal, tropological and anagogical.

Literally and to some extent allegorically, the voice of the narrator is that of the presenter, fabricator, creator, manipulator, revealer, exposer, arranger, joketeller, ironizer, perhaps even distorter. Typically it is a voice of ebullience and glee, heightened and delighted with its sudden access of glory in discovering, creating, revealing this microcosm of incongruity, inconsistency and discrepancy, tickled to see and speak double - the literal voice of the comic and ironic. In fact this voice may suggest from the dim glimmers of anthropology F.M. Cornford's *eiron*, the witty protagonist of Attic comedy who exposes and puts to rout the impostor. It is this tonality, this wicked delight in creating and discovering, in showing and telling the comic ugly which is the basis of John Hawkes' theory that O'Connor's fictional voice is the Devil (HB p. 464), which she admits is the case in "The Lame Shall Enter First."

The voice of the jokester is authoritative, dominating, and manipulative and is precisely defined in O'Connor's comments on Hulga Hopewell as projection of herself, Flannery O'Connor: "Hulga in this case would be a projection of myself...presumably only a projection, because if I could not stop short of it myself, I could not write it. Stop short or go beyond it, I should say. You have to be able to dominate the existence that you characterize." (HB p. 106). It is in the voice of the jokester that we hear distortion, such rearrangement of the usual as to seem unnatural but a necessary license for narrator and artist: "If we admit, as we must, that appearance is not the same thing as reality, then we must give the artist the liberty to make certain rearrangements of nature if these will lead to greater depths of vision." (MM p. 98). "I think I approve of distortion but not abstraction." (HB p. 115).The omniscient narrator as comic maker typically functions as a conscious ironist setting up characters to become victims of their own unconscious irony. Bailey says: "get this: this is the only time we're going to stop for anything like this. This is the one and only time." (CS p. 124). Mrs. May: "This is the last night I'm going to put up with this." (CS p. 329). Mary Fortune Pitts: "Nobody's ever beat me in my life and if anybody did, I'd kill him." (CS p. 340). "A Late Encounter with the Enemy" and "The Partridge Festival" are instances of the comic omniscient narrator in high spirits while "The Enduring Chill" is a relentless exercise in comic bathos in which the arch narrator reduces everything to the comic ridiculous; everything that sinks must also converge. The crowning achievement in this vein is "Good Country People," that lavish anecdote of how one arrogant intellectual loses her footing and having had her leg pulled by a wandering *eiron* sits finally in a pile of dusty straw recalling perhaps some famous death-bed words: "It's all straw." (HB p. 93). In fact Robert Giroux' suggestion that a new ending be written may have reminded our author that her narrator could have one more laugh, this time at Mrs. Hopewell's expense when in the onion field she judges Manley Pointer as simple: "but I guess the world would be better off if we were all that simple." (CS p. 291). I must confess that I've never quite believed O'Connor on the genesis and evolution of "Good Country People:" "When I started writing that story I didn't know there was going to be a Ph.D. with a wooden leg in it...As the story progressed, I brought in the Bible salesman, but I had no idea what I was going to do with him. I didn't know he was going to steal that wooden leg until ten or twelve lines before he did it." (MM p. 100).

In its second and tropological signification the omniscient narrator is the voice of a rational and moral norm, evaluator, appraiser, assessor, judge. It is here that the bludgeoning force of the grotesque is felt. In her essay "The Grotesque in Southern Fiction" O'Connor states:

It's considered an absolute necessity these days for writers to have compassion.... Usually I think what is meant by it is that the writer excuses all human weakness because human weakness is human. The kind of hazy compassion demanded of the writer now makes it difficult for him to be anti-anything. Certainly when the grotesque is used in a legitimate way, the intellectual and moral judgments implicit in it will have the ascendancy over feeling. (MM p. 43).

In an attack on André Gide she pronounces: "I believe that the writer's moral sense must coincide with his dramatic sense and this means that moral judgment has to be implicit in the act of vision." (HB p. 147). Since it is the narrator in a fictional microcosm who performs the act of vision, it is the narrator who is in the position of moral judgement. In O'Connor's fictions the narrator is shockingly hostile to the characters, a reaction verified by her dictum: "To be great storytellers, we need something to measure ourselves against." (MM p. 202). It is through the omniscient narrator that this alienation articulates itself in what amounts to a snipe attack, a moral hostility toward characters not unlike A.J.A. Waldock's description of Milton's technique of degradation of Satan: "a long line of automatic snubs, of perfunctory jabs and growls...the running fire of belittling commentary."[8] In O'Connor's fiction these snubs, jabs and growls veil themselves in the narrator's Olympian snobbery and pungent condescension as in this stunning instance of narrator *sang froid* toward Mr. Shiftlet:

"I'm a man," he said with sullen dignity, "even if I ain't a whole one. I got," he said, tapping his knuckles on the floor to emphasize the immensity of what he was going to say, "a moral intelligence!" and his face pierced out of the darkness into a shaft of doorlight and he stared at her as if he were astonished himself at this impossible truth. (CS p. 149).

The omniscient narrator's voice in its moral capacity is targeted at two accommodations of human weakness: one accommodation is a banal aggressive rationalizing and another is a fugitive regressive subjectivism. O'Connor's narrators contemptuously mock the rationalizing of a character; in the following three instances the narrator speaks in the third person. Mrs. McIntyre congratulates herself on her magnanimous treatment of Mr. Guizac: "She was sorry that the poor man had been chased out of Poland and run across Europe and had had to take up in a tenant shack in a strange country, but she had not been responsible for any of this. She had had a hard time herself. She knew what it was to struggle. People ought to have to struggle." (CS p. 219).

Sheppard complacently justifies his indulgent treatment of the delinquent Rufus Johnson and neglect of his own son Norton though the rationalizing is interrupted by his own voice saying "I have nothing to reproach myself with," thus emphasizing the narrator's account of the rationalizing: "His every action had been selfless, his own aim had been to save Johnson for some decent kind of service, he had not spared himself, he had sacrificed his reputation." (CS p. 481). Mark Fortune's pragmatic rationalizing on the advantages of selling the "lawn" to facilitate progress culminates in fatuous moralizing and foolish altruism:

They would not have to go any distance for gas. Anytime they needed a loaf of bread, all they would have to do would be step out their front door into Tilman's back door. They could sell milk to Tilman...Tilman would draw other business. The road would soon be paved. Travelers from all over the country would stop at Tilman's. If this daughter thought she was better than Tilman, it would be well to take her down a little. All men were created free and equal. When this phrase sounded in his head, his patriotic sense triumphed and he realized that it was his duty to sell the lot, that he must insure the future. (CS pp. 348-349).

What is insured is Mark Fortune's own damnation. It is a paradox that O'Connor's characters who most live inwardly in their private worlds of moral and emotional subjectivism are most savagely judged by the omniscient narrator. It is necessarily inside that moral judgment occurs, yet fugitive innerness is held in extreme judgment, at most in scathing contempt, at least in amused mockery and icy condescension. An instance is Mrs. Shortley. Though the peacock might have been a map of the universe for her, she didn't see it for she was having an inner vision instead. These fatuous inner visions culminate in an ultimate one of mayhem that shall befall the children of wicked nations:"Legs where arms should be, foot to face, ear in the palm of hand." (CS p. 210). The narrator judgmentally and ironically turns this against Mrs. Shortley in the comic scene of her death in her overfreighted leaking ark. Another example is Thomas in "The Comforts of Home" who hears voices especially that of his father: "The old man - small, wasp-like...appeared to have taken up his station in Thomas's mind and from there, usually squatting, he shot out the same rasping suggestion...." (CS p. 395).

Of all the stories which project the abuse of the inner moral faculty, contemptuously mocking both rationalizing and subjectivism, "Everything That Rises Must Converge" is the most insistent, and Julian, the central consciousness, is the most radical subjectivist to haunt O'Connor's pages:

Behind the newspaper Julian was withdrawing into the inner compartment of his mind where he spent most of his time. This was a kind of mental bubble in which he established himself when he could not bear to be a part of what was going on around him. From it he could see out and judge but in it he was safe from any kind of penetration from without. It was the only place where he felt free of the general idiocy of his fellows. His mother had never entered it but from it he could see her with absolute clarity. (CS p. 411).

In a narrative passage of extreme complexity the moral and rational and ironic voice of the narrator ironizes the irony of Julian:

The further irony of all this was that in spite of her, he had turned out so well. In spite of going to only a third-rate college, he had, on his own initiative, come out with a first-rate education; in spite of growing up dominated by a small mind, he had ended up with a large one; in spite of all her foolish views, he was free of prejudice and unafraid to face facts. Most miraculous of all, instead of being blinded by love for her as she was for him, he had cut himself emotionally free of her and could see her with complete objectivity. He was not dominated by his mother. (CS p. 412).

The moral judgment here of Julian is another instance of the narrator mocking the verbal idiom and hollow rationalizing of the comic victim, but here there is that added dimension of the moral, the wilful moral blindness and deafness of a character with eyes and ears but who sees and hears not, but lives only within.

I propose that this narrator voice of moral and rational norm is effectually a choral voice functioning precisely like the chorus in Greek tragedy: a voice of traditional moral and religious values which responds, reacts, comments, generalizes. abstracts, and warns but one that rises even higher. William Arrowsmith declares that "the normal mode of choral utterance is a characteristic group speech... rising from sheer banality to the apocalyptic gnomic richness"[9] of Aeschylus. It is here that we arrive at the ultimate deployment of the omniscient narrator; in its anagogical signification the voice is apocalyptic, that of the avenger, prophet, and perhaps oracle, the voice of the Terrible, of judgement, condemnation, destruction, doom; it is final, irrevocable, inexorable, eschatological, eternal. Before taking wing for this apotheosis, however, a note on multiple meanings is in order. The medieval notion of ascending multiple meanings has been presumed throughout this discussion. This presumption is solidly based, however, in O'Connor's own criticism as when she asserts the grandmother's gesture to be "on the anagogical level." (MM p.111). In "The Nature and Aim of Fiction" she describes the medieval exegetical technique as "the kind of vision that is able to see different levels of reality in one image or one situation." (MM p.72). For medieval readers there had been three levels of meaning implicit in the literal: "One they called allegorical, in which one fact pointed to another; one they called tropological, or moral, which had to do with what should be done; and one they called anagogical, which had to do with the Divine life and our participation in it." (MM p.72).

But to the anagogical signification of the omniscient narrator; it is the voice of the prophet. O'Connor has written feelingly of prophetic vision and the writer as prophet: "prophecy is a matter of seeing near things with their extensions of meaning and thus of seeing far things close up. The prophet is a realist of distances." (MM p.44). The prophetic vision is a quality of the imagination, not the moral life of the prophet, held St. Thomas Aquinas (*De Veritate*, vol. II), a notion cited by O'Connor in a letter of 1959 (HB p.365). The subject matter of prophecy is the Terrible, the other side of which coin is the Comic: "everything funny I have written is more terrible than it is funny, or only funny because it is terrible, or only terrible because it is funny." (HB p. 105). The tone of prophecy is oracular and the vision is apocalyptic, that is, of the nature of revelation or disclosure especially of violent upheaval.

Many of O'Connor's stories are apocalyptic. "The Enduring Chill" concludes with an implacable descent of the Holy Ghost, emblazoned in ice instead of fire. The Atlanta hoodlums dance as prophets in the circle in the fire cleared by the angel. Obadiah Elihu Parker sees a burning bush to which he responds "God above." There is a descent into a metropolitan hell in "The Artificial Nigger" while Mr. Shiftlet flees the crouching cyclone in "The Life You Save May Be Your Own." Could we include Mrs. May's goring dreams of penetration and Mark Fortune's hallucination of trees bathed in blood and his death vision of gaunt trees in dark files marching across the water? From its title through its last word "hallelujah" the story "Revelation" is O'Connor's largest apocalyptic canvas in which three episodes are both illuminating and ominous. There is the attack by Mary Grace upon Ruby Turpin with the big book; armed with the revelation "Go back to hell" Mary Grace sees with pleasure that her message has struck its target. Ruby has no doubt of the authenticity of the revelation or that the bearer of it "knew her in some intense and personal way, beyond time and place and condition." (CS p. 500). Then there is Ruby's violent colloquy with God at the pig parlor, a scene haunted by allusions to the sacrament of baptism and echoes of the exorcism of Legion of devils into a herd of swine. Finally there is the crowning vision of the procession to Heaven in which the first are last and Ruby "could see by their shocked and altered faces that even their virtues were being burned away." (CS p. 508).

In sum O'Connor's omniscient narrator voice, though not intrusive in the usual sense, is a complex aggregate: the comic and ironic voice of the *eiron*; the rational and moral voice of the chorus; the prophetic and apocalyptic voice of the oracle. These speak in turn of the comically distorted, the morally grotesque, and the mystically Terrible. The *eiron* creates; the chorus judges; and the oracle condemns, though sometimes it redeems. In plain words the voice is amused, engaged, and delighted; solid, stable, and reliable; arch, a little smug, perhaps a touch vindictive. To my ear the complex voice is incarnated in the witty but sardonic comment on the dedication of her first story collection to the Fitzgeralds: "Nine stories about original sin, with my compliments." (HB p. 74). Finally after a superficial ransacking of prose fiction searching for an analogue or comparable narrative voice, I found it in a poem, the voice of Jove in Swift's "The Day of Judgment":

> Offending Race of Human kind,
> By Nature, Reason, Learning blind;
> You who thro' frailty, step'd aside;
> And you who never fell- *thro' Pride?*
> You who in different sects, have shamm'd,
> And come to see each other damn'd...
> The World's mad business now is o'er,
> And I resent these Pranks no more,
> I to such Blockheads set my Wit!
> I damn such Fools! Go, go, you're bit.[10]

Notes

1. *The Republic, The Dialogues of Plato*, III, 398, trans. B. Jowett, New York, 1937).
2. "Introduction," *Henry James: Selected Fiction*, New York, 1953, p. xii.
3. *The Republic*, III, 394-397.
4. *Poetics*, xxiv, trans. Leon Golden, 1968, p. 44.
5. James Boswell, *The Life of Samuel Johnson*, Random House, 1952, p. 161.
6. Robert Scholes and Robert Kellogg, *The Nature of Narrative,* Oxford University Press, 1966, p. 272.
7. Wayne Booth, *The Rhetoric of Fiction*, Chicago, 1983, p. 265.
8. *Paradise Lost and Its Critics*, London 1947, p. 78, p.83.
9. *Princeton Encyclopedia of Poetry and Poetics*, 1965, p. 125.
10. *Gulliver's Travels and Other Writings*, ed. Ricardo Quintana, p. 543.

Narration and the Grotesque in Flannery O'Connor's Stories

Marshall Bruce Gentry

Most readings of Flannery O'Connor assume that the narrator of the typical story is O'Connor herself, authoritatively stating the truth about event and character. These readings also consider O'Connor's characters grotesque in an entirely negative sense; that is, the grotesquerie of characters is considered to reflect their separation from spiritual well-being. And it generally follows that when O'Connor characters achieve redemption, it results from grace that the characters have done all they can to avoid. While these predominant readings describe adequately a few works, most of O'Connor's works require different approaches to her narration and to her use of the grotesque. Only with a new look at these topics can we discover how her stories reinterpret and dramatize redemption. O'Connor's typical story sets up a battle between an authoritarian narrator and a character who sees the world grotesquely, a battle often won by the character's unconscious maneuvers for redemption.

Before illustrating what I think O'Connor makes of redemption, I would like to point out that a character whose experience fits the usual readings - the grandmother in "A Good Man Is Hard to Find" - also illustrates the necessity of a complex strategy in dramatizing the psychology of redemption. Apparently O'Connor felt that is what this story dramatizes; in *Mystery and Manners* she says to look for "the action of grace in the Grandmother's soul." (MM p.113). And it is tempting to say that when the grandmother acknowledges The Misfit as one of her children, she achieves a redemption of a traditional sort: a conscious acceptance of grace. The problem is that we cannot see inside the grandmother's mind. Insofar as the grandmother is conscious at the climax, her actions can be taken as attempts to subjugate The Misfit, to make him a weak, manipulable child like Bailey. The Misfit's reaction to the grandmother's assertion of kinship - shooting her - is partly a response to his feeling that the grandmother attempts to dominate him.

Our doubt about the grandmother's redemption indicates the need for a strategy to give clues about the character's psyche so that redemption becomes believable. O'Connor found two such strategies, one more powerful than the other. The lesser strategy is to use completely innocent characters such as Harry-Bevel Ashfield in "The River." We believe in Harry's redemption, if we do, because his life prior to redemption is a vacuum; he grasps religion unhesitatingly once it enters his simple mind. The more intriguing strategy for dramatizing redemption involves more sophisticated and corrupt characters. In this strategy, O'Connor gave the grotesque a deeply psychological dimension, thus transforming an obstacle to redemption into a means of redemption.

I need now to explain two ideas basic to my reading of O'Connor: how the grotesque becomes positive, and how characters become more than the corrupt figures the typical O'Connor narrator makes of them. The term "grotesque" generally refers to images of degraded physicality with an effect at once humorous and disturbing. The notion of degradation, of descent from a higher to a lower grade, is important to the term; the grotesque always depends upon an attraction to the ideals from which the grotesque declines. Although it may seem that grotesquerie is primarily a state of being - as with the hermaphrodite in "A Temple of the Holy Ghost" - such physical abnormality is less important to this paper than the use of the grotesque as a mode of representation and its use as a mode of perception. These two forms are most commonly found in the actions, respectively, of the narrators (who create comparisons to represent characters as degraded) and of the characters (who often perceive themselves or the world around them as degraded). The most common critical attitude to the grotesque is in line with the narrators' use of it to express negative judgments, to reveal the characters' fallen state from which they seem incapable of rising. When the characters use the grotesque, however, it can become positive.

The primary critic who argues that the grotesquerie of a character can have positive qualities is Mikhail Bakhtin, who says the grotesque degrades abstract ideals to a physical level, thus producing a "regenerating ambivalence" that leads to a sense of communal wholeness and to rebirth.[1] Bakhtin challenges the negative version of the grotesque, described by Wolfgang Kayser, who says the grotesque "instills fear of life" by producing an "awareness that the familiar and apparently harmonious world is alienated under the impact of abysmal forces."[2] Bakhtin's explanation for the difference between his theory and Kayser's is that Kayser explains only "Romantic and modernist forms," while Bakhtin accounts for "the archaic and antique grotesque...and the medieval and Renaissance grotesque, linked to the culture of folk humor."[3] My claims about O'Connor's grotesque, of course, call into question Bakhtin's restriction of the positive grotesque to early literature and folklore; although one might agree that the positive grotesque has been almost dead for well over a century, O'Connor revives it.

It may seem that the grotesque cannot become positive so long as O'Connor's narrators are in control. Her narrators use the techniques at the disposal of any narrator - structuring the story to provide emphasis, describing setting, character, action, etc. - in a manner emphasizing the characters' wrongheadedness, which can only be transformed by the intervention of an outside force, presumably grace. The typical O'Connor narrator is so strict and authoritarian as to seem puritanical. Many O'Connor characters, however, refuse to remain merely isolated individuals incapable of acting to bring about redemption. Rather than accepting O'Connor's stories as rigid works in which narrative authority is clear, I suggest we give more importance to individual characters' world-views and discover the ways in which those views rival the narrators' for authority. What I have in mind is Bakhtin's model of the novelistic literary text as a battleground, where characters fight the authoritarian narrator's rigid standards. In such a model, the narrator's voice becomes one voice in a shouting match. The more authoritarian and infallible the narration presents itself as, the more conspicuous the narrator's incompletions, failures, and distortions appear.[4] To illustrate how O'Connor characters use the grotesque to rival the narrators and to bring about redemption, I shall examine two characters: Mrs. Turpin in "Revelation," and Hulga/Joy Hopewell in "Good Country People." Both these characters escape the role assigned to them by the narrators and unconsciously prepare for their redemptive entrance into a bodily community. After explaining my view of how these two characters work, I shall summarize the particulars of O'Connor's version of redemption.

Mrs. Turpin in "Revelation" manages to experience a revelation that also suggests, somewhat paradoxically, physical annihilation. The precise significance of her vision of hordes on a fiery bridge, consequently, is not altogether a matter of agreement. Most critics feel that the vision shows Mrs. Turpin following her social inferiors on the way to heaven, but some critics see her on her way to hell.[5] Perhaps one reason for the uncertainty is that if Mrs. Turpin is responsible for her vision, we are inclined to say that her vision must be corrupt, that only a revelation entirely supernatural in origin can be genuine. The narrator, of course, encourages such an inclination by ridiculing Mrs. Turpin, but I believe Mrs. Turpin is herself responsible for a genuine, redemptive revelation.

To see how Mrs. Turpin brings about her transformation, we must examine her psyche before Mary Grace's attack appears to begin Mrs. Turpin's awakening. Such an examination shows Mrs. Turpin to desire her own demotion in the chain of being and to have practiced bringing it about. One of Mrs. Turpin's nighttime fantasies, even as it shows her bigotry and self-righteousness, comes to a conclusion in which she is demoted. As she names the hierarchy of social classes - an abstracted version of the ideal community - she also disrupts the hierarchy:

...the complexity of it would begin to bear in on her, for some of the people with a lot [of] money were common and ought to be below she and Claud and some of the people who had good blood had lost their money and had to rent and then there were colored people who owned their homes and land as well. There was a colored dentist in town who had two red Lincolns and a swimming pool and a farm with registered white-face cattle on it. Usually by the time she had fallen asleep all the classes of people were moiling and roiling around in her head, and she would dream they were all crammed in together in a box car, being ridden off to be put in a gas oven. (CS pp.491-492).[6]

Many readers assume that Mrs. Turpin wants this fantasy to establish a stable hierarchy but that reality intrudes on her; the stability of Mrs. Turpin's other ridiculous fantasy denies this explanation, however. In the other fantasy, Jesus tells her she must be "a nigger or white-trash," and Mrs. Turpin brings the fantasy to a neat conclusion: "finally she would have said, 'All right, make me a nigger then - but that don't mean a trashy one.' And he would have made her a neat clean respectable Negro woman, herself but black." (CS p.491). When Mrs. Turpin imagines herself on the way to physical annihilation, the most reasonable conclusion is that Mrs.Turpin's hierarchy collapses because she desires the collapse. Her oven fantasy transforms her banal prejudices about class and race into a force for redemptive reentry into the communal body. It is interesting that even before Mrs. Turpin's hierarchy collapses, she refers to the people she is categorizing as a "heap," a word which implies that collapse is inherent in the process of categorization. Consequently, when Mrs. Turpin enters the doctor's office and, carefully noting everyone's shoes, begins building the hierarchy, she must know the result of such hierarchical ordering. And her thoughts and actions in the waiting room do reveal an unconscious desire for disruption.

One violation of the class hierarchy is Mrs. Turpin's agreement with a gospel hymn on the radio. When she hears the hymn "When I looked up and He looked down," her mind supplies the last line: "And wona these days I know I'll we-eara crown." (CS p.490). In this particular instance Mrs. Turpin imagines that a disruption of the usual hierarchy of classes would move her up, but in her handling of Mary Grace, Mrs. Turpin works to move herself down. When she first notices Mary Grace reading, Mrs. Turpin thinks that Mary Grace is "annoyed that anyone should speak while she tried to read." (CS p.490). The next thing Mrs. Turpin says - "That's a beautiful clock" (CS p.492) - seems intended merely to upset Mary Grace. As the conversation strays on, Mrs. Turpin projects her own destructiveness onto the girl. One indication that Mrs. Turpin invests Mary Grace with importance is the description of Mary Grace's eyes as "lit all of a sudden with a peculiar light, an unnatural light like night road signs give." (CS p.492). These words clearly are from Mrs. Turpin's perspective, since they follow a sentence expressing a thought which only Mrs. Turpin can have, that Mary Grace "looked straight in front of her, directly through Mrs. Turpin and on through the yellow curtain and the plate glass window which made the wall behind her." (CS p.492). The wording is the narrator's, but the thought is Mrs. Turpin's, for she "turned her head to see if there was anything going on outside that she should see." (CS p.493). The comparison of the light in Mary Grace's eyes to the light of road signs, consequently, suggests that what Mrs. Turpin sees is a reflection of her own metaphorical headlights. A related projection of Mrs. Turpin's thoughts occurs as Mary Grace makes an ugly face. Mrs. Turpin feels certain that the girl had "known and disliked her all her life - all of Mrs. Turpin's life, it seemed too, not just all the girl's life." (CS p.495).

When Mary Grace does become destructive, Mrs. Turpin is immediately convinced that the girl should be heeded. Mrs. Turpin even makes an extra effort to ask the disturbed, partially sedated girl for a message. And when she receives that absurd message - "Go back to hell where you came from, you old wart hog" (CS p.500) - she decides it contains the truth about her. Mrs. Turpin's awed response to the girl's attack is not an involuntary one. The white-trash woman personally insults Mrs. Turpin almost as nastily as Mary Grace insults her, but Mrs. Turpin is able to dismiss the white-trash woman's insult simply by "considering where it came from." (CS p.496). Thus Mrs. Turpin should easily be able to dismiss Mary Grace's attack. Mary Grace may appear to be of a higher class than the white-trash woman - and therefore a greater threat - but Mrs. Turpin has demoted the ugly girl by revising the fantastic offer from Jesus into "All right, you can be white-trash or a nigger or ugly." (CS p.492). Her fascination with the destructive Mary Grace comes from Mrs. Turpin's ability to imagine in her the disruptions of hierarchy that she desires. When she receives the curse from Mary Grace, she becomes totally serious, and she spends the rest of the story bringing up to consciousness the revelation she has prepared.

Her conscious protests at home confirm her real convictions: "'I am not,' she said tearfully, 'a wart hog. From hell.' But the denial had no force." (CS p.502). Only after she has returned home does it occur to her that there were others in the waiting room who might also deserve condemnation. (CS p.502). For confirmation of the truth of Mary Grace's accusation, she uses the black workers on the farm to offer the sort of rejection of the girl's message that will make Mrs. Turpin certain of the accusation's validity. As she gives water to the black workers, Mrs. Turpin knows that they will flatter and defend her excessively, responding with praise that Mrs. Turpin herself will reject: "Mrs. Turpin knew exactly how much Negro flattery was worth and it added to her rage." (CS p.505). After talking to the workers, Mrs. Turpin is ready at last to defeat her conscious mind.

David Eggenschwiler says that when she goes to the pig pen, Mrs. Turpin must "confront a Jesus who is more than a reassuring echo of her self-righteousness."[7] She gets more than trivial reassurance, but she does indeed hear an echo; when she asks God, "Who do you think you are?" (CS p.507), her question "returned to her clearly like an answer from beyond the wood." (CS p.508). That Mrs. Turpin controls her awakening is also suggested by the fact that she reinterprets Mary Grace's accusation. She does not merely ask how she is like a hog, but asks, "How am I a hog and me both? How am I saved and from hell too?" (CS p.506). Mary Grace's charge suggests a grotesque process of degradation and redemption, but it needs Mrs. Turpin's adjustment. Mrs. Turpin is like a hog, and she is going back where she came from, but her real origin, Mrs. Turpin senses, is the communal body, and her residence in hell is a stopover on her path back to heaven. Thus Mrs. Turpin achieves redemption in two related ways: she escapes the limited self that the narrator ascribes to her, and she disrupts the hierarchy that separates her from the physical community.

This essay is too short to demonstrate that many other O'Connor characters complete grotesque processes ending in a form of redemption in which the character is freed from a narrator's constraints. I want now to suggest that many characters who do *not* complete their redemption also use the grotesque as a means of working toward redemption. I shall use Hulga/Joy Hopewell as an illustration.[8] Several critics of "Good Country People" take the ending as an indication that Hulga is despicable, and some critics condemn the entire world of the story.[9] The narrator of the story is certainly a demon of consistent moralism who reduces Mrs. Freeman to a truck in the opening paragraph and who seems to delight in Hulga's embarrassment. The narrator does not lead us to consider the possibility that I believe is crucial to the story: that Hulga desires her betrayal by the Bible salesman and the redemption it could bring. The key to understanding Hulga's plan for enlightening herself is her choice of the name "Hulga." While she consciously believes the name is appropriate because it reminds her of Vulcan's powers, on a deeper level the name sets a trap. When Hulga explains the appropriateness of the association with Vulcan, she thinks of him as one "to whom, presumably, the goddess had to come when called." (CS p.275). The important word is "presumably," a word that hides and reveals a slip in Hulga's thought with which she will trap herself. The notion of a goddess having to come when summoned refers to the myth of Hephaistos/Vulcan and Aphrodite; although they were married, Aphrodite repeatedly deceived her husband with Ares. The goddess "presumably" had to come to her husband, but, as Hulga knows, Aphrodite often did not.

The myth on which Hulga bases her choice of her grotesque name itself illustrates the necessary connection between the grotesque and the ideal. In Book Eight of the *Odyssey*, a singer tells about Hephaistos/Vulcan's use of a fine net to capture his adulterous wife with Ares. He leaves the couple trapped in the net until the gods arrive to see the captured lovers. Mixed with the viewers' laughter and condemnation is a considerable portion of desire, however; Apollo and Hermes agree that they would like to be caught in bed with Aphrodite.[10] The entire story is relevant to Hulga's choice of her name, I believe; the trap that Hulga sets for herself could lead to such an enviable capture. In her relationship with Manley Pointer, Hulga plays two roles: consciously she is Vulcan, and unconsciously she is the captured Aphrodite. Hulga is victimizer and willing victim.

The value to Hulga in making herself grotesque through a name change is that the grotesque process can produce a return to the ideal, in this instance the bodily community of physical beings like Mrs. Freeman's daughters. Hulga's shock at Manley Pointer's actions at the end may indicate that she is unaware of what she has done, but unconsciously she expects that in the barn she will become Joy as goddess. One obstacle to the notion that Hulga controls her own capture is the reader's sense that the characters in this story are quite different from one another and that Hulga does not understand the others well enough to control anything about them. A set of puns, however, encourages us to investigate the possibility that beneath superficial differences, they are members of a community. The key term for these puns is the name of the philosopher that Hulga quotes approvingly - Malebranche.[11] Hulga's wooden leg is a "mal-branch" or bad limb, the addition of which seems to make her "male." Manley Pointer's name suggests a phallus, a "male branch." Mrs.

Freeman's name connects with the notion of detachableness in Hulga's bad limb as well as containing the word "man." Even Mrs. Hopewell is involved in the wordplay when Manley mistakenly calls her by a name suggesting wood - Mrs. Cedars.

These connections suggest that the story's characters have much in common. The most important similarity for Hulga's purposes is that between Manley Pointer and Mrs. Freeman, both of whom are fascinated by her artificial leg and the grotesque. If Hulga sees the similarity, she should have some idea of what will happen in the hayloft. Hulga seems slow to make the connection, but she does see the similarity among the other characters as they trade trite expressions, and I think that the most significant quality that the characters share, and that Hulga must tap, is banality. Here as in "Revelation," banality expresses radical ideas with a cloak of conventionality; the literal meaning of a cliché always threatens to break through the conventional meaning. More generally, the mind frame necessary for operating on a level of cliché implies that everything which can be known is already known. The idea that new knowledge is impossible implies that the most profound insights are always present in some form before the events in which they reach consciousness. And to some extent, Hulga does succeed in tapping her group's well of banality. In remaining conscious only of trite reasons for naming herself Hulga, she allows her unconscious to use the profound implications of the myth she associates with that name.

Despite all of these connections and Hulga's opportunities to transform herself, it is difficult to see a successful transformation in Hulga's "churning face" at the end. (CS p.291). Some critics see conversion as the step following Hulga's fall, but I am inclined to agree with Louise Westling that in this story, the handling of the sexual issues ultimately conflicts with such an interpretation.[12] Whatever freedom Hulga achieves from the narrator's constraint is limited by her failure to recover an ideal. Perhaps the problem is that her goal of goddess retains the notion that she is superior to her community. Nevertheless, the numerous similarities between the unconscious maneuvers of Hulga and Mrs. Turpin suggest that most characters in O'Connor's works are on a grotesque, unconscious path toward redemption.

My use of the word "redemption" in this essay may seem peculiar, but I think O'Connor reinterprets - even redeems - the concept. *The Catholic Encyclopedia* defines redemption as "the restoration of man from the bondage of sin to the liberty of the children of God through the satisfactions and merits of Christ."[13] In the traditional definition, redemption is a natural conclusion to a process, redemption is experienced consciously by the individual, and redemption results primarily from the actions of Christ and of grace - the individual's role being one merely of cooperation. Most of the time, however, redemption in O'Connor's works seems untraditional. O'Connor's redemptions are most often momentary states in a process that has no natural end, the consciousness of the individual is nearly irrelevant to redemption,[14] and redemption results primarily from the workings of the individual's unconscious. What is traditional about the redemptions in O'Connor is that they involve the discovery of freedom in the communal ("the liberty of the children of God"). Although many O'Connor characters seem to achieve ideals only through submission, their achievement of these ideals actually involves, paradoxically, the attainment of freedom. They free themselves from the narrator's puritanical restriction of them, and as they give up their restricted selfhood, they join the body of the redeemed community.

The readings I have presented here suggest a new explanation of how O'Connor is a Catholic writer. In focussing on her characters' works that bring about their redemptive return to a community, O'Connor brings her fiction toward the Catholic art she said it was. Although the O'Connor narrator is puritanical, although most of her characters are Protestant, and although there is an apparently Protestant emphasis on private religious experience in O'Connor's works, the characters' Protestantism and even Hulga's atheism ultimately function as grotesquely enlivening forms of Catholicism. The majority of her characters lead themselves toward a Catholic sense of the communal body, and part of the message of O'Connor's art is that the most extremely individualistic religious experience can bring humans back to Catholicism. Another implication of this essay is that a psychological approach to O'Connor's works is compatible with a theological one. O'Connor contrasted her religious explanations of behavior to psychological ones, but I think that psychology in O'Connor's works exists in a grotesque relationship to dogma. As characters live out their religious conflicts, they produce through personal psychology enlivened forms of religious formulae.

Notes

1 *Rabelais and His World*, trans. Helene Iswolsky (Cambridge, Mass., 1968), pp.20-21.
2 *The Grotesque in Art and Literature*, trans. Ulrich Weisstein (1963; rpt. Gloucester, Mass., 1968), p.185, p.37.
3 *Rabelais and His World*, p.46.

4 See Bakhtin's "Discourse in the Novel," in *The Dialogic Imagination: Four Essays*, ed. Michael Holquist, trans. Caryl Emerson and Michael Holquist (Austin, Texas, 1981), pp.259-422. I consider Bakhtin's theory of the novelistic text applicable to more literature than he says; in this regard, see Roger Fowler's "Anti-Language in Fiction," *Style*, 13 (1979), 259-78.

5 In his *Flannery O'Connor* (Minneapolis, Minnesota, 1966), p.36, Stanley Edgar Hyman says that the final vision is one of "hellfire" and that Mrs. Turpin "seems destined for hell." Samuel Irving Bellman argues in "The Apocalypse in Literature," *Costerus*, 7 (1973), 17, that the final vision shows Mrs. Turpin that she is "NOT among the Elect."

6 The inserted word, omitted in *The Complete Stories*, is from the text in *Everything That Rises Must Converge* (New York, 1965), p.196.

7 *The Christian Humanism of Flannery O'Connor* (Detroit, Michigan, 1972), p.44.

8 Characters similar to Mrs. Turpin include Mrs. Cope, Mrs. Shortley, the child in "A Temple of the Holy Ghost," Mrs. May, Asbury Fox, Calhoun, and several characters from the novels. Characters I consider similar to Hulga/Joy Hopewell include The Misfit, Mr. Shiftlet, Mrs. McIntyre, Mr. Fortune, and Thomas.

9 Carol Shloss, in *Flannery O'Connor's Dark Comedies: The Limits of Inference* (Baton Rouge, Louisiana, 1980), p.47, says that the story is unchristian: "The grounds for construing a specifically Christian idea of 'the whole man' are not adequately developed." Constance Pierce says in "The Mechanical World of 'Good Country People'," *The Flannery O'Connor Bulletin*, 5 (1976), 30, that all the characters have "a mechanistic way of dealing with the world, a façade that covers their underlying 'neutrality', or 'nothingness'."

10 See Robert Fitzgerald's translation of the *Odyssey* (Garden City, N.Y., 1963), pp.132-136. Anneliese H. Smith, in "O'Connor's 'Good Country People'," *Explicator*, 33 (1974), item 30, uses Vulcan's failures to argue that Hulga's "understanding is deficient." Smith asks, "When in classical mythology was Vulcan ever successful as an autonomous figure?" I would argue that Hulga knows Vulcan is sure to fail.

11 "Malebranche" is also the name of the demons in Circle VIII, Bouge V of the *Inferno* (Cantos XXI and XXII). In Canto XXII the Malebranche try to tear the limbs off a Barrator, but the story ends in a reversal that suggests a connection to O'Connor's story. The Barrator tricks the demons, and, as he escapes, makes the demons fall into a stream of pitch.

12 "Flannery O'Connor's Mothers and Daughters," *Twentieth Century Literature*, 24 (1978), 519-520; compare Westling's *Sacred Groves and Ravaged Gardens: The Fiction of Eudora Welty, Carson McCullers, and Flannery O'Connor* (Athens, Georgia, 1985), pp. 149-153.

13 J.F. Sollier, "Redemption," *The Catholic Encyclopedia* (New York, 1913-14), XII, 677.

14 Mrs. Turpin may seem fully conscious of her redemption. She does, after all, hear joyous sounds from the saved even after her vision fades. She remains unconscious, however, of the sense in which her redemption lies in her freedom from the narrator's version of her individuality. Mrs. Turpin's experience after the story ends surely involves a fall from her moment of redemption as consciousness regains control.

Image Maker

Comic Imagery in the Fiction of Flannery O'Connor

Sheldon Currie

Henry Bergson in his precise essay, "Laughter,"[1] reduces the comic to four essential characteristics: it is exclusively human, purely intellectual in that it requires absence of feeling, socially significant or corrective, and is the result of something mechanical encrusted on the living: we laugh when a person gives the impression of being a thing. Reading Flannery O'Connor after Bergson a reader might suspect she had set out in her fiction to illustrate his theory of the comic. In "The Life You Save May Be Your Own," Mr. Shiftlet proclaims himself endowed "with a moral intelligence": he has meditated on the mystery of life and the potential of the human spirit. "Lady," he tells Mrs. Crater, "a man is divided into two parts, body and spirit.... The body, lady, is like a house: it don't go anywhere; but the spirit, lady, is like a automobile: always on the move, always, .." (CS p. 152). Mr. Shiftlet is practical as well and can fix a roof, build a hog pen, restore a fence and teach a deaf and dumb girl to speak, so Mrs. Crater negotiates a marriage between Shiftlet and her daughter, Lucynell: he gets the girl and the car in return for looking after the farm. It is the car he wants. He loves it and sleeps in it during his short courtship.

'I told you you could hang around and work for food,' she tells him, 'if you don't mind sleeping in that car yonder'. 'Why listen, lady...the monks of old slept in their coffins!' (CS p.149).

Mr. Shiftlet's moral intelligence does not keep him from deserting his wife in a roadside café. The car becomes his moral coffin. The warning sign beside the highway, "The Life You Save May Be Your Own," mocks Mr. Shiftlet for his missed opportunity, and the imagery in the final paragraph shows his hypocrisy.

'Oh, Lord!' he prayed. 'Break forth and wash the slime from this earth!'...there was a guffawing peal of thunder from behind and fantastic raindrops, like tin-can tops, crashed over the rear of Mr. Shiftlet's car. Very quickly he stepped on the gas and...raced the galloping shower into Mobile. (CS p. 156).

The Lord broke forth, as requested, but Mr. Shiftlet was protected from the cleansing raindrops by his car, that moving spirit for which he had traded his soul. No wonder God laughed. Car imagery, whereby, in Bergson's terms, "something mechanical is encrusted on the living," and "a person gives us the impression of being a thing," is also used to describe Mrs. Freeman in "Good Country People":"Besides the neutral expression that she wore when she was alone, Mrs. Freeman had two others, forward and reverse..." (CS p. 271) and the main character in this story, Joy, renamed Hulga, meaning ugly hulk, presumably, is "encrusted" by the mechanical in a fundamental way because she has become a thing. She stalks around her mother's house, pounding her wooden leg into the floor, defiant, hostile, and full of pride; she has "the look of someone who has achieved blindness by an act of will and means to keep it," (CS p.273) a woman who "looked at nice young men as if she could smell their stupidity;" (CS p. 276) she considers herself superior; she has a Ph.D; she is in love with her wooden leg. A wooden leg is not comic, but a wooden soul is. A wooden leg makes a person "walk funny" because he appears to be a puppet, a robot, a mechanical thing, whereas we know the person, by definition, to be a spirit. Henri Bergson explains:

To sum up...our imagination...in every human form...sees the effort of a soul...shaping matter, a soul...infinitely supple and perpetually in motion, subject to-no law of gravitation.... This soul imparts...its winged lightness to the body it animates: the immateriality which thus passes into matter is what is called gracefulness. Matter, however, is obstinate and resists. It draws to itself the ever-alert activity of this higher principle, would fain convert it to its own inertia and cause it to revert to mere automatism. It would fain immobilise the intelligently varied movements of the body in stupidly contracted grooves, stereotype in permanent grimaces the fleeting expressions of the face, in short imprint on the whole person such an attitude as to make it appear immersed and absorbed in the materiality of some mechanical occupation instead of ceaselessly renewing its vitality by keeping in touch with a living ideal. Where matter thus succeeds in dulling the outward life of the soul, in petrifying its movements and thwarting its gracefulness, it achieves, at the expense of a body, an effect that is comic. [2]

The makers of wooden legs do their best to keep their products from appearing "immersed and absorbed in the materiality of some mechanical occupation," and usually their clients cooperate and dress them up and direct them to appear to be vital and animated adjuncts of a spirited person, and we who watch hope the partnership succeeds, so we won't be tempted to entertain uncharitable thoughts, and perhaps even snigger behind our hands. Hulga, however, does not cooperate. Watching her graceless stomp, the maker of her leg would think himself a clumsy failure. Hulga is far from trying to incorporate her leg, to spiritualize it, to make it a vital and animated adjunct. She herself becomes the adjunct, and the leg becomes her center and she its satellite, like Mr. Shiftlet who, instead of making the car a part of his life, becomes part of the life of the car, which runs off with him to Mobile. "...she was as sensitive about the artificial leg as a peacock about his tail." (CS p. 288). In the outrageously comic seduction scene the truth about Hulga's condition becomes abundantly clear. She sits with Manley Pointer in a hayloft. Between them are a pint of whiskey and a package of condoms hidden in a box disguised as a Bible: He leaned over and put his lips to her ear.

'Show me where your wooden leg joins on,' he whispered. The girl uttered a sharp little cry and her face instantly drained of color.... 'No,' she said.'I known it,' he muttered sitting up. 'You're just playing me for a sucker.' 'Oh no no!' she cried. 'It joins on at the knee. Only at the knee. Why do you want to see it?' The boy gave her a long penetrating look. 'Because,' he said, 'it's what makes you different. You ain't like anybody else.' ...This boy, with an instinct that came from beyond wisdom, had touched the truth about her. When after a minute, she said in a hoarse voice, 'All right,' it was like surrendering to him completely. It was like losing her own life and finding it again, miraculously, in his. (CS pp. 288-289).

There is a struggle then for control of the leg and O'Connor shows that the struggle is not simply for a limb, but for something fundamental to Hulga's being. "She gave a little cry of alarm but he pushed her down and began to kiss her again. Without the leg she felt entirely dependent on him. Her brain seemed to have stopped thinking altogether and to be about some other function that it was not very good at." (CS p. 289).O'Connor's short stories are full of characters like Hulga and Shiftlet who have not developed into the animated beings nature intended. The relationship between body and soul is defective; the body is not, as it should be, the satellite of the soul; so the person appears not as a body animated by spirit, but rather as spirit trying, unsuccessfully, to overcome the animal, vegetable or mechanical aspects of its nature. O'Connor sees the human as a defeated spirit, dominated either by the mind or by the body; that is, by being too much like the angels whose mental nature man shares, or by being too much like the animals whose corporeal nature he shares. The difference between humans and angels, in the Christian view, is simple, and the inverse of the difference between humans and beasts. Humans, like angels, are spirits, and humans, like beasts, are animals. Heart and head, body and mind, instinct and reason, are the two great spheres of human being and activity. Angels don't have to brush their teeth because they don't have any; animals have them but don't have to think about them. Only humans both have teeth and must consciously decide to look after them. Consider the following conversation: Brush your teeth! No! Brush your teeth! No! Brush your teeth or they'll rot and fall out! I don't care. Neither Fido nor Gabriel is up to such conversation, and the idea of replacing rotten teeth or missing legs with imitations would never occur to either. If it did they would be amused, but neither angels nor dogs are ever amused. Hulga and Shiftlet are ludicrous figures because something is profoundly wrong; they have willingly abandoned what makes them human. One way to express their problem is to say they have become things, another way to express it is to say they have abandoned their animality; they are no longer social, no longer involved in the network of relationships we call society, but rather have stepped beside it, are alone, cold, intellectual observers. In effect they have become disincarnate, existing as minds rather than bodies, and have become part of the technology they admire, no longer animated, but woodenized and metallized.

Flannery O'Connor's novel *Wise Blood* is rich in images that lead us to an understanding of two comic characters, Hazel Motes and Enoch Emery, each in a different way a deficient person, and by his deficiency showing what a complete human being should be. Hazel Motes has in common with Shiftlet his affinity for the automobile, in which he attempts to escape his destiny, and he has in common with Hulga her cold, rational, intellectual nature. Motes lacks animality, is as nearly disincarnate as a human can be. He has no use for food, sex, sleep, death, birth, or any of the animal events in human life or for any of the rituals or ceremonies that go with them. His body appears as an awkward mechanism. When we first meet him "He looked as if he were held by a rope caught in the middle of his back and attached to the train ceiling." (WB p. 12). After his sexual encounter with Leora Watts, the author comments: "When he finished, he was like something washed ashore on her," (WB p. 59) a piece of driftwood, a man made of wood. The imagery consistently characterizes Motes as wooden, metallic, angular, awkward, cold-blooded, humorless, mechanical. There is little or none of the beast in Hazel Motes; even his sexual life is cerebral and not encouraged by animal instinct. When he is in the room with the prostitute, Leora Watts, the author describes him this way: "His throat got dryer and his heart began to grip him like a little ape clutching the bars of its cage." (WB p. 60). His little beast, his heart, is safely locked up in jail and his sexual activity is asensual and has one purpose - to prove that he does not believe in God. And his behavior shows the same kind of man as the imagery. His relationships with Sabbath Hawkes and Enoch Emery, who would like to be his friends, are without tenderness, and his way of dealing with his competitor, Solace Layfield, was simple; he deliberately ran him down and then backed over him. And when the poor man tried to make a last minute confession, Motes told him to shut up. His first deliberate act in town was to find a woman, but like Hulga in "Good Country People" he had no interest in sex for itself, he simply wanted to prove there was no such thing as sin, and that it is silly to believe in Christ, a Savior, and therefore, nonsense to think he had a preaching vocation. He preached the Church without Christ, that is, without the sacrifice of blood, and hoped by indulging himself in sensuality to forget what was in the back of his mind. But in spite of Leora Watts' best efforts he was unsatisfied, and rose in the morning from his bed with "only one thought in his mind: he was going to buy a car. The thought was full grown in his head when he woke up;" (WB p. 67) where sex failed, technology might succeed. "Nobody with a good car needs to be justified," (WB p. 113) he said. But he didn't find riding cars a sufficient distraction either; technology, the machine, failed him. His car is later destroyed by a highway patrolman and Hazel Motes walks back to town and his tragic death.

Hazel Motes is disincarnate; O'Connor describes him as an angel: "He pushed through them with his elbows out like sharp wings." (WB p. 54). Enoch Emery, on the other hand, is all carnation. Hazel is bloodless; Enoch is all blood, and his talent, his genius, his wisdom, limited as it is, is in his blood, his heart, whereas Hazel's wisdom is in his head. Hazel is all mind, Enoch all body; Hazel is all reason, Enoch all instinct, one is spirit, the other body. ("His blood was more sensitive than any other part of him." (WB p. 129)). What Hazel disdains, Enoch revels in: food, sex, sleep, all the animal events in human life, and the rituals and ceremonies that go with them. And his actions are automatic, unsupervised by intellectual discretion. "...[Enoch] didn't think, he only wondered, then before long he would find himself doing this or that, like a bird finds itself building a nest..." (WB p. 129). Only infrequently does Hazel Motes appear as an animal and when he does he resembles a lone eagle or a lofty hawk, but Enoch always appears or behaves like an animal with four legs very attached to the earth. Once he appears as a horse but usually we find him in the guise of the less noble dog. "He looked like a friendly hound dog with light mange," (WB pp. 43-44) and although Enoch is hungry for society,.and craves friendly relationships, his attempts to communicate lead him into confrontations resembling dog fights.

A little man...jostled him, 'Whyn't you look wher you going?' Enoch growled.The little man stopped and raised his arm in a vicious gesture and a nasty-dog look came on his face. 'Who you tellin' what?' he snarled. 'You see,' Enoch said, jumping to catch up with Haze, 'all they want to do is knock you down. I ain't never been to such a unfriendly place before.' (WB pp. 46-47).

If images reflect an author's opinion about characters Flannery O'Connor leaves no doubt about what she thinks of Enoch Emery. She presents him near the swimming pool hiding in the bushes, spying on a young woman who is diving and swimming. "...he appeared on all fours at the end of the abelia and looked across the pool." (WB p. 84). And just before this incident Enoch himself comments: "Well, I'll be dog.... Well, I'll be dog...." (WB p. 83). The object of Enoch's affection is also presented as an animal:

The woman was climbing out of the pool chinning herself up on the side...sharp teeth protruding from her mouth. Then she rose on her hands until a large foot and leg came up from behind her and another on the other side and she was out squatting there, panting. She stood up loosely and shook herself, and stamped in the water dripping off her...she padded over to a spot of sun. (WB p. 85).

Shortly after the pool incident Enoch and Hazel stopped by the bear cage where "Two black bears sat...facing each other like two matrons having tea, their faces polite and self-absorbed. 'They don't do nothing but sit there all day and stink,' Enoch said," (enviously). (WB p. 93). Earlier he had looked in awe and hate at the caged animals being fed T-bone steaks. The woman who absorbs Enoch's attention is presented as an animal, and his animals are presented as women. It is not only that these animals have servants and eat well that excites Enoch's envy, but that they sit like matrons having tea, that is, they have a settled, social, civilized, ritualistic life that he longs for. It is a longing lost on Hazel Motes, the rationalist who seeks only truth. For him truth is the only good; ceremony and ritual are mere packages for goods that don't interest him, (birth, food, sex, death) and are best left to dogs and bears and the likes of Enoch Emery. Flannery O'Connor stated that *Wise Blood* "is a comic novel about a Christian *malgré lui*, and as such, very serious, for all comic novels that are any good must be about matters of life and death." (WB p. 5). Indeed the novel is comic, because its characters are comic, and serious because it attempts to define human beings and to understand human behavior. Motes and Emery are comic because, as Bergson notes, the comic effect results when something mechanical is encrusted on the living. "We laugh every time a person gives us the impression of being a thing." The soul or spirit *should* animate a person's being and his behavior. As Hulga is dominated by her leg, Shiftlet by the car, Motes and Emery too are dominated by things, Emery by his blood, Motes by his brain. The soul, Bergson notes, is infinitely supple and perpetually in motion. It "imparts...its winged lightness to the body it animates," and "the immateriality which this passes into matter is...gracefulness. Matter, however, is obstinate and resists." When matter rules over spirit, the person becomes a thing, and is reduced to the dominating matter, in Enoch's case to his blood, his heart, his instinct; in Hazel's case to his head, his brain, his intellect. The human soul depends for its integrity on a balance between mind and heart; if mind dominates, the person tends to be rational, intellectual, unmodified by blood, emotion, sympathy, in other words, angelic, pure spirit; if heart dominates the person tends to be emotional, sympathetic and undirected by reason, in other words, animal. In either case they become things: their behavior, because unanimated is graceless, automatic, mechanical, robotic. Like stick men, they are wooden, awkward, comic.

But *Wise Blood* is a tragic as well as a comic novel because of the unrealized potential of each major character. Hazel and Enoch are incomplete human beings, and each lacks what the other has. Hazel's head needs Enoch's heart, and Enoch's heart needs Hazel's head. Just as Enoch's instinctive behavior is unsupervised by reason, so Hazel's rational behavior is untempered by emotion. Enoch runs to the zoo and steals the mummified relic because he needs a god, and any god will do; Hazel, when confronted with a rival preacher, runs him over because the man "ain't true," (WB p. 155) a perfectly rational act, but man can not live by reason alone. Hazel and Enoch are comic because they are incomplete. But Bergson further defines the comic as "socially significant" or "corrective." O'Connor's novel illustrates this aspect of the comic as well, for she intends us to understand that these caricatures, her characters, Hulga, Shiftlet, Enoch Emery and Hazel Motes, are not essentially different from you or me. Commenting on Hazel Motes in her introduction to *Wise Blood*, she said: "Does one's integrity ever lie in what he is not able to do? I think that it usually does, for free will does not mean one will, but many wills conflicting in one man." (WB p. 5).

What is it that Hazel Motes is not able to do? He is not able to achieve perfection, in Christian terms to become a saint, because he has only part of the necessary equipment; but he goes as far as he can on what he has, and so succeeds, making mistakes because of what he lacks. And we are all in the same predicament, according to Flannery O'Connor. If, like Mr. Shiftlet, we have enough sense to know that something is up, even if we are puzzled by it, then we are in pursuit of perfect being and consequent perfect behavior, but hampered in our pursuit by imperfect equipment and missing parts. So our integrity does lie in what we are not able to do. Human beings are all caricatures, none of us is matter perfectly animated by spirit, and insofar as we are not, we are awkward, wooden, stereotypic, rigid, graceless, mechanical, robotic, and of course, comical. Miss O'Connor is laughing at herself, and of course, that's what we are supposed to be doing.

In chapter seven of *Wise Blood*, Sabbath Hawkes comes upon a cage with a sign on it that says: TWO DEADLY ENEMIES. HAVE A LOOK FREE.

[In it] there was a black bear about four feet long and very thin, resting on the floor of the cage; his back was spotted with bird lime that had been shot down on him by a small chicken hawk that was sitting on a perch in the upper part of the same apartment. Most of the hawk's tail was gone; the bear had only one eye. (WB p. 125).

Sabbath does not comment so we don't know what she's thinking as she watches these deadly enemies cohabiting their prison, the intelligence of the hawk and the strength of the bear neutralized by their inability to co-operate and make their prison a home; their abilities are unexploited except when used to combat each other, and their personalities are misunderstood as contrary rather than complementary. Who knows what Sabbath thinks as she watches those two disturbed beings in their mutual prison; she might be thinking of Hazel Motes the Hawk and Enoch Emery the Bear, one without a head, the other without a heart. They are both like Hulga in "Good Country People" who became her leg; the mechanical thing had been encrusted on the living.

Notes

1 Henri Bergson, "Laughter," in *Comedy*, edited by Wylie Sypher. New York, 1956, pp. 61-146.
2 Ibid. pp. 78-79.

Archetypes of the Child and of Childhood in the Fiction of Flannery O'Connor

Mary V. Blasingham

The fictional world of Flannery O'Connor is peopled with many children in broad life-spectra: child-saints and child-satans, the whole and the deformed, the voyeurs and the unseeing, the exuberant and the passive, the sober and the sacrilegious, protagonists and minor characters. These children display the many aspects of two major psychological phenomena: *the complex primordial archetype of the child*, and the *situational archetype of childhood*. O'Connor's children, singly and collectively, are integral to their author's profound message — her invitation to psychic transformation toward a synthesized Self. The sense of the rightness, of the synthesis, of O'Connor's work may to a large extent be attributable to her comprehension of basic patterns of the unconscious human psyche from which these two archetypes spring eternally to renew and to be renewed in life. Her children, read in the literal dimension, are indeed fully real, but, interpreted archetypally, are myth-children, symbolic rather than humanized, and therefore "divine" in the psychological use of the term.

On concepts earlier delineated by the Germans W. Wundt and C.G. Carus, C.G. Jung and the Greek scholar Karoly Kerényi built studies of the child archetype, [1] the child fantasy of the collective unconscious psyche; while Gaston Bachelard, Michael Fordham, and others have recognized a more general archtype of the state of childhood — the two archetypes having certain elements in common. Archetypes are involuntary manifestations of unconscious processes, O'Connor's children being evidence of those processes at work on or in her adult characters' psyches. They invite correction of conscious psychic extremes, but, whenever their transforming roles are denied, they rise and erupt in sudden and sweeping violence. For archetypal forces are by nature autochthonous, autonomous, and autocratic. When an individual or a collective violates the instinctual forces extensively, it piles up a "Promethean debt which has to be paid off from time to time in the form of hideous catastrophe." [2]

Jung wrote, "A special position must be accorded to those archetypes which stand for the goal of the developmental process" [3], in other words, those which forster the process of individuation. And he included among these the archetype of the child, which preserves the link (*religio* means "linking back") to the primordial forces of the human psyche; which preserves the unselfconscious, the instinctual, and the affective life; and which simultaneously urges reconciliation of conscious and unconscious forces. The child archetype has all-pervasive functions in man to prevent the unbasing of the individual, to revalue the past when society has devalued it, to prepare for a new god when a god has been destroyed. It is the source of instant reverence and religious devotion. Functionally, the child archetype appears in the pre-conscious psyche to promote that process of individuation toward final maturity. The child archetype as a myth-child is, then, called the "divine child" because of its supernatural status and function as a "savior" force. This single purpose is served even though the child figure may appear in behavioral patterns in fictional plots as either godly or monstrous, as apparent good or apparent evil.

A second usage of the term "divine child" applies to the positive figure of the child-god, one face of the child archetype. The recurring vision of the child-god ensures that such concepts as the value of the instinctual life and the needed reconciliation of conscious and unconscious psyches not be forgotten; it compensates for the heavily one-sided rational modern consciousness with its arrogance, its rigid "planning," its perfectionism, its narrow individualism, and its failure of love; and, again, it serves as unifying symbol for each new synthesis occurring with personality transformation — the *vereinigen* (unite, combine) function. In this unity/futurity aspect, the archetype anticipates the coming transformation and so serves as a unifying figure of wholeness. It is, then, the principle of salvation and unity. In short, it serves as the "mechanical governor" of the psychic engine of both the individual and society, its functions integral to the overall fictional purpose of Flannery O'Connor.

Concomitant details reveal the multifarious complexity of this archetype. The variant forms of the symbolic "divine child" in *positive* aspect are a "treasure" such as a flower, a golden egg, or gold ball; a gold child or a king's son or a god or the center of the mandala; a "smaller than small" as a hidden force of nature or an individual in the form of an elf or Tom Thumb; a "bigger than big" as a giant, indicating the individual's capacity for miraculous deeds as well as the broad scope of the cosmos — these latter two representing the contrast of the small individual and the vast cosmos or godhead. Other possible forms include an *androparion* (a mannikin metal man), a protective animal, a jewel, a pearl, the chalice, the quaternity, a hermaphrodite, or Mercury reborn in perfect form. In *negative* aspect, the so-called "divine child" may be configured as an imp, a vicious animal, a miniature satan or manipulator with a deformed foot, a "Radiant Boy," a *puer aeternus,* a witch's child, a troop of unholy boys, or *homunculi* in swarms.An additional element in the portrayal of the child archetype is the use of the analogue method, which implies a core meaning as an irrational third, a central truth shrouded in *mystery.* This parabolic method accounts for the heavy emphasis in O'Connor's work on an ultimate "mystery," a non-rational implied synthesizing force of truth created through, but beyond, the images. Meaning configured in archetypes is always implicative, rather than denotative.Further, an adult may experience a vision of him/her self as a child, indicating dissociation, such as dissociation between the individual character's conscious and unconscious psyches, or conflict of the original self with current forced actions. When a child in literature is configured in single form, a unity in the relevant character(s) is implied; when the "child" appears in plurality without individualizing characteristics, then psychic dissociation and/or dissolution in the relevant character(s) is implied. Plural children in normal personalities indicate as-yet-incomplete synthesis of those personalities.

In the portrayal of the half-divine, half-humanized child-hero figure, the life phenomena include, among others, the following: unnatural or accidental birth, abandonment, struggle for survival amid dangers (paralleling the genesis of the human self), heroic actions and serving through *athla* (works or deeds), conquest of the dark, and final triumph — all elements brought to viability in the children of various O'Connor narratives.The remaining and highly significant elements of the child archetype include numinosity, invincibility, hermaphroditism, and the beginning-and-end concept, or *renatus in novam infantiam.* Brief comment will identify these elements. Numinosity surrounds all archetypes, the child archetype having a high degree. Further, in dreams, a governing principle clinically evidenced is that the younger the child and the lower his level of ego-consciousness, the more numinous the archetypal images that he envisions. The quality of light surrounding such images is, then, a point of literary analysis in works inhabited by children, for numinosity as a value inheres in all archetypes. Regarding invincibility, Jung wrote, "The urge and compulsion to self-realization is a *law of nature* and thus of invincible power...."[4] In spite of incredible impediments, the child persists in his purposes. Hermaphroditism is an ancient symbol of synthesis, of the creative union of opposites. The beginning-and-end concept includes the reappearance of the dead in new life and is always associated with sea-forms. The child, in this concept, symbolizes the unconscious state of earliest childhood and the post-conscious anticipation of immortality or rebirth after death as a "child" again — thus both beginning and end.

Let us now turn to the archetype of childhood, a situational archetype. Classifying childhood in general as an archetypal energy and claiming in *The Poetics of Reverie* that all images drawn from the archetypal fund of childhood experience preserve their suggestive power for the imagination, Gaston Bachelard writes: "Every archetype is an opening upon the world...when through a dream the archetypal power of childhood has been revived, all the great archetypes of paternal and maternal power resume their potency...."[5] This archetype's functions are, then as follows: the awakening of indigenous and inter-related patterns of images, the retention of values through images, and the continuing adherence to the natural wellsprings of the racial and preconscious childhood experiences. The child's unconscious psyche dominates long after the incipient development of ego-consciousness sets in, his unconscious predisposing him to live in a world of the timeless, the sensory, and the symbolic. Children have forces of freedom and creativity, of balance and centricity or integration about which "enlightened" adults should be wiser. The unconscious in general, however, also promotes the principle of non-resistance to superior forces, a naivete causing some children to fall prey to dangers.

Children project assorted images upon parents, so that the parental imagos in children's psyche-eyes are not pure reality or precisely realistic; in fact, the younger the child, the more the parents are to him only primitive archetypes little differentiated as realistic beings. The mother appearing to the child archetypally is often envisioned as upraised arms or as a ship. Daughters are usually equated with mothers and often the daughter-goddess is sculptured as placed above the mother-goddess with her feet on the mother's shoulders — this figure appearing in perverted form in O'Connor's "A View of the Woods" with Mary's feet on her grandfather's shoulders. Although Jung delineates sensation, intuition, feeling, and thinking, yet in the child these are diffused and undifferentiated, as observed in the confused reactions and interactions in "A Temple Of the Holy Ghost." Anxiety and fear of both life and death, as in O'Connor's Nelson and Tarwater particularly, pervade most young child psyches, as well as confusion of good with evil and easy intimidation by adult "giants." All these fears may normally be relieved in dreams, for there is an inner *iatros* (physician), or agency of self-healing.

The child psyche is still interfused with its primal source; so that, as with primitives, magnificient, unexpected archetypal images often spring forth from children's psychic depths. Dreams' uncomprehended quality of "futurity" refers to their power to forecast and to fore-condition children's entire lives. Dreams and fantasies apparently pre-form and pre-shape a child's destiny, as demonstrated in young Tarwater. Jung states: "...those farseeing dreams and images appear before the soul of a child, shaping his whole destiny."[6] Child visions have full symbolic meaning, as the artful glimpses offered in "The Lame Shall Enter First," "A Temple of the Holy Ghost," and *The Violent Bear It Away* . The visions often include animals and O'Connor recognized the child's theriomorphic world with personifications in lions, cats, dogs, mules, hogs, snakes, and so on. In the child's world, there are present both "protective" and "dangerous" animals, as well as humans disguised as animals — the child's psyche bearing an innate content of animal imagery laden with un-comprehended primordial symbolism. For example, all frightening parents transmute to animal images, as Mrs. Turpin to a wart hog. O'Connor's animals are often indifferent or vicious, yet the configuration of the child-and-animal is present as well as a surrounding mass of the natural world.The above characteristics inter- and intra-relate to the central psychic condition of childhood: a governing unity or Oneness. Childhood drawings, if allowed full course, resolve into red and white fused mandalas of eight spokes; of all the figure-and-shape preoccupations of children, the circle predominates, and children's many archetypal dreams display these and other symbols of wholeness.

The phenomena of the children in O'Connor's stories range from the simplest suggestion of child judgment upon the adult to the complete and complex figure of the child-hero archetype in *The Violent Bear It Away*. But selected examples must suffice. In "Greenleaf" three dogs emerge like hounds of hell and a clutch of silent children pass sullen judgment upon the self-righteous and unrelated Mrs. May, whose artificiality and over-conscious personality compose a different world from theirs. The natural here judges the unnatural. And with unmistakable foreshadowing as to where her soul is likely to be "hounded"!

In "Everything That Rises Must Converge," an authentic child archetype is the imp taunting the arrogant, the dark gnome with the pointed hat, prototype of imps, gnomes, and goblins of fairy tale. Greek manifestations of this figure included the Cabiri, to whom mighty wonder-making powers were ascribed. They were usually deformed dwarfs with small magic feet and the symbolic peaked hat, the *pileus*, the identification of the Cabiri tradition. The black child of this story is a "little boy" wearing "a Tyrolean hat with a blue feather in it." (CS p.415). Julian's mother's individuation process, arrested years ago, reverses into the dependency and diffused bewilderment of the state of childhood, this retrogressing mother-child then sparking the psychic trauma of Julian, who suffers a negative initiation deeper into childhood. The impish child archetype functions as a symbol of transformation, though negative.

In "A View of the Woods," the role of mother is usurped and perverted by Mr. Fortune, so that Mary appears as the goddess-daughter to a goddess-mother, this Koré figure normally representing the life/fruition/fertility of earth and the continuity of generations. Here there is, finally, in ironic reversal, bitter enmity, destruction of earth, and discontinuity of generations. Mary serves as her grandfather's long-lost mother and as his unheeded conscience;she is an "angel," a "saint," a sometime princess, and a mirror of her grandfather's Self — a frustrated symbol of transformation. It is as if "he were being attacked not by one child but by a pack of small demons...." (CS p.354). She is, thus, both the holy child Mary and the unholy demonic, a child-god archetype driven into this dual condition. When a single child figure breaks down into multiple figures, the unity/plurality of the child archetype is demonstrated and symbolizes the lack of or loss of synthesis of personality as in Fortune, and as in Mary herself in the breakdown into which she is driven. The "woods" represent eternal mystery, the link to nature, the depth of the unconscious to which the child is attuned; it is, further, self-respect and repudiation of the grossly limited, vulgarly materialistic, power-hungry "monster" that technological consciousness has bred. Repudiation of the "morality" of unconscious values causes the eruption of violence.

In "Revelation," O'Connor portrays a *puella aeterna* parallel to the well-known *puer aeternus*; in fact, it offers several, Mrs. Turpin, Mary Grace, and Mary Grace's mother. Mrs. Turpin enjoys her child-state and even uses a term of exclamation familiar in the early part of this century, "child, yes," but Mary Grace has been forced against her will into the role of *puella aeterna*. She seeks to rise above the permanent infantilism but is blocked and disoriented. The "dirty" children, the delivery boy, and the "grinning" boy on Turpin's farm all reflect the affinity in unconsciousness of all childhood for natural grace and earthiness. The story presents many facets of the state of childhood: its passivity, its rebellious sense of rightness, its honesty even unto bodily grace and integrity, and its unconscious affects, in contrast to the perversions of these by the story's strained and meddling adults. Childlike joy in the innocent and faithful - "shouting and clapping and leaping like frogs" - sharply contrasts with the "shocked and altered faces." (CS p.508).

In "A Good Man Is hard To Find," two unnatural children, John Wesley and June Star, simply reflect the vulgarities, the spiritual limitations, and the drifting, unimpassioned, quarrelsome purposelessness of modern society — characters who are not really children at all but grotesques of arrogant and opinionated abandon. The helpless baby, however, is a rudimentary divine child-god, and it forecasts the shocking transformation of consciousness for both the grandmother and the reader. Grandmother and The Misfit are, respectively, the *puella aeterna* with inflated ego and simplistic unrealism, and The Misfit, a demonic witch's child in a weird criminal extension. The accompanying animal is of course the cat serving as a dragon, both felines and dragon-serpents being common mythically in this archetypal configuration.

In "A Temple of the Holy Ghost," archetypal conditions of childhood predominate: a sense of timelessness, irreverence resulting from slowly developing ego-consciousness, archetypal dreams, candidness, a search for individuation and for the as-yet-unattained transcendent, red and white symbolism, and diffused night reality. However, the reversed archetypal configuration of the girl from child-hero to child-non-hero or, better, child-non-heroine comes to the fore, as well as the implied comparison of her to a hermaphrodite. The wrong-sexed-if-sexed-at-all archetypal child-heroine should, by all mythical propriety, slay the lions, then sacrifice *herself* by burning for a rebirth to save mankind. Instead, although this child thinks she wishes desperately to serve mankind, she entertains an inflated ego and sees herself as taming the lions with no effort at all, in fact, identifies with them by sleeping with them, the lions being normally symbols of transformation associated with the archetypal hero but here representing evil and danger. She cannot be burned and, finally, though she fancies herself a hero-saint with numinosity, she fails to reach a state of heroism at all. Childlike mankind here searches for the transcendent Self or God, but fails dismally because of ego-centeredness.

"The Artificial Nigger" presents two elements in the phenomenology of the child — the reversion of the adult in the "Radiant Boy," and transformation lost through traumatic disillusionment in Nelson, a Hero Manqué. Nelson has the unknown origins and abandonment in infancy of the true child-hero; and he distinctly serves as Head's ego-deflator and the instrument of the onset of Head's supposed humility. Head's Peteresque denial of Nelson throws Nelson into the Christ-image and thus automatically into the role of a symbol of transcendence, but Head's denial of him arrests Nelson's development. Mr. Head, meanwhile, is "slowly returning from the dead," for there can be no rebirth without preceding death. At the sight of the plaster statue, each serves as the other's symbol of transformation, now ironically retrogressive. Mr. Head abnegates responsibility and casts himself upon God's mercy, though alas he still judges himself — and favorably. Night, the elemental unconscious with feminine implications, produces a high numinosity. This uncanny light, accompanying the return of an adult to the childhood state, manifests the archetype of the "Radiant Boy," an apparition that came with the centuries to be considered an evil omen. Through life, Nelson will be, psychically, as "artificial" as the plaster "nigger."

Little Harry-Bevel of "The River" is a child abandoned on life's journey, called "old man" by his father and by the guest. As the true child-hero-god archetype he suffers and struggles with enemies — boys, dogs, shoats, the "wild animal," and such serpents as his mother. Actually Bevel survives all these. He dies, primarily for the reader, a sacrificial death. There is a picture of Christ on the wall! For the boy, the young preacher as well as the river water become mother-images as when the preacher "lifted his head and arms and shouted...." (CS p.165). The sun, "like a diamond," (CS p.164) is the accompanying light. Mr. Paradise as a river monster should be a Wise Old Man archetype, in antiquity the advisor to heroes, but actually he fails in this role. Little Harry sees fragmented light, "broken pieces of the sun knocking the water," (CS p.168) his shattered hero-life. Little Harry with his eye and nose picking and his treading or kicking motion in the water enacts the frustrated, retrogressive infantile sexual response in a starved attachment to the absent mother. The river then substitutes for the mother, and he becomes the child-fish, symbol of renewal and redemption — an archetypal savior only "four or five" years old. Red and gold indicate respectively his blood sacrifice and the central spiritual meaning.

The "prophets" in "A Circle in the Fire" are of course an "unholy" child archetypal configuration. The girl voyeur displays well the state of childhood, with undifferentiated reality, animosity to adult thought patterns, direct action in opposition to Mrs. Cope's evasive hypocrisy, and unfrightened affinity for fields and woods in diametrical opposition to Mrs. Cope's exploitive attitude toward nature. Although the sun flames and the sky looks as if it is trying to push through a fortress wall, Mrs. Cope resists the offered symbols of love and salvation. As for the concept of the-small-and-the-large, the boys with Powell reinforce the interpretation that the three are simply one archetypal evil devil/saint futilely inviting Mrs. Cope to enlarged insight. The crowing irony is, of course, that the young three-devils-in-one dance in the circle reserved for the "men of God"! Nevertheless, in function, they *are* men of God.

The child phenomenology of "The Lame Shall Enter First" configures another demonic child and false prophet in Rufus Johnson. Jung writes: "The foot...is possessed of magical generative power.... Ugliness and deformity are especially characteristic of those mysterious chthonic gods...the Cabiri..."[7] as in Johnson's small stature, deformity, magical power over Norton, "possession by the devil," and face like an "old man's." He comprehends the imbalance in the over-conscious manipulative psyche of Sheppard. In a psychological transmittal, Sheppard suddenly sees Norton's face as the archetypal divine child in its numinous halo, but it has seemingly been the satanic Rufus who has performed the function of a symbol of transformation throughout the story. Since emphatic positions of opening and closing are reserved for Norton, we interpret that O'Connor has created a double child archetype: the demonic and the angelic, the one with "thin, dark hair" and the "stocky blond," as opposites in two bodies but with a single rhetorical function.

The Violent Bear It Away demonstrates the required elements of the complete child-hero archetype as follows: insignificant beginnings, miraculous birth, divine origin followed by abandonment and exposure, extraordinary upbringing with persecution, a protective natural world with animals, a numinous child image, unity and plurality, hermaphroditism symbolizing union of opposites, red and white fusion symbolizing the synthesis of father and mother forces, deeds or *athla* performed but with a small object or flaw being the hero's temporary undoing, an obligatory bondsman role, suffering producing opposites of megalomania and its compensating inferiority feeling, invincibility with ultra-survival power, and final triumph. Further elements are: the above-named irrational and redemptive third force generated out of the collision of opposites; self as *coincidentia oppositorum* containing both dark and light, often the marriage of sun and moon; preconceived symbols of wholeness such as the circle and the quaternity; and beginning-and-end, death surrounded by the sea, with *renatus in novam infantiam*. *The Violent Bear It Away* appears to be a unique but authentic version of this complete configuration. Tarwater is illegitimate and born at the scene of an accident. He is of near-divine origin in the Judao-Christian tradition, his uncle being an "Old Testament prophet." He is "abandoned" by his mother and his natural father; by Rayber who lacked the courage to take him; and even by old Tarwater when the old man went into the woods for days to wrestle with his soul. Tarwater's exposure to danger includes kidnapping, isolation, snakes, bears, bobcats that spring in the kitchen window, Rayber's atheism, and rape. Other animal references are

O'Connor's favorites, dogs, bull, fowl, and lions with heroic and Christian implications. He is, however, protected by the flora, the pine, birch, and fig trees, the poor road, the thorns, and the tall corn. The child remains in touch with nature, the sky, the sun and the moon, and the animals. The unruliness of nature is a protector of a certain wildly independent and impassioned spirit.

The numinosity of the child image is strong. The collision of the opposing forces of the secular and the transcendent tears Tarwater, but yet light, fire, sunshine, and the heat of rage constantly bathe him. He is split in personality during the visitations of the stranger, his doppelgaąnger shadow, but, when the boy is functioning as an integrated personality, the shadow is not present. Hermaphroditism is suggested in the homosexual attack which combines his maleness with a female role. Red and white symbolism predominates — a mass of red is punctuated regularly with white daylight or moonlight. The concluding scene combines the burning woods with moonlight. The bondsman or thrall service, is, of course, Tarwater's sacred obligation to baptize Bishop. The boy was held in bondage by his great-uncle. His temporary undoing is associated with a trivial bottle-opener when young Tarwater takes up with the stranger. The loss of the bottle-opener symbolizes his being prevented from ever savoring fully the "wine of mortal life." His hat also is stolen, that is, his role in wholly unconscious orientation. And Tarwater has temperamental shifts from megalomania to feelings of inferiority. As for the circle and the quaternity, it seems that the "roots" of the cross would "encircle all the dead;" there are "halos" and Tarwater's round hats. In fours, there are four key characters, two "fathers" and two "sons," and the spiritual call of the wood thrush in four notes. "With the same four formal notes it trilled its grief against the silence." (VBIA p.326). These only suggest the many circle and square references in the novel. As for a key symbol in the archetype: "The sun, from being only a ball of glare, was becoming distinct like a large pearl, as if sun and moon had fused in a brilliant marriage." (VBIA p.221). The pearl is an alternate of the child, and the marriage of sun and moon a symbol of the unity of opposites which the child archetype presages. Tarwater's night prowling is, in one of its meanings, a search for conquest of the "dark." His final sense of dedication becomes overt just at the onset of darkness, the tree "would consume the darkness in one tremendous burst of flame," and "...his face set toward the dark city...." (VBIA pp.242-243). The final element in the configuration of the child archetype is the "rebirth" of Tarwater following the drowning of Bishop and the sleep/death following the rape. Though the drowning is technically a crime, nevertheless a new child is born out of that death, Bishop *renatus in novam infantiam* Tarwater, Bishop with his halo of white hair, an innocent unconsciously oriented, a divine child-God. At the point of the synthesizing symbols of the child-God and the androgyne, when he is reborn hermaphroditic, Tarwater reconciles his former wholly unconscious orientation — which extreme he had to modify — with the "city" or conscious psychic orientation, and thus he achieves his unified Self and his mission in life.

O'Connor's phenomenology of the child, in both her short stories and her second novel, is validated by clinical findings and invites the reader to a rich psycho-fictional experience of imaging and re-imaging the child.

Notes

1 C.G. Jung, "The Psychology of the Child Archetype," *Psyche and Symbol*, ed. V.S. de Laszlo, Anchor Books (New York, 1958), p.124.
2 *Ibid.*, p.126.
3 C.G. Jung, *Two Essays on Analytical Psychology*, trans. R.F.C. Hull, Bolligen Series Vol. 7 (Princeton, N.J. 1953), p.110).
4 C.G. Jung, "The Special Phenomenology of the Child Archetype," *Psyche and Symbol*, p.136.
5 Gaston Bachelard, *The Poetics of Reverie*, trans. Daniel Russell (Boston, 1971), pp.107-108.
6 Jung, "On Psychic Energy," *On The Nature of the Psyche*, trans. R.F.C. Hull, Bolligen Series XX, Vol. 8 (Princeton, N.J. 1960), par.98, p.52.
7 Jung, *Symbols of Transformation*, p. 126.

Cold Comfort: Parents and Children in the Work of Flannery O'Connor

Helen S. Garson

Her world was narrow, said the poet, Elizabeth Bishop, of Flannery O'Connor's stories. A limited number of themes interested O'Connor; and certain character types and relationships appear and reappear to form a pattern in the two novels and the two short story collections.More than half the stories focus on parents and children: fathers and sons, mothers and daughters, mothers and sons. Rarely are there two parents. Sometimes there are surrogate parents, grandfathers, uncles, granduncles. Just as most of the families have a single parent, almost always there is only one child, very rarely siblings.

The family in O'Connor's stories bears no resemblance to most we associate with Southern fiction, although unquestionably they are of the Gothic, grotesque school. There is, as one critic states, "horror...at the core of family life,"[1] in the stories of O'Connor. In all her work, parents and children want and expect things of each other that can never be given. Either the parents are cold, calculating, selfish, or totally indifferent to the child, as in her stories of parents with small children; or the children are people who are grown up only chronologically, who remain adolescents, totally dependent, hostile, and filled with a sense of self-importance and superiority. In the smoldering atmosphere of anger, rejection, and repulsion, violence usually erupts. If the child does not kill himself or the parent directly, something he does leads to an act which is a type of violation. Fear and repression often bring about a displacement of anger. Sometimes, but this is rare, the result of the explosive act is the beginning of understanding. But more often, the reader is left to sort out the effects of the final deeds on the characters.

Because there are too many stories to discuss in a short paper, I have chosen a few which seem to me to represent major character types as well as significant concerns about relationships in O'Connor's stories. In some of the stories the parent-child relationship is central; in others it is peripheral. Yet, whether or not the focus is on the family, the basic behavior remains unchanged."I really don't know much about children,

that is...what goes on in their minds. I like to watch them from outside."
(HB p.529). O'Connor wrote in a letter to a friend. But a number of her
stories concern small children. In "The River" and "The Lame Shall Enter
First" the central theme pertains to the failures of the parents to care for
or about their sons, so that both boys commit suicide. In an ironic
contrast, although both children want to escape, Harry, *away* from his
mother, Norton, *to* his dead mother, both seek the same thing basically.
They want escape, but more than that, Harry longs for an unknown
kingdom of love that has been promised him, and Norton longs for
reunion with the loving dead mother he knew. For each child, life as it is
contains coldness, emptiness, and cruelty. Although both boys are too
young to have any comprehension of death, nevertheless, death holds
more expectation for them than life does. The fact that Norton has only a
father, and Harry has two parents, or that Norton's father is ostensibly
an upright man, whereas Harry's parents seem to have no purpose
whatsoever, does not alter the resemblances between the families. In
each, the boy appears to be little more than a nuisance that the adult has
to bother with. Not that much is done for or given to the child, but his very
existence interferes with the parent's life. The burdensome children have
no place in the world. Harry is sent off with baby sitters so that the
parents are free of responsibility; Norton's father sees him as a trial he
must put up with. Harry's mother, Mrs. Ashfield, speaks of her child as a
liar; Norton's father, Mr. Sheppard, constantly refers to his son as selfish.
Neither parent seeks or finds anything of value in the child. Mrs. Ashfield
and Sheppard remain locked in their own lives, and the lost children find
a way out of the dread of the emptiness of daily existence. Without
conscious recognition that he is seeking death because he longs for love,
each child kills himself: Harry by drowning, Norton by hanging - violent,
and Gothic choices, but logical for the child. Harry has been promised by
a preacher the "River of Faith, ...of Life, ...of Love, ...the rich red river of
Jesus' blood." (CS p.165). In seeking that love the child chooses literally to
become a part of the river. Norton, promised by an older boy that he will
be reunited with his mother in heaven if he does not live long enough to
become a sinner, tries to launch himself into space, where he is certain he
has seen his mother. When Harry tells his mother about his baptism he
states: "...I'm not the same now...I count." (CS p.171). The disinterested
mother makes no effort to learn what he means, and the next morning,
Harry returns to that "strange country" he had been baptized in,
determined to baptize himself again, but without the help of anyone, and
to continue until he "found the Kingdom of Christ in the river." (CS p.173).
Sheppard, like Mrs. Ashfield ignores the signals. He either misses, or

underestimates, or is hostile to what he perceives to be his son's view of religion, space, and most of all the child's continuing grief over the loss of his mother. The father finds the boy's sorrow excessive and unnatural. For his child has no charity.

Many critics have pointed to O'Connor's ironic naming of the father in "The Lame Shall Enter First." Sheppard, the father, does not protect his own flock, but seeks others to shepherd. In "The River," the family name of "Ashfield" stands in stark contrast to the natural environment where the boy seeks and finds his death, "the strange woods" that he has never seen before - the woods a symbol of the mystery of religion, - and the muddy river in which he seeks the love he has never known. The fact that O'Connor has a four year old boy take another name needs to be noted, because the writer stresses it at several points in the story and because it is something she does also in "Good Country People" and "The Comforts of Home." Name changes tell us about the other self the character wants to be. Difficult as it is to acccept even the unconscious desire for such change in a small child, it is significant in the structure of the story, "The River." Harry, upon hearing the preacher's name, decides to adopt it. He renames himself "Bevel." Since name changes are made not only for their own sake - that is, as an indication of conflict in the character - but also because they hold a particular meaning in a story, we find some interesting possibilities in the name Bevel. Bevel is the slant of a line when not at right angles with another; a bevel gear cuts into a surface; a bevel square is an adjustable instrument for drawing angles or adjusting the surface of work to a particular inclination. The fact that the preacher's full name is Bevel *Summers* serves to reinforce the difference between Harry Ashfield, the child, and Bevel Summers, the boy preacher. When Summers takes hold of Harry to baptize him, the child recognizes in the preacher deep intent and seriousness of a kind he has never encountered before. Thus, symbolically, the name suggests what Harry seeks. O'Connor stresses the importance of the name change in a subtle way throughout the story. At the beginning, as soon as the baby sitter takes him from the family apartment and asks his name, the child tells her it is Bevel; from that point on, the author speaks of him as Bevel, until the sitter returns him to his home that night. There, Mrs. Ashfield speaks of him as Harry, and she mocks his change of name. When Harry leaves the apartment the next morning, intent on returning to the river, the author gives him no name at all: he is neither Harry nor Bevel, but only "he" for the remainder of the story. Harry/Bevel, the lost child is the seeker, the slant of line, the adjustable instrument.

The endings of the two stories are different in ways that are characteristic of changes between the early and later stories. Where the story "The River" concludes with the death of Harry, "The Lame Shall Enter First" bears a resemblance at the end to another parent child story, "Everything That Rises Must Converge." In that story, at the moment of his mother's death, the son feels a rush of love for her - too late of course - and we are told that a burden of guilt and sorrow lies before him. In that same collection of stories, the father in "The Lame Shall Enter First" recognizes that he has done more for a stranger than for his own son. Three times he repeats that statement - which is an affirmation of his betrayal, yet ironically, recognition comes too late. Thinking he can make it all up to the boy, and filled with "a rush of agonizing love" (CS p.481) he rushes to tell his son that he loves him, and that he will never fail him again. But for Sheppard as for Julian in "Everything That Rises Must Converge" self-knowledge comes too late. Both Sheppard and Julian will live out lives in sorrow and guilt. O'Connor strikes the perfect chord, poignant and melancholy in both endings. She touches the reader's deepest feelings, the recognition of the might-have-been's of human relationships.

Another type of parent child dissociation is seen in two stories in which the parent child figures are mother and daughter. In one, "Good Country People," they are central; in the other, "Revelation," the mother and daughter are significant in the role they play for the major character, who has the revelation.

"Good Country People" has a familiar type of O'Connor character, the "thirtyish adolescents [who] do battle with their old mothers."[2] Each is a grown single child who lives with his or her parent. In "Good Country People," Mrs. Hopewell and her daughter, Joy, live together on a rural Southern farm. Like the boy, Harry, in "The River," Joy tries to change her identity by changing her name to Hulga, a name whose sound and connotation suggest the heavy physical ugliness which she emphasizes as well as the heaviness of spirit which is hers. Joy/Hulga sees the change of name as a major triumph in her lifelong battle with her mother, for "her mother had not been able to turn her dust into Joy," but she "had been able to turn it herself into Hulga." (CS p.275). Hulga has an artificial, wooden leg, a weak heart, a Ph.D. in philosophy, and very little to do in her life. The wooden leg has deformed "her whole character,"[3] states Miles Orvell. Her body, says Josephine Hendin, "has formed her mind, shaped her identity, and turned her life into a reaction against her own body."[4] Carter Martin sees the artificial leg as the symbol of Hulga's soul.[5] On the other hand, Stanley Hyman sees Hulga as an intentional self-caricature, of the "cruelest" kind.[6]

In addition to her obvious resemblances to O'Connor Joy/Hulga has attributes that relate her to Mary Grace in "Revelation," to Julian in "Everything That Rises Must Converge," to Mrs. May's two sons in "Greenleaf," and to Asbury in "The Enduring Chill." Hulga despises or denies everything her mother values; yet for the mother the daughter "becomes a symbol of everything Mrs. Hopewell wants to deny."[7] The mother's world is the life of the farm, which she, a divorced woman, runs with the aid of a tenant family. Her perceptions are so limited she cannot understand human suffering, certainly not her daughter's. She is certain that if her daughter looked on the bright side of things she could be beautiful. Instead, her glum daughter, who is "brilliant" but "without a grain of sense," dislikes what the bright side holds: " dogs or cats or birds or flowers or nature or nice young men." (CS p.276). Although Joy/Hulga is a grown woman, Mrs. Hopewell treats her as if she were a child. And while the daughter resents the mother's overprotection, she continues to play the role of the child. She is dependent, does not work on the farm, behaves badly with guests, is sullen and rude, and childishly calls attention to herself constantly by needlessly dragging the wooden leg across the floor. Her clothing is that of an adolescent; and when she meets a Bible salesman, thirty-two year old Joy/Hulga tells him at first that she is seventeen. Literally crippled in her physical body, Joy is also crippled by her mother's "love." Mrs. Hopewell's views are uttered, as Orvell says, "with a force...staggering in its banality."[8] All the cliches and platitudes one can think of are Mrs. Hopewell's: "It takes all kinds to make a world," she tells Mrs. Freeman, the tenant farmwoman. "Nothing is perfect." "Other people have their opinions too." (CS pp.272-273). But her sweet banalities are only surface expressions, for the irony is that Mrs. Hopewell doesn't accept her daughter's difference. Mrs. Hopewell, certain that she knows what a lady is, wants her daughter to fit that description. Equally convinced that she knows what good country people are, Mrs. Hopewell identifies the Bible salesman as one of that breed, thus indirectly and unwittingly encouraging her daughter to take up with the man. Hulga, thinking to deceive him, is left deceived and helpless at the end, a victim not only of her own making and his, but also of her own childlike, though hidden, acceptance of her mother's views.

The mother-daughter relationship in "Revelation" bears multiple similarities to the earlier story. The unnamed mother of Mary Grace is like almost all of the mothers in O'Connor's stories; they are women who expect "their children to conform to stereotyped, though alien, patterns of behavior and outlook."[9] And Mary Grace, herself, resembles the other daughters of the fiction; she is unattractive, overweight, clumsy looking.

117

Her face is blue with acne. Her clothing while different reminds us of Hulga's. Further, Mary Grace is another daughter who is an intellectual. Like Hulga, she reads constantly. But reading for both of the young women is more than a desire for knowledge. Each tries desperately to escape the mother, to close out sight and sound of the person she wants to be freed of and cannot be. Hulga is not free because of her illness, and Mary Grace is still a student. Dependency on the parent is so great that it plays an important part in the contempt with which each of the young women regards her mother

Mary Grace's mother, well-dressed, well-mannered, speaks the same banal language as Mrs. Hopewell. She chats meaninglessly at first with the central character of the story, Mrs. Turpin, in a doctor's reception room, where she waits with her daughter, and Mrs. Turpin waits with her husband. As the wait becomes longer, the mother-daughter relationship becomes well-defined. A strong hostility exists between the two, one that neither voices directly, but the tension is obvious. As the daughter focuses her anger on Mrs. Turpin, rather than on her mother, who is the real source of it, the mother uses Mrs. Turpin as a means of talking indirectly about her daughter. Mary Grace is a bookworm, who goes to a college her mother does not approve of. And she spends all her time reading, never going out to have fun, something the mother, like Hulga's mother, thinks the daughter should be doing. The mother turns remarks of Mrs. Turpin's about tempers and pleasantness to her advantage so that she can needle her daughter. "'I think the worst thing in the world,' she said 'is an ungrateful person.'" (CS p.499). She continues, more pointedly and explicitly with each statement, as she mentions knowing "a girl" who has everything anyone could want, and who is an unpleasant, critical complainer. No matter that the Turpins ignore her, as the mother does. The intimacy between her mother and total strangers, making her the target, becomes unbearable for Mary Grace and she strikes out. But Mary Grace cannot attack the real focus of her anger, her mother; in fact, she cannot even admit to herself that it is the mother she would like to injure. No longer able to contain her rage, she hurls her book at Mrs. Turpin. A twin of Hulga, who protects herself from her relationship with her mother by using the tenant farm woman, Mrs. Freeman, as a deflector of sorts, Mary Grace avoids any direct encounter with her mother. Her infantile dependency is revealed as the girl lies on the floor, her fingers "gripped like a baby's" (CS p.501) around her mother's thumb. Though the mother moans as she sits on the floor next to her daughter awaiting an ambulance and then leaves quietly with her as Mary Grace is taken out, nothing has changed or will change. The temporary friendship the mother struck up will be forgotten, but Mary Grace has once more proved, this time more forcefully and devastatingly, that she lacks all the qualities the mother prizes. Further, her dependency on her mother has only been reinforced. The damage she has done has been to herself.

"The indefatigably optimistic mother," a phrase used by Josephine Hendin, appears even more obvious in those stories in which the relationship is that of mother and grown son: "A Good Man Is Hard to Find," "Greenleaf," "The Enduring Chill," "The Comforts of Home," and "Everything That Rises Must Converge." Although the mothers are different in various ways, their similarities far outnumber the differences. Julian's mother, Mrs. Chestny, resembles the grandmother, in "A Good Man Is Hard to Find," in her concern about proper clothing, about recognition of social status, in her distorted memories of an elegant past, and her sense of racial superiority. Their focus on appearance, on correct behavior, on class structure is also akin to that of Mrs. May in "Greenleaf." The five women live with their children; all have a blindness to their offspring's failings and failures; all have a kind of innocence about the world (although Mrs. May has less than the others); and all, except Asbury Fox's mother in "The Enduring Chill," die as the result of violent action.

Just as the women remind us of one another, so do the sons. With the exception of Bailey, in "A Good Man Is Hard to Find," the sons are unmarried and dependent on their mothers, physically and financially. Yet, the mothers take considerable pride in the children, exaggerating their achievements and praising them to anyone and everyone, to friends, relatives, neighbors, and total strangers they encounter. The sons appear to take the exaggerated pride of the mothers as their due, even when they themselves have moments of doubt and recognition about their limited abilities. Filled with a sense of superiority to their mothers, they not only accept the excessive regard in which they are held, they feel misunderstood and unappreciated by those very parents.

Like the mothers in "Good Country People" and "Revelation" these women dominate their children, who respond with acts of deflected hatred. The politeness and platitudes infuriate the sons. They long to rebel, yet fear it. They live in an atmosphere of silent fury, of repulsion, and impotence. Direct confrontation must be avoided and rage displaced. The sons long for freedom which can come only with their own deaths or their mother's; ironically, they are too weak, too unprepared for a life on their own, too dependent on others, to be able to function without the strong mother. But, directly, or indirectly, the sons play some role in the death of the mother, as the fathers do in the death of the sons in "The

River" and " The Lame Shall Enter First." Bailey's inability to assert himself against his mother's pressures leads the family to the fatal area in which they are all murdered by The Misfit; Julian's deliberate provocation of his mother and the subsequent attack on her by a black woman lead to her death; Wesley and Scofield May's refusal to help their mother capture the Greenleaf's bull brings about the death Mrs. May has predicted would come to her at any moment; and Thomas, in "The Comforts of Home," accidentally shoots his mother, while aiming to kill the young woman he sees as the rival for his mother's affections.

Only in "The Enduring Chill" is there no death, although Asbury Fox, because of serious illness which he thinks is a prelude to his imminent death, has come home reluctantly and angrily to die. Asbury's relationship to his mother, as well as her views of him, their physical surroundings and the ironic turn at the end of the story, remind us of the mother and daughter in "Good Country People." Each, wanting to thwart the mother, yet afraid of direct confrontation, takes action which injures him or her, not the mother. Warned by the blacks on the farm of his mother's injunction about drinking unpasteurized milk, yet not knowing the scientific reasons for it, Asbury defiantly breaks the rule. Hulga, constantly told by her mother about young girls having a good time with nice young men, sets out to seduce the apparently simple, apparently religious Bible salesman. In each situation, they pay a heavy price for their actions: Asbury ruins his health and will be dependent on his mother for the rest of his days; Hulga loses her artificial leg, the symbol of her freedom, the loss is a mocking reminder of her dependency.

The most complex of the mother-son relationships is that of Thomas and his mother in "The Comforts of Home." As in the father-son story, "The Lame Shall Enter First," a third person becomes involved in the situation. But the complexity is greater here because in this instance the son is a grown man in his thirties and the outsider is a woman. A name change occurs also in this story; however, in "The Comforts of Home" it is the outsider who rejects her original name for a new one. Sarah Ham becomes Star Drake; from hog to male duck, the suggestion is made. But a drake is also a term for an eighteenth century cannon. The name suggests a masculine force that Thomas himself lacks. Sarah/Star's presence undermines Thomas in ways that become more and more untenable. Like a child, he is unwilling to share his mother with anyone; he is jealous of the loss of complete attention, and he insists that his mother choose between him and the stranger. He has an ever growing sense of panic and rage when his mother ignores his ultimatum. Feeling threatened to the core of his being, Thomas begins to sense the constant taunting presence of his dead, violent, and exploitive father. The father's physical power and force are referred to both specifically and obliquely in ways that outline Thomas' own lack of these. In the final scene, in the struggle between Thomas and Sarah/Star, it is the father's voice that yells "fire" in Thomas' ear, when the mother thrusts herself in front of the younger woman "to protect her."

As the reader looks at the quick sequence of events, it is easy to read the violent conclusion as an accident. Surely, Thomas did not mean to shoot the mother he has loved, the one whom, as we are told earlier in the story, "He loved because it was his nature to do so." Yet, we are also told "there were times when he could not endure her love for him...times when...he sensed about him forces, invisible currents entirely out of his control." (CS p.385). At the end of the story, it is not Sarah/Star in front of him as he holds the gun and hears his father's words, but his mother. And he shoots. The deliberate listing of the order of events leads the reader to the fact that on some level the son wants to, *acts to* rid himself of the mother, to destroy finally and irrevocably all that she represents; his dependency on her, his endless childhood, his impotence. Only through her death can he free himself. It is a strange turn of the oedipal cycle. Thomas, through his violent action, unconscious though it appears, does what other adult children long for, but never do. They insult or provoke, as Julian does in "Everything That Rises Must Converge;" they snarl and quarrel, as the May boys do in "Greenleaf;" they are sullen, like the children in "A Good Man Is Hard to Find;" or they write secret Kafka-like letters, like Asbury does in "The Enduring Chill." But only in "The Comforts of Home" is the confrontation a direct one.

One comes to the end of an examination of parent-child relationships in O'Connor with the recognition that here, perhaps more than anywhere else in the narrow world with which she dealt, as one critic has said of her general approach, "she found the human heart a pretty dark place."[10] From the ties and bonds of blood there is no escape. Entrapped and dependent emotionally or physically because of age, or inability, or malaise, or illness, the child struggles in a circle from which there is no way out except death; and the darkness of death becomes preferable to the darkness of life. On O'Connor's darkling plain where there is neither joy nor love nor certitude, nor peace nor help for pain, it is not human love that protects, saves, or heals; there is only the light one must reach beyond the far, dark tree line.

Notes

1 Josephine Hendin, *The World of Flannery O'Connor* (Bloomington, Indiana, 1970), p.150.
2 Hendin, p.31.
3 Miles Orvell, *Invisible Parade: The Fiction of Flannery O'Connor* . (Philadelphia, 1972), p.139.
4 Hendin, p.72.
5 Carter Martin, *The True Country: Themes in the Fiction of Flannery O'Connor* (Kingsport, Tennessee, 1969).
6 Stanley Hyman, *Flannery O'Connor* (New York, 1970).
7 Hendin, p.73.
8 Orvell, p.137.
9 Martin, p.223.
10 Warren Coffey, "Flannery O'Connor," *Commentary* 5, vol. 4 (November 1965), 99.

The "Feeder" Motif in Flannery O'Connor's Fiction: A Gauge of Spiritual Efficacy

Delores Washburn

The topic that has consumed my interest for a number of years is one ignored for the most part by other readers: Flannery O'Connor's treatment of the rites of feeding. The rituals of feeding are part of the fabric of Southern life: antebellum letters, diaries, journals, and belletristic literature delineate the purposeful services of the table as observed by the family feeder, typically wife and mother, who prepared or oversaw the preparation of life-sustaining food, no matter what her station in society, and offered it to her family as well as to any servants, hired hands, or visitors whose presence required her services. According to the means of the family, the fare provided was simple or elaborate; also, the manners with which the food was served were determined by family prosperity. The common aim of the feeders of that body of literature was to provide for each individual a sense of well being with respect to both bodily and social nourishment. Of necessity, nursing was a corollary skill cultivated by the feeder. Typically, devoted love and a firm respect for life were associated with these rites. In turn, her services were rewarded by the establishment of bonds of respect, love, and appreciation, all of which contributed to the cultivation of both social harmony within the community and a personal sense of contentment. *The Children of Pride* , Robert Manson Myers' edition of the letters of the family of C. Colcock Jones, is a treasure-trove of primary material on the subject.

As points of reference, we find within modern Southern fiction evidence of this kind of feeding tradition being sustained by William Faulkner's Granny Millard and Aunt Jenny Du Pre, Katherine Anne Porter's Grandmother Rhea, Eudora Welty's Ellen Fairchild, and to some degree by Flannery O'Connor's Mrs. Pitts. Additionally, in the large plantation homes, the matriarch was frequently assisted in the kitchen and garden by a competent black woman who developed her mistress' loyalty to the ritual of the table. If the mistress of the household were temporarily ill or absent, or perhaps died, the black woman became an able surrogate as long as she was needed. Literary representatives of this helper or successor are Faulkner's Louvinia, Elnora, and Dilsey; Porter's Old Nannie; and Carson McCullers' Berenice and Portia. We find no actual counterpart in O'Connor's fiction, chiefly because of the time in which her stories are set; however, in "Everything That Rises Must Converge," as she dies, Julian's mother calls for her old nurse Caroline, remembered for the sense of well being provided through her services, and the household in "A Temple of the Holy Ghost" includes a Negro cook.

In the course of time, as the extended family of the stable agrarian society was succeeded by the technological nuclear family (typically the subject of O'Connor's canon), feeding rites altered, sometimes drastically, as individuals drifted or fled to urban locales, where they were obliged to depend upon their own resources for sustenance. Simultaneously, commercial feeding establishments began to assume a considerable part of the task of nourishing. The boarding house and small town café serve the needs of such fictional characters as Faulkner's Bayard Sartoris and Joe Christmas, McCullers' John Singer and Cousin Lymon, and O'Connor's Hazel Motes. In addition, the hotel dining room, the urban restaurant, and the roadside rest stop cater to the needs of others, like the Clay community and Powerhouse in Welty's fiction; Miranda in Porter's; and George Rayber, Bailey and his family, and Mr. Shiftlet in O'Connor's. Moreover, as the family disintegrated, a new surrogate feeder - this time male - was obliged to cultivate feeding skills in order to nurture a motherless kinsman. He is particularly evident in O'Connor's fiction and is represented as being relatively effective by old Mason Tarwater in *The Violent Bear It Away*, a little less effective by Mr. Head in "The Artificial Nigger," and as ineffective by younger men, George Rayber in the novel just named and the case worker Sheppard in "The Lame Shall Enter First." At the same time, the traditional matriarchal feeder survives at the center of the home, though the household is shrunken and the nature of its occupation altered. Often, however, either the matriarch's devotion to the well being of her family or her skills in nourishing, or both, are diminished, impeded, or negated by her own character or by certain other circumstances. When such conditions occur, the matriarch fails to provide a sense of well being for those she serves, and their dissatisfaction is in turn mirrored in her own discontent. Consequently, social connections are severed, and members of the family become alienated, somewhat freakish, in fact, and even violent.

Furthermore, when the stable society of the former century was operable, personal and national piety were general. Christianity was viable. The matriarch who then served as feeder was intrinsically religious and derived both guidance and comfort from the Bible. However, with the development of wide-spread technology, not only did the family unit and its feeding practices deteriorate, but also its religious beliefs. The decline in religious faith is marked in this era of Southern fiction by intellectualism, the substitution of scientific humanism for traditional Christianity, the standardization of secular taste, and a marked increase in violence.

How Flannery O'Connor sketches the nature of feeders and their patterns of feeding is remarkable in that their observances are demonstrative of their own state of grace or absence thereof. In this fact O'Connor is positively consistent. Two of her stories contain the extended families common to the earlier era. Contrary to convention, however, the authoritarian older adult, the grandparent, disrupts the natural feeding order and ultimately invites violence and destruction. In "A Good Man Is Hard to Find," the grandmother has usurped authority from her son and, apparently, the matriarch's position in the household from her daughter-in-law. Unobtrusively, the feeding episodes take place on vacation inside the family automobile and The Tower, a roadside barbecue establishment, where the grandmother insists that tidiness and good manners be exerted but is chiefly unconcerned about the food itself. Simultaneously, in a perversion of traditional Christianity, the grandmother invests her faith in superficial respectability; and her family seeks its own material pleasure, comfort, and security. The two older children are prideful and sophisticated little individuals, who like the grandmother crave sensual and exciting experiences. Neither Bailey nor his passive wife possesses a vital spirit, both being overshadowed by the sheer energy of the others. Walter Sullivan has observed that the family's "belief in their own virtue is a sign of their moral blindness. In pride they have separated themselves from God, putting their trust in modern technology: in paved roads and automobiles...; in advertising messages...and tapdancing lessons for children and in motels and pampered cats."[1] Moreover, the grandmother is deceitful, as demonstrated by her hiding the family cat on the journey, the cat becoming the agent that causes Bailey to wreck the car; and she manipulates the children in order to get her own way. Ironically, the grandmother proclaims that she would not take her children "in any direction with a criminal like [The Misfit] aloose" from the Federal Pen (CS p.117), but through error guides the entire family into his path and certain death. Her erroneous judgment signifies her erroneous spiritual guidance, her identification with The Misfit being declared when she addresses him: "Why you're one of my babies. You're one of my own children!" (CS p.132). Though she does not intentionally direct her family into physical and spiritual destruction, the grandmother's faith in appearance and other temporal qualities brings death to all. In contrast to the family, The Misfit knows he is not good and cannot save himself. We recognize that he alone has suspected that spiritual dimensions exist in the universe.

Old Mark Fortune in "A View of the Woods" is the grandmother's male counterpart. Before the story begins, his daughter, concerned about the old man's health, convinces her husband that they and their children should move to the farm owned by Fortune in order to care for him. Fortune chooses to misconstrue their intentions, believing that his son-in-law, Pitts, is both worthless and a fortune-hunter. For ten years, Fortune treats his own family like hired hands, refusing to allow Pitts to make any capital improvements on the land, lest he attempt to exercise the rights of ownership. Neither will he sell any of the land to Pitts. Moreover, from time to time, "as a practical lesson" (CS p.337) to the Pittses, Fortune sells off acreage, even that which Pitts laboriously clears of bitterweed. Like the grandmother in "A Good Man Is Hard to Find," Fortune is spiritually bereft, dreaming of the future development that may occur on his land, "a paved highway in front of his house with plenty of new-model cars on it,...a supermarket store across the road from him,...a gas station, a motel, a drive-in picture-show within easy distance" (CS p.337) - all as prelude to a town that will bear his name. Moreover, through Mary, the one grandchild he cares for - because she is a mirror image of himself - Fortune expects to exert control over both the Pittses and his property from beyond the grave.

In contrast to Fortune, the Pittses are protective of the land, seeking to use it in the natural ways, especially to produce food. In particular, they favor the "lawn," which provides a play area for the children, grazing space for the calves, and a view of the woods across the field. For them, the woods are especially expressive of the glory and wonder of nature and symbolize the divine force in the universe. The Pittses hallow the woods and despair when Fortune announces his intention to sell the lawn for commercial development. His decision precipitates the action that leads to violence and death for both Fortune and his favored grandchild.Throughout the story, Fortune's power over the household is repeatedly demonstrated at the table. Mrs. Pitts is unable to exercise the natural rites of the table, though she has a regard for them, because Fortune sits at one end of it, affirming his authority by subordinating Pitts to a position on the side along with the children. Because Mrs. Pitts can do nothing to alleviate the underriding current of distrust and discontent, mealtime is often the occasion when Fortune chooses to exert his authority, such occasions leaving Mrs. Pitts more worn and languid than before. Despite Pitts' hard work, admirable character, and toleration of abuse, his ten years' loyalty to his father-in-law amounts to nothing in Fortune's heart. Therefore, Pitts' own manhood is provoked at mealtime when Fortune displays his prerogatives; at such occasions, Pitts exerts the only authority he possesses that can express his frustration: he whips Mary, after signalling her to leave the table with him. In being favored by Fortune, Mary becomes a scapegoat for her father. As these acts demonstrate, instead of love and devotion experienced within the household and happiness and contentment shared at table, estrangement and hostility are registered among the three generations. "A View of the Woods" dramatizes through the action of the Pittses and Fortune the destructive effects of a conflict between the traditional agrarian ways, in which the pious feeder was viable, and the modern technological society, which is devoid of respect for the supernatural as well as the natural. In such a conflict, the feeder is rendered ineffective and consequently may even become hostile to members of her own family, as Mrs. Pitts is to Mary; for she mistakenly blames Mary for Fortune's decision to sell the lawn: "She [Mary] put you up to it.... She puts you up to everything." (CS p.344). Much more assertive than the parents in the household rendered in "A Good Man Is Hard to Find," the Pittses are thwarted in their purposeful pursuits in rearing children and raising crops by the capitulation⁻ of Fortune to a standardization of secular taste that embodies a desire for inordinate power, wealth, and recognition. These two stories expose the loss of spiritual values in the extended family as it survives today. The absence of a truly effective feeder is a register of spiritual decline.

In the modern nuclear household, the matriarchs with full families - that is, husband, wife and children - are few, and they have spiritually degenerated in O'Connor's short fiction; none appear in her two novels. Feeding patterns in these women's households are often corrupted, the family members piecing together snacks or utilizing the vague services of commercial feeding institutions at mealtime. Such behavior is symptomatic of the feeder's abnegation of the nurturing role and reveals a general disregard for both the physical and spiritual well-being of the family, the substituted trade services merely operating on a profit motive. As points of reference, the Ashfields and Hills, families in "The River" and "A Stroke of Good Fortune," contain young matrons whose faith is placed on the one hand in abstract art, fashionable clothing, parties, liquor, and cigarettes, and on the other in suburban subdivisions that offer bungalows, drugstores, picture shows, and supermarkets "right in your own neighborhood." (CS p.97). Mrs. Ashfield's young son, Harry, has become adept at discriminating among scraps of party remnants, eating peanut butter and raisin bread heels, or waiting for his hungover parents to get up to take him to a restaurant for lunch. Clearly, Mrs. Ashfield - though tender in her conversations with Harry - lacks the ministries of the feeder. She neglects her duty to provide both physical and spiritual nourishment for her family, thus rendering Harry vulnerable to the seduction of Mrs. Connin, the Reverend Bevel Summers, and the river.

In comparison, Ruby Hill values her youthfulness and what she calls her "get." She disdains motherhood altogether, disparages her two sisters "who married four years have four children apiece" (CS p.97), and deprecates her own mother's ignorance in having given birth to eight children by the time she was thirty-four: "Her mother had got deader with every one of them." (CS p.97). In keeping with her system of thought, which condemns natural procreation, Ruby disapproves of her visiting brother's request for common collard greens for dinner; for she considers the gritty vegetable uncivilized. Thematically, Ruby's disregard for the food preference of her younger brother indicates her disapproval of the old, more natural, ways of living: "She and Bill Hill hadn't eaten collard greens for five years and she wasn't going to start cooking them now." (CS p.95). Despite all she affirms, however, Ruby is part of organic nature. Her husband has deceived her with regard to the use of contraceptives, and she is pregnant and must endure her condition as well as her mortality. Complementing her nature, Ruby's head is described as being "like a big florid vegetable at the top of the sack" of groceries she carries, and her body as being "shaped nearly like a funeral urn." (CS p.95). Ruby Hill seems destined to become the same kind of feeder for her child as Mrs. Ashfield is for Harry.In contrast to the two urban women, Harry's babysitter, Mrs. Connin, is an uncouth country woman; she holds Harry on her lap while feeding him the breakfast she herself prepares. In addition, she shows Harry a picture of Jesus, reads to him from "The Life of Jesus Christ for Readers Under Twelve," and takes him to a river baptizing. Ultimately, Harry's experiences under the auspices of the substitute feeder lead to his drowning; but, despite the violence of the conclusion, we recognize that Mrs. Ashfield is one of the godless ones while Mrs. Connin yet strives to do God's will.

In the four stories just examined - in which husband and wife are still part of the family's composition, no effective feeder emerges, save the outsider Mrs. Connin, though Mrs. Pitts can perhaps become one with the removal of the restraints of her willful father. In all four families, the absence of the feeder's strength is paralleled by marked materialism; in three of them violence results in a death toll of four adults and five children. Significantly, as indicated in the details just cited, both Mrs. Pitts and Mrs. Connin are country-dwellers whose rhythms of daily life are yet associated with the land and animals. They accept the constraints of nature signified by such things as weeds, disease, mutability, human cynicism; and they remain open to mystery and Grace.

Country life does not ensure the adoption of Christian morality, however; nor does the family that lives in the country necessarily escape the dissolution of the feeder impulse or family unity. In fact, most of O'Connor's protagonists belong to single-parent households, and many of these are established in either rural areas or small towns surrounded by farming districts. A group of females associated with such households who fail to observe acceptable feeding rites includes Mrs. Crater in "The Life You Save May Be Your Own," Mrs. Cope in "A Circle in the Fire," Mrs. May in "Greenleaf," and Mrs. Hopewell in "Good Country People." A foil to these women is the pious mother in "A Temple of the Holy Ghost," who still adheres to meaningful offices in the kitchen and enjoys the aid of "the thin blue-gummed cook." (CS p.241). This last woman is given no name, and her one offspring is simply called "the child." The four formerly named women are involved in some phase of what is currently called agribusiness, and all are either widowed or divorced. Similarly, the mother in "A Temple of the Holy Ghost" is without a husband, but her means of livelihood is not explained, though a female schoolteacher boards in her home.

By her boarding of Miss Kirby and her playing weekend hostess to two teenage girls from a nearby convent, the mother demonstrates her healthful nurturing skills. She is a woman with a generous heart, a sense of humor, and a sincere respect for others' welfare. She observes particularly the loneliness of Miss Kirby, who tolerates the courtship of the aged Mr. Cheatam and will "ride in [his] car that smells like the last circle in hell." (CS p.239). True to traditional practices, the mother expends additional effort to entertain her youthful guests by providing them escorts and an outdoor dinner under Japanese lanterns. This feeder is a whole woman - one of the few in O'Connor's fiction. The final evidence of the mother's wholeness is found in her daughter, a young girl frank to confess her own pride and errors or spirit when she meditates upon her nature:"...she was a born liar and slothful and she sassed her mother and was deliberately ugly to almost everybody." (CS p.243). At the end of the story, the child perceives the sun as "a huge red ball like an elevated Host drenched in Blood" that leaves in its sunset " a line in the sky like a red clay road hanging over the trees." (CS p.248). Because of the wholeness of her mother - her holiness, if you will - the child is developing a unified perspective of matter and spirit that compose the universe. Her own eye is whole.

In contrast, with the exception of the innocent Lucynell Crater, the off-spring of the other women possess many of the unfavorable characteristics confessed by the child without admitting them. Indeed, since most of them are mature adults, their ugly behavior is blatantly outrageous. All of these offspring - Sally Virginia, Joy-Hulga, Wesley and Scofield - are unhappy, bitter, disoriented human beings. Joy-Hulga has adopted a rationalistic philosophy that denies the efficacy of the soul; Wesley and Scofield are ill-natured, impotent, self-pitying, defiant, and hostile; and Sally Virginia shows signs in her scowling demeanor of being a younger version of these unhappy beings. All together, these offspring reflect in their natures the spitirual deficiencies of their mothers. Though they can speak of dedication to Christianity, both Mrs. Cope and Mrs. May ascribe wholly to the work ethic as a means of salvation; and both feel their vulnerability to economic ruin. While, as her name suggests, Mrs. Hopewell hopes for the best in every circumstance, she trusts in her own craftiness to run things satisfactorily on her farm. In feeding scenes, all three women reveal their self-centeredness in unconscious ways.

For example, Mrs. Cope, when obliged to offer food to the city boys who come to her farm, provides only Coca-Cola, soda crackers, and guinea sandwiches (which the boys deplore) outside the house. Though she conceives of them as being hungry, she uses food as a bribe, hoping that once the boys are fed, they will depart. Imagery of hunger threads the scenes together, the boys ultimately being discovered to carry their own food in a suitcase. Clearly, the boys hunger for more than food - for genuine social fellowship, family stability and devotion, a bond with nature, and an alliance with the Creator. The smallest of the three disputes the hired man's statement that Mrs. Cope owns the woods by proclaiming, "Man, Gawd owns them woods and her too." (CS p.186). Similarly, Mrs. May abuses the rites of the table; she does so by withholding her fellowship from her grown sons. While she sits with them at mealtime, she does not eat, using the occasion instead to complain about her difficulties with Greenleaf and the dairy farm. In the climactic table scene, Wesley and Scofield instigate a fight, upset the table, and scatter food, dishes, and silver across the floor. In like manner, Mrs. Hopewell and Joy-Hulga are estranged at table episodes. Joy-Hulga especially resents her mother's toleration at mealtime of the hired woman, Mrs. Freeman, who "always managed to arrive at some point during the meal and to watch them finish it." (CS p.273). Like Mrs. May, Mrs. Hopewell particularly abuses the order of the table by using the time to lecture Joy-Hulga (usually about her negative attitude), using clichés repugnant to her well-educated daughter. Most corrupt of all, Mrs. Crater exploits both her feeding services and her retarded daughter, trading both for the hoped-for services of the vagabond Tom T. Shiftlet, whom Mrs. Crater trusts to restore the value of her property. Appropriately, Shiftlet abandons his innocent bride in a roadside diner.Violence, materialism, intellectualism, and secularity are emblems of both the decline of religious faith and the feeder impulse in the four stories just explored. Especially significant is the resultant schism between parents and children. The tales conclude in scenes of arson, death by goring, theft of a wooden leg and desertion of the victim, and abandonment of a mentally retarded bride. In contrast, as previously noted, the story containing a genuinely pious feeder, "A Temple of the Holy Ghost," concludes with an image of nature that represents God's mysterious incarnation of matter, the eucharistic *bread* offered to believers.

Further aberrations of the structure of the family are recorded in the novel *Wise Blood* and in the works that include male surrogate feeders. In the former, the homeless Hazel Motes provides food for himself, encountering hostile commercial feeders in the dining car of a train and the Frosty Bottle refreshment stand. Later, Mrs. Flood exploits him in her boarding house. Uncomfortable when others nourish him, Haze is also dissatisfied with the secular philosophies he attempts to imbibe from the urban populace. Ultimately, he fends for himself in the matter of salvation, reverting to the traditional Christianity of his dead grandfather; and food takes on less and less meaning for Haze as he grows more dedicated to achieving spiritual sustenance.

More important than in *Wise Blood* is the feeder motif in the works in which motherless youngsters are dependent upon a male kinsman. Rayber in *The Violent Bear It Away* and Sheppard in " The Lame Shall Enter First" are counterparts: both are devoted to rationalism and secularity, both are city-dwellers, both are associated in their jobs with the psychological analysis of youth. While the divorced Rayber nourishes his mentally defective son, Bishop, and for a time his visiting nephew Tarwater, the widower Sheppard has the care of his son, Norton, and temporarily that of the delinquent juvenile, Rufus Johnson. Both fathers surrender a portion of the feeding acts to their sons, who manage as does Harry Ashfield to endure a meagre or spoiled kitchen fare. Significantly, when Tarwater arrives, Rayber offers him convenience food that is unappetizing and restaurant fare that seems "slop" to the boy.[2] In both works, the typical activity of the kitchen is perverted. While Rayber uses the table as a desk where he administers aptitude tests to Tarwater and writes a case study of old Mason Tarwater, Sheppard disregards his eleven-year-old's natural state of bereavement caused by the mother's recent death. In addition, like Mrs. May and Mrs. Hopewell, both men combine mealtime with lectures on Good Samaritanism or rationalism that emotionally or psychologically upset those being fed; in such an instance with his father, Norton vomits into his plate, while, in the case of Tarwater and Rayber, Tarwater disgorges into the lake from the side of a boat. Finally, both men's sons endure violent and untimely deaths as the result of their entanglement with the visiting lads, both of whom reject their temporary guardians along with their beliefs, which are false or insincere.It is doubtful that Rayber achieves any spiritual insight from his experiences; but Sheppard, just before his discovery that Norton has hanged himself, undergoes a revelation that is expressed in feeding terminology: "His heart constricted with a repulsion for himself so clear and intense that he gasped for breath. He had stuffed his own emptiness with good works like a glutton. He had ignored his own child to feed his vision of himself." (CS p.481). Too late, Sheppard proclaims that he will "be mother and father" (CS p.482) and find the image of his salvation in Norton's face.

Still another of these male feeders who act as false guides to kinsmen but experience spiritual insight in so doing is old Mr. Head in the popular tale "The Artificial Nigger." Head and his grandson, Nelson, share the rites of the table in their country home, the fare being the hearty, common sort typical thereof. Thematically relevant, Head leaves behind them on the train the lunch prepared for the two when they arrive in Atlanta, a loss that contributes to the day's agony. Head's failure to keep track of the foodstuff is emblematic of his failure to cultivate certain spiritual traits, notably humility; but in an epiphany before the statue of the Negro, Head is restored to community with his estranged grandson and, we think, with the Lord.

Finally, among the male feeders, old Mason Tarwater in *The Violent Bear It Away* - though relatively extreme in theology and behavior - is the most admirable and effective. In the absence of a matriarch, he observes at Powderhead the traditional feeding role, preparing wholesome but simple food for his grand-nephew, young Tarwater, and providing congenial fellowship at the table as well. In all ways, old Tarwater is a foil to his nephew Rayber. The conflict in the novel rests in Tarwater's choice of either the traditional faith of old Tarwater - Christianity - or the modern secular rationalism of Rayber. Consistently, the feeding habits of the primitive Powderhead are contrasted with the sophisticated ones of the city, the latter being associated with expedience, convenience, and artificiality. By this comparison, Rayber's rationalism is represented as a conveniently adopted secular faith without substance. The novel's conflict is resolved when young Tarwater, seeing a vision of his old uncle partaking of the loaves and fishes along with other believers, adopts Christianity. He ascribes to his great-uncle's chief teaching, "Jesus is the Bread of Life," and thereby finds the hunger of his body and soul assuaged. Through the novel, food imagery abounds, the feeder motif being central to the imagery. For example, copious references to bread echo old Tarwater's conception of eternity as being a feast day when Jesus serves loaves and fishes to the assembled multitude. Old Tarwater expects to be one of the group because he has remained faithful, particularly being certain to nourish his family's offspring on the Bread of Life, the immortal feeder.

Since human values and their sustainment are inextricably bound to the work of Flannery O'Connor thematically, as a part of the motivation of her art, her fiction is consequently controlled by thematic emphasis and her plots best catalogued as theme plots. Moreover, this integration of theme and plot design involves as well the whole question of characterization. The feeder is a motif that clarifies both character and theme. Because of the central position of the feeder in O'Connor's plots, this character becomes an important technical device by which we may gauge the contemporary state of individual and family life. The consistency of the delineation in her work is a noteworthy corollary to our modern ethos. With more frequency than when O'Connor wrote her tales, families reflect the constitution of her fictional milieu, single-parent households having particularly multiplied. The schism between generations is obvious in contemporary homes, the bond of fellowship and mutual respect suffering disruption as a result. Most notable, perhaps, is the capitulation of the family to commercial feeding, whether food is taken home for consumption or eaten in the restaurant. A consequent lack of appreciation for nature's role results. The supermarket or dining hall is perceived as the source of nutriments rather than the earth or its creator. Those feeders in O'Connor's fiction who subordinate their kindred's sustenance to their own personal, secular goals - profits, a sense of power, security, or affirmation of a particular self-image - prove to be ineffective and devoid of grace. On the other hand, those who maintain effective feeding rites embody love; and because they honor others' needs before their own, they find joy and grace in God's spirit. Thus, the motif consistently operates as a gauge of spiritual efficacy. Those who maintain the traditional feeding roles maintain a close association with God; those who fail to do so are estranged from Him. The legacy of the former is wholeness, while that of the latter is various forms of disintegration and demise.

Notes

1 "Flannery O'Connor, Sin, and Grace: *Everything That Rises Must Converge*," in *The Sounder Few: Essays from the Hollins Critics* , Eds. Richard H.W. Dillard, George Garrett, and John Rees Moore (Athens, Georgia, 1971), p.104.
2 My essay published in *The Flannery O'Connor Bulletin* ("The 'Feeder' in *The Violent Bear It Away*," 9 [1980], 112-119) elaborates on the nature of the food Rayber provides, as well as on the nature of feeding both in Powderhead and in Rayber's household.

Aesthete

Flannery O'Connor's Poetics of Space

Christiane Beck

Flannery O'Connor's poetics of space has not so far given rise to any controversy among the critics of her eccentric and baffling fiction. Unlike other fields of investigation, O'Connor's sense of place as well as her use of space have either received little attention from the critics or have been universally praised as an unmistakable stamp of her Southernness and a felicitous effect of her pictorial gift. It is beyond dispute that the function of space, in her work, is essentially traditional in the sense that the settings of her weird tales provide an impression of secure familiarity of everyday life, whereas, her glaring suns, her ominous woods point to the apocalyptic strain which subverts the smooth surface of her deceptively mimetic fiction.

This brief study of O'Connor's poetics of space will only allude to her settings in their relationship to the narrative structures or the thematic patterns of her work; it will primarily be concerned with the writer's imaginary creation of her spatial figures. This study will also try to bring out the texture of various connotations that contribute to make of space a subjective, existential experience of the characters and/or the narrator. This approach may lead us a long way from O'Connor's fiction as a text, it may, however, help us to perceive the major trends of the writer's imagination, and how these go to inform the work, and how, ultimately, they help us to grasp the underlying logic of O'Connor's imaginary world.

O'Connor's use of space, however, cannot be divorced from her themes or from that other pole of fiction, related to space: temporality. As in many modern works of literature, space has predominance over time in her fiction in so far as the temporal element, which is predominant, is not duration but the instant, and more particularly that crucial instant when the scheme of time is broken up by the sudden eruption of timelessness: the moment when through a dramatic climax the protagonist undergoes a shattering inner experience that brings about a radical change in his very being. The only possible way of expressing, in fiction, this experience compressed in the instant, is to disclose its effects in terms of visual perception, i.e. to translate it into spatial terms. The characters' sudden displacement to the frontiers of their 'true' and 'strange' country which retains, however, its elusive mystery, is one instance of this recurring spatial theme. If not rendered explicitly in those terms, the ending of a great number of O'Connor's short stories as well as that of her last novel is nevertheless expressed in spatial figures, as the stupefied protagonists are subjected to a disrupting and often hallucinatory vision of their familiar surroundings.

Moreover, O'Connor's most pregnant religious theme is certainly the absolute transcendence of a divine power, a theme that conveys the most primitive and most awesome connotations of the Holy, and which refers explicitly to spatiality in its very etymology since transcendence can only be rendered by means of spatial images. Although O'Connor's fiction can hardly be said to belong to the 'spatial form novel' analyzed by Joseph Frank in his influential essays on the subject[1], her treatment of space is far from being unique in contemporary literature.

As shown by sociologists who have studied human space in modern culture, space itself has become a major theme in contemporary literature. Georges Matoré[2] has been led to conclude that this new awareness of space has resulted from all the uncertainties of our age, as man has become haunted by the problem of his precarious position in a world where he has continuously to look for landmarks which can no longer be taken for granted. Postwar existentialist literature has explored a number of spatial themes that stress man's exile in the world. We know partly through her letters, partly through Frederick Asal's recent study[3] that O'Connor was attuned to this general mood of uncertainty of her age. If one senses some desolate, ghostlike quality about her wandering loners, suggesting a kinship with existentialist anti-heroes, her themes as well as her typology of space are, however, undeniably derived from traditional sources. Her typology is largely indebted to literary pastoralism with the difference that she does not share the sense of nostalgia which characterizes the Southern Agrarians of the 30's. Taking up the time-honored opposition between town and nature, she alters it radically by integrating it and submitting it to the central archetype of the sun which becomes the ultimate reference of her spatial and fictional world. The sun is not only the source of light, it is often given in O'Connor's work the form and the function of an eye, capable of seeing the world, of judging the ways of man, of spying on his most secret acts, thus assuming the power of an·All-Seeing God, the absolute Master of the world and of man, from whom all judgment comes.

The most conspicuous characteristic of space in this work is its pervasive hostililty invariably aimed at man. The human world is shown to be an essentially homeless place, a world where children are left motherless as soon as they are born and doomed to face the aggressions of a hostile universe without ever having known the protective warmth of love. O'Connor's world is one where man is fated from his birth to live as the prey of hostile spatial powers. This spatial antagonism is mostly generated by the sun, activated by its ocular nature. Whenever the sun is shown as propitious to man, this particular characteristic significantly vanishes to give way to the coruscating luminosity of the sun as a pearl or a diamond.

If sun and sky represent the most powerful cosmic forces that confront the human being, spatial antagonism is, however, not restricted to them. One can denote a strain of hostility in the writer's very way of representing space, its effects being less overtly polemical and perhaps more subtly disturbing and uncanny as it tends to de-realize space. O'Connor's familiar landscape of the hilly farmland with its chequered expanse of fields, pastures and woods, carefully separated by the hand of man, suggesting the geometrical outline of a cadasteral survey, stands out sharply against the wide empty sky, either blank or glaring, with its defensive dark treeline, rigidly erect like a 'sentinel', a 'wall' or a 'fortress-line'. What this mode of spatial delineation leaves out altogether is the dimension of depth that usually characterizes space to the human eye; we no longer recognize it through our visual sense, memory or common sense.

This mode of spatial representation has become, since the beginning of our century, the characteristic innovation of modern painting with the elimination of perspective, and it can to some extent define O'Connor's spatiality. Whereas the flatness of her characters has often been mentioned, her frequent use of two-dimensional space has not been noticed, yet both partake of the same imaginary mode of representation. "Some times the last line of trees was a solid gray-blue wall a little darker than the sky but this afternoon it was almost black and behind it the sky was a livid glaring white." (CS p.175).These opening lines of "A Circle in the Fire" strike a note of hostility in the very disposition of the landscape, which is sharply divided by the treeline into two surfaces set side by side. It is further dramatized by the chromatic black-white contrast, whereas a threatening note is conveyed by the single word "glaring" that betrays the explosive dynamism of the apparently absent sun. This setting is taken up at crucial moments throughout the story, as it is experienced by a young girl, with a more and more ominous urgency, so that the reader is left with the feeling of an active cosmic power set up against the child. What characterizes O'Connor's setting, here and elsewhere, is, first, clear distinctness. There is a definite urge in her essentially visual imagination to distinguish, to separate different elements, to disconnect things and often to oppose them. This disjunctive turn of the writer's imagination can be seen operating in her way of representing space, leading her to emphasize clear outlines, neat segregation of different planes, which tends to suppress the sense of depth, harshness of straight or broken lines, as well as violent contrasts of colors. It may even be more stylized and lead to a kind of geometrism which is particularly striking when applied to the human figure or face, but the same impulse informs her settings of juxtaposed surfaces. This tendency of O'Connor's imagination may even assume a more aggressive form when the urge to segregate turns into that impulse to cut things up, that Gaston Bachelard has called 'complexe du glaive' (literally: the sword complex). O'Connor is famous for her relish for mutilating human bodies; she has a similar relish for mutilating space: in *Wise Blood* "A boxcar roared past, chopping the empty space in two." (WB p.16). In the same novel, the skyline of Taulkinham reveals a harsh ruggedness: "The smokestack and square tops of buildings made a black uneven wall against the lighter sky and here and there a steeple cut a sharp wedge out of a cloud." (WB p.198).Space retains this two-dimensional quality when it functions as a background with characters simply stuck on; thus Julian in "Everything That Rises Must Converge:" "[He] appeared pinned to the door frame, waiting like Saint Sebastian for the arrows to begin piercing him." (CS p.146).This aspect becomes more arresting when the character is silhouetted against the blank sky, as is the case with Mr. Shiftlet in "The Life You Save May Be Your Own:""He turned his back and faced the sunset. He swung both his whole and his short arm up slowly so that they indicated an expanse of sky and his figure formed a crooked cross." (CS p.146).This disposition of the human imagination to strive for visual distinctness and sharp segregation has been analyzed by anthropologists, who consider it as a primary and major operational mode of the human imagination.

Gilbert Durand[4] has named it the 'schizomorphous' structure of the imagination, opposing it to the 'mystical' structure, both terms being taken in their etymological sense. This mode of perceiving reality as it is revealed in its extreme form of abstracting things totally from their mundane environment is usually strongly dualistic, leading to a world view in which two opposing forces are seen to contend for domination, which often accounts for the polemical tone, distinctive of this mode. According to Durand's analysis, this mode characterizes, to a high degree, the Western imagination and culture, where it has given rise to the heroic myths of conquest and the victory of light over darkness.

This mode often seems pertinent to a study of O'Connor's dualistic imaginary world as a whole. We have tried to show it operating in her settings of natural space; it may also be perceived in her representation of urban space. The town of Taulkinham, in *Wise Blood*, with its harsh linear design, its dark tunnel-like alleys, its box-like houses, its "glary" lights and its sky flat "like a piece of thin polished silver with a dark sour-looking sun in one corner of it," (WB p.68) can hardly fail to remind the reader of T.S. Eliot's "Unreal city." It constitutes one of numerous instances in modern literature where space, deprived of its third dimension, is deliberately de-realized and no longer bears any reference to our 'natural' vision.[5]

What makes the experience of the town particularly terrifying is its confinement; the town is one of the many dark enclosing spaces of this world. Urban space is steeped in a lugubrious semi-darkness which reveals the absence or the weakness of the sun and conveys to it the spectral quality of a space cut off from the cosmic vitality of sunlight. The dangers of the town never come from the sky as in the country, but from its confinement and its labyrinthian configuration, generating the characters' haunting anguish of being "sucked along endless pitchblack tunnels," down into chthonian depths. Young Tarwater's fear of engulfment is further associated with his obsession of different imaginary themes (inefficiency of the sun 'too far to ignite anything', claustrophobia, the image of metal as a destructive substance which reinforces O'Connor's general pessimism as regards matter), which makes of the town a space indelibly doomed to entropy. This is clearly suggested in *The Violent Bear It Away* on young Tarwater's arrival in town:

...He was sitting forward on the seat, looking out the window at a hill covered with old used-car bodies. In the indistinct darkness, they seemed to be drowning into the ground, to be about half-submerged already. The city hung in front of them on the side of the mountain as if it were a larger part of the same pile, not yet buried so deep. The fire had gone out of it and it appeared settled in its unbreakable parts. (VBIA pp.54-55).

Entropy is the ultimate law of man-made space because the sun can neither reach it nor purify it with its fire. The town constitutes one spatial pole, totally negative, of the writer's typology while the opposite pole is the remote clearing in the woods, inaccessible to the mechanized world of modern life, protected by its impregnable primitivity. Powderhead is its most significant example, opposed to the town, but also to the cultivated rural space; there the surrounding trees lose their geometrical design and are seen to run "in grey and purple folds" whereas the last line of trees is softened into a light blue. If Powderhead is safe from the evils of modern progress, it is, by no means, an edenic space; it is a stronghold which old Tarwater is prepared to defend with his loaded gun against the intrusion of townspeople, but it is neither safe from bobcats nor from divine wrath: the old prophet has occasionally to thrash out his peace with the Lord in the nearby woods. But as the name aptly suggests, it is endowed with a potentially explosive energy, with cosmic vitality, being open to the light and the power of the sun. "...when I'm gone, you'll be better off in these woods by yourself with just as much light as the sun wants to let in than you'll be in the city with [the schoolteacher]," (VBIA p.24) old Tarwater advises his great-nephew and spiritual heir.

Between these two poles lies O'Connor's favorite battleground that of most of her stories, the self-enclosed farms run by her domineering and struggling widows forming a threatening space, relentlessly spied and preyed upon and claimed by the sun. As the sun assumes essentially the judging and castigating function of the eye, its most frequent position is in the middle of the sky, just above the characters, and it is hardly surprising that the predominant dynamic movement of space should be vertical and strike from above, and that most characters should be haunted by the fear of being struck by lightning and by the fear of fire. Yet they feel as much threatened by the absence as by the presence of the sun, space itself generating an overwhelming sense of awe, no longer related to the theme of solar transcendence. This spatial anguish concerns particularly O'Connor's spiritual anti-heroes Hazel Motes, The Misfit and O.E. Parker, and it takes them wandering around the world. It represents one of the writer's most pregnant spatial themes with which, very much in the manner of Kafka, she conveys a compelling metaphysical or possibly religious dimension, by associating a great archetypal spatial image - the sea, the desert - with the concrete details of everyday reality. Parker's experience at sea suggests this tone remarkably:

After a month or two in the navy, his mouth ceased to hang open. His features hardened into the features of a man. He stayed in the navy five years and seemed a natural part of the gray mechanical ship, except for his eyes, which were the same pale slate-color as the ocean and reflected the immense spaces around him as if they were a microcosm of the mysterious sea. In port Parker wandered about comparing the run-down places he was in to Birmingham, Alabama. (CS pp.513-514).

Haze Motes undergoes a comparable experience in the desert where the authorities forget him, while he is contemplating his soul and the empty space around him. This elusive threat, inherent in immense spaces, is likewise felt by Parker: "Long views depressed Parker. You look out into space like that and you begin to feel as if someone were after you, the navy or the government or religion." (CS p. 516).

Toward the end of *Wise Blood*, after the dismantling of his car, Haze Motes has an uncanny experience of space as a reality of its own, without any kind of referential value attached to it, an experience of absolute space: "Haze stood for a few minutes, looking over at the scene. His face seemed to reflect the entire distance across the clearing and on beyond, the entire distance that extended from his eyes to the blank gray sky that went on, depth after depth, into space." (WB p.209).

This fascination with absolute space, which mysteriously captures the look of the haunted man, may suggest the fascination of 'the invisible' conceived as infinite distance, as an inaccessible transcendence. One cannot help being struck by the great number of negative connotations used to define this transcendent power as Hazel Motes is pathetically dispossessed while he stands staring into this space, and one cannot help feeling how absolutely 'the numinous' is equated with nothingness in this novel.

O'Connor's second novel shows less ambiguously this annihilating experience of 'the numinous'. Marion Tarwater is the only one of the writer's spiritual anti-heroes who is granted the mystical vision of 'numious' space. As the clearing of Powderhead is being transfigured into vast grey spaces, he cannot but submit to this vision, so that the boy's ultimate religious experience also takes on the extreme form of total dispossession. The sun is significantly absent from this final scene, its active power being no longer needed, the scene is endowed with a passive and sublime mysticism, symbolized by vastness, semi-darkness and silence. According to Rudolf Otto, these are the only ways of suggesting 'the numious', which is the non-rational element of the Holy, the irreducible and primitive feature of the sacred in all religions.[6] Echoes can be found in the Old Testament, and this seems the most remarkable and eccentric aspect of the religious, compellingly revived in O'Connor's fiction.

Space is also more powerfully active in *The Violent Bear It Away* and its dynamism derives from the sun: we may remember the cosmic convulsions, experienced by Marion Tarwater, as the whole sky seems to fall down and smother him. Compare also the tree of fire which Parker feels is about to seize him. These apocalyptic climaxes are often foreshadowed by an atmosphere of spatial threat, generated by the sun seen as a spy, an intruder or an outraged master. O'Connor's second novel is particularly governed by this obsessive presence of the sun whose ocular character is almost systematically stressed.[7] O'Connor has even imparted new vigor to the theme of solar transcendence in using two striking metaphors: the sun as a "silver bullet" and as a "ball of glare." Besides being expressive in itself, each metaphor revives significant aspects of the eye metaphor: the image of the silver bullet connotes the projectile and piercing power of the eye while the ball of glare suggests the explosive sense of outrage which the eye can express. In "Greenleaf," Mrs. May twice perceives the sun in this threatening way:

The light outside was not so bright but she was conscious that the sun was directly on top of her head, like a silver bullet ready to drop into her brain. (CS p.325).

When she first stopped it was a swollen red ball, but as she stood watching it began to narrow and pale until it looked like a bullet. Then suddenly it burst through the tree line and raced down the hill toward her. (CS p.329).

Even O'Connor's first use of colors must be examined in its relation to the sun and its igneous element, fire. Her often violent colors are definitely pictorial in their purity and contrasting effects. Her crimson suns, her black woods unfailingly acquire a dynamic or polemical quality; yet colors tend to be often less significant than brilliance and luminosity. The dramatic climaxes, the crucial experiences of her protagonists are recurringly signaled, in space, by a chromatic transmutation: colors become more intense and glassy as through the secret purifying action of fire, gaining a quality of unreal transparence and sheen. This chromatic change is noted in "A Circle in the Fire" by the child at the approach of the three boys: "The sun burned so fast that it seemed to be trying to set everything in sight on fire. The white water tower was glazed pink and the grass was an unnatural green as if it were turning to glass." (CS pp.184-185).In the second novel, as the two children make for the lake, Rayber notices a similar change: "The sky was a bright pink, casting such a weird light that every color was intensified. Each weed that grew out of the gravel looked like a live green nerve." (VBIA p.197). So, more than colors themselves, it is intense brightness and, as we shall see, white radiance which always imply positive connotations in O'Connor's fiction. This is clearly evinced in her second novel, when the image of the sun as a "silver bullet" or a "ball of glare" is transformed into the image of a pearl or a diamond to signify a positive change in the protagonists. Thus, after young Tarwater has accomplished his first mission, he witnesses the metamorphosis of the sun: "The sun, from being only a ball of glare, was becoming distinct like a large pearl, as if sun and moon had fused in a brilliant marriage." (VBIA p.221). However, O'Connor seldom resorts to this kind of complete symbolic reversal. The metaphor of the sun as a diamond is normally used in scenes of natural beauty, which are not totally absent from her work, and in which, significantly, perspective is restored. These scenes act on the protagonists as a revelation or an illumination and form what could be called an epiphanic space. The most obvious one occurs in *The Violent Bear It Away*, as Marion Tarwater watches Bishop in the pool in the city park:

The sun, which had been tacking from cloud to cloud, emerged above the fountain. A blinding brightness fell on the lion's tangled marble head and gilded the stream of water rushing from his mouth. Then the light, falling more gently, rested like a hand on the child's white head. His face might have been a mirror where the sun had stopped to watch its reflection." (VBIA p.164).

In "The River," Bevel, the child protagonist, is given to contemplate another scene, set in nature, open to the sunlight: "At the bottom of the hill, the woods opened suddenly onto a pasture dotted here and there with black and white cows and sloping down, tier by tier, to a broad orange stream where the reflection of the sun was set like a diamond." (CS p.164). If the first scene strikes the reader as epiphanic mainly through its use of dazzling sunlight and whiteness, its unusual sense of exuberance and delicacy of forms, the second landscape has all the marks of O'Connor's style of representation, but somehow subtly toned down; the woods no longer form a wall and all the pasture is gently sloping down to the expanding river, while the whole scene is directed toward the sun's scintillating reflection in the stream, conveying to it a sense of spatial openness and freedom, seldom encountered in this work. The final scene of "The Artificial Nigger" succeeds even more fully in expressing a sense of resolution and harmony which remains unique in O'Connor's fiction:

...the moon, restored to its full splendor, sprang from a cloud and flooded the clearing with light. As they stepped off, the sage grass was shivering gently in shades of silver and the clinkers under their feet glittered with a fresh black light. The treetops, fencing the junction like the protecting walls of a garden, were darker than the sky which was hung with gigantic white clouds illuminated like lanterns. (CS p.269).

O'Connor has, perhaps, never more brilliantly combined visual accuracy and vigor with a fine sense of natural gracefulness: the dominant impression is, indeed, one of radiant luminosity that is softened by two graceful notations of light and movement ("the sage grass was shivering gently in shades of silver") and the final scene brings to the story a resolution that is largely expressed in spatial terms.These scenes of natural beauty, however infrequent, may well betray a striving, if not for any dialectical resolution in her harshly dualistic world, at least for a lessening of the extreme tension that shapes her fiction, when conflicts are not actually resolved, but simply toned down, or "euphemized."

One of her most impressive achievements in the use of space, light, color and movement in relation to the conclusion of the story, can be found in the last pages of "Revelation" where she brings into harmony, through unusually muted effects, her often jarring elements of violence, satire and sudden enlightenment. In a scene which combines O'Connor's sense of the ludicrous and the uncanny with her high moral seriousness, Mrs. Turpin gazes down at her pigs when "a red glow suffuses them" and they are panting "with a secret life." (CS p.508). This final vision shows a sense of spatial reconciliation between heaven and earth, as a purple streak merges the crimson of a field with the dark blue of the sky at dusk building a bridge between the two worlds:

She saw the streak as a vast swinging bridge extending upward from the earth through a field of living fire. Upon it a vast horde of souls were rumbling toward heaven. There were whole companies of white-trash, clean for the first time in their lives, and bands of black niggers in white robes, and battalions of freaks and lunatics shouting and clapping and leaping like frogs. (CS p.508).

This ending of one of O'Connor's last stories may well be an artistic triumph over her habitual "Imagination of Extremity," a story where her stern sense of judgment seems more in accordance with the human sins she denounces, while space is brilliantly used as the sole means of harmonizing her starkly divided world.

In concluding with this story, we do not mean to imply that O'Connor had, at last, found her true voice and a new way of using her exceptional talent that might have proved more palatable to her modern audience. The style of her imagination is, undoubtedly dualistic and polemical, and her religious sensitivity, as reflected in her work is so strangely attuned to a primitive, pre-Christian view of the sacred that it is hardly comprehensible either to the Christian or to the secular audience of our times. Yet there are some spatial figures, some scenes of nature that tend to reveal at least a tendency of her imaginary world toward "euphemization," tuning down her relentless sense of strife and her too frequently. triumphant conspiracy with the sun against man. And this undertone of her fiction has found its most convincing expression in her aesthetics of space.

145

Notes

1 Joseph Frank, *The Widening Gyre: Crisis and Mastery in Modern Literature*, Rutgers, 1963.
2 Georges Matoré, *L'Espace Humain*, Paris, 1962.
3 Frederick Asals, *Flannery O'Connor, The Imagination of Extremity* , Athens, Georgia, 1982.
4 Gilbert Durand, *Les Structures Anthropologiques de l'Imaginaire* , Paris, 1969, pp.209-215.
5 This modern aspect of O'Connor's representation of space may be accounted for by Wilhelm Wo°rringer's theory concerning the alternation between the naturalistic and non-naturalistic styles in the plastic arts. In eras dominated by disharmony between man and the cosmos "the artist abandons the projection of space entirely and returns to the plane, reduces organic nature to linear-geometric forms, and frequently eliminates all traces of organicism in favor of pure lines, forms and colors." Joseph Frank, p.51.
6 Rudolf Otto, *The Idea of the Holy*, translated by John W. Harvey, New York, 1958.
7 Cp. VBIA pp.24-25, p.42 The ocular characteristic is also applied, in this novel, to the moon and the stars without any significant change in its symbolism. VBIA p.85.

"The Meanest of Them Sparkled": Beauty and Landscape in Flannery O'Connor's Fiction

Carter Martin

"'We've had an ACCIDENT,'" the children cry gleefully. "'But nobody's killed,' June Star said with disappointment." (CS p.125). Within a few minutes, June Star is dead, and so is the rest of her family. This extraordinary irony informs the story in several ways. Like Eliot being surprised that so many have crossed the bridge or Ransom's characters being astonished at a child's death, we as readers of "A Good Man Is Hard to Find" are awed by the swiftness and finality of the six deaths effected by The Misfit. I think we come back to the story time and again to experience this awe and to inquire into it. We are, in this, somewhat like Mrs. Greenleaf, who clips stories of grotesque deaths and bizarre suffering so that she can wallow in the dirt and pray over them. There is a medieval quality about the centrality of death in O'Connor's fiction.

There are, however, other dimensions to the irony of "A Good Man Is Hard to Find," specifically, that the automobile accident and the swift deaths following it constitute an opening up, a movement of this fiction to a moment when Flannery O'Connor shows us, as she so often does, the landscape of eternity. Rather than showing us, as Eliot does, "Fear in a handful of dust,"[1] she shows us *beauty* in the most horrible of human experiences. This journey of the imagination from the horrible to the truth of God's grace has been an important response often noted by O'Connor's readers. Nevertheless, there is a wallowing in the dirt about it all, for we too often assume that it is only through the ugly and the grotesque, through suffering and pain, through loss and death that the grand truths of the universe emerge from *Wise Blood, A Good Man Is Hard to Find, The Violent Bear It Away,* and *Everything That Rises Must Converge.* However, O'Connor presented the beauty of this world as vividly as sunlight through the stained-glass window of a Gothic cathedral or the brilliant icons of the churches of Byzantium. It is this beauty I want to show in its importance in the total perception of O'Connor's fiction. It is one reason for her popularity - not just among academics but among readers everywhere of every persuasion and personal circumstance.

In his introduction to *Everything That Rises Must Converge*, Robert Fitzgerald took issue with those who complained that O'Connor's fiction "lacked a sense of natural beauty and human beauty."[2] In refutation, Fitzgerald cites a line from a beautiful story, which is actually also O'Connor's most notoriously violent story, "A Good Man Is Hard to Find." The line reads: "The trees were full of silver-white sunlight and the meanest of them sparkled." (CS p.119). More generally but relevant to this passage, Fitzgerald says: "Beyond incidental phrasing and images, beauty lies in the strong invention and execution of the things, as in objects expertly forged or cast or stamped, with edges, not waxen and worn or softly moulded."[3] For this quality he uses the term *ascesis* because of its economy, its spareness and brevity. Further, he contends that the wife in "A Good Man Is Hard to Find" carries out a beautiful action when she politely says "Yes, thank you," (CS p.131) to her murderer, as he leads her away into the woods. Such actions, he contends, are beautiful, "though as brief as beautiful actions usually are."[4]

In spite of Fitzgerald's pointing the way, too little has been written about the very real beauty to be found in O'Connor's fiction. She herself does not use the word often, but in her nonfiction she makes it clear that beauty is very important to her view of the world. In a letter to "A" she states: "I am one, of course, who believes that man is created in the image and likeness of God. I believe that all creation is good...." (HB p.104). And when reviewers failed to see that there was (according to her) no bitterness in her stories but a cherishing of the world, she took their failure to be a moral one and tantamount to "what Nietzche meant when he said God was dead." (HB p.90). She admits that her stories in *A Good Man Is Hard to Find* contain "...many rough beasts now slouching toward Bethlehem to be born," but contends that reviewers have "hold of the wrong horror." She insists that "you have to cherish the world at the same time that you struggle to endure it." (HB p.90).

I want to demonstrate in several of O'Connor's works a pattern of beauty which I take to be an important part of the rhetorical structure of her fiction. These patterns happen to be at one with the narrative structure, and they are at one with her own statements in regard to what the works are "about." She once complained in a letter to Sister Mariella Gable that critics too often do not see what is really there, and she invoked Gerard Manley Hopkins' notion of "inscape" to explain what she meant. (HB p.517). Her method is at one with so many other writers who have, like Hopkins, written in 'Pied Beauty' about:

All things counter, original, spare, strange;

Whatever is fickle, freckled (who knows how?)
With swift, slow; sweet, sour; adazzle, dim;...(ll. 8-10).

It is a method of indirection that nevertheless is especially about the beautiful. One thinks of Emily Dickinson, who spoke of this matter in one of her poems:

Tell all the truth but tell it slant -
...The truth must dazzle gradually,
or every man be blind - ("Tell all the truth", ll. 1;7-8).

She carries out what Robert Browning's painter "Fra Lippo Lippi" claimed was one of the artist's functions:

...We're made so that we love
First when we see them painted, things we have passed
Perhaps a hundred times nor cared to see;
...Art was given for that;...(ll. 300-304).

O'Connor was herself a visual artist as well as a literary one. Robert Fitzgerald describes some of this graphic art: "They are simple but beautiful paintings of flowers in bowls, of cows under trees, of the Negro house under the bare trees of winter."[5] Her literary work is also highly visual, and when this visualization is specifically beautiful it often constitutes a special form of punctuation that gives rhythm and shape to the structure of her narrative. One must look carefully to appreciate this aesthetic, for it is similar to what Auden perceives about Breughel and the old masters in his poem "Musée des Beaux Arts": Those painters understood, he says, the human position of suffering,

...how it takes place
While someone else is eating or opening a window or just walking dully along,
...That even the dreadful martyrdom must run its course
Anyhow in a corner, some untidy spot
Where the dogs go on with their doggy life and the torturer's horse
Scratches its innocent behind on a tree (ll. 3-4, 10-13).

The beauty in O'Connor's stories is that way: it occurs casually, is understated, characterized by the spareness of *ascesis*, and is usually surrounded by ugliness, banality, or violence. The result, however, is not necessarily an impression that beauty is chimerical or accidental but instead that it is the reality that informs the entire structure of the affective world she portrays. "For the almost blind," she wrote, "you draw large and startling figures." (MM p.34). Which is to say that she, like

149

Dickinson, doubted the capacity of her audience to look directly and consistently upon the beauty that she herself perceived in the universe. Breughel's "The Blind People," portrays in the foreground a single file of stumbling, wildly disoriented blind men; but in the background landscape is the church. The rhetoric could not be simpler or clearer. In his "The Fall of Icarus" the rhetoric is similar; the great tragic drowning is proportionately minuscule in comparison to the coarse farmer, his ox and plow cutting fresh furrows in the foreground. In "The Hunters in the Snow" Breughel creates unusual beauty from a severe, colorless and cold landscape by investing it with meaning that comes from the shape of life and activity and the sense of returning home or coming into the open. The village and the frozen lake lie below the men and their slender dogs.

O'Connor's use of such forms of beauty is found throughout her work. I would like to examine it in "The Life You Save May Be Your Own," "A Good Man Is Hard to Find," and in *The Violent Bear It Away*, which represent examples of her increasingly complex technique. In "The Life You Save May Be Your Own," we find what might be called a brief conceit of grotesque beauty: "A fat yellow moon appeared in the branches of the fig tree as if it were going to roost there with the chickens." (CS p.148). The poetic adequacy of this sentence is as fully realized as Ezra Pound's poem, "In a Station of the Metro":

> The apparition of those faces in the crowd;
> Petals on a wet, black bough.

O'Connor's sentence achieves what Pound himself claims for his poem and his concept of *Imagisme* and vorticism: that the image when presented directly transforms an outward and objective thing "into a thing inward and subjective," but he goes on to say that "the image is not an idea. It is a radiant node or cluster,...a *vortex*, from which, and through which, and into which, ideas are constantly rushing." Pound quotes Thomas Aquinas, *Nomina sunt consequentia rerum* ,[6] that is, names are the consequence of things. O'Connor's sentence permits the reader to find beauty where it would not have been perceived without the intervention of art; she permits the beauty and objective propriety of the moon/fig tree/chickens image to emerge. The entire matter illustrates the meaning of a passage she underlined in her copy of Croce's "A Breviary of Aesthetics": "Art is an ideal within the four corners of an image."[7] In this case the ideal is linked with the actual and is made flesh by the linking of heavenly bodies with earthly ones - a converging of actualities in one plane of perception. Another fleeting but beautiful image in an unlikely context is Mrs, Lucynell Crater's perception of the evening sun in "The Life You

Save May Be Your Own": it "appeared to be balancing itself on the peak of a small mountain." (CS p.145). Mrs. Crater sits "with her arms folded across her chest as if she were the owner of the sun." (CS p.146). The sun, from her perspective, is indeed on the mountain, and as seen from her porch it is indeed her sun. Just as she is confident that *her* chickens are roosting in *her* fig tree, so the moon *must* be there and be hers. Her literal-mindedness and simplicity are counterbalanced by Mr. Shiftlet's mechanical rationality and calculatingly evil opportunism. The flashes of beauty, brief though they may be, enable the reader to understand the wholeness of the world portrayed by O'Connor - its depth and its contradictions and its multiple realities.

When a reader enters an O'Connor story by looking through such windows that open onto beauty - particularly when he feels that the narrative house from which he looks is filled with darkness and terror and malignity - he is experiencing what Martin Heidegger referred to as "coming into the open." Heidegger asserts that "Meaning is...not a property attaching to entities, lying 'behind' them, or floating somewhere as an 'intermediate domain.'" It is the field upon which "something becomes intelligible as something." [8] Heidegger contends that the poet experiences the abyss (the "default of God," he calls it) [9] and causes readers to reach into the abyss to discover divine radiance shining "in everything that is" and also to realize that absence is presence, "the ancient name of Being." [10] In "What are Poets For?" Heidegger says that they "sense the trace of fugitive gods" [11] and trace for others the way toward the turning. In the midst of the unholy, he claims, the songs of the venturesome poets (those who take dangerous risks) turn "our unprotected being into the Open." [12]

A reader's experience of coming into the open by way of O'Connor's punctuation of beauty is more elaborately realized in one of her most violent and disturbing stories, "A Good Man Is Hard to Find." The pattern of this story is a series of scenes in confined space which are seen in the context of unbounded space - light, sky, clouds, and woods seen from above so that they stretch out as the blue tops of trees. The story moves from the unpleasant circumstances of three-generational family life to the awesome absence of the lives so recently present. Yet this movement is one that leads us from the beauty of the world to the beauty of death or perhaps to the beauty of grace attendant upon death. The key lines form an image cluster that controls this meaning. Significantly, the perception originates with the grandmother, just as the presence of grace is understood only with reference to her at the time of the mass murder. When the family is setting out on their Florida trip, the grandmother tries

151

to share the beauty she sees with the ill-tempered children, Wesley and June Star:

She pointed out interesting details of the scenery: Stone Mountain; the blue granite that in some places came up to both sides of the highway; the brilliant red clay banks slightly streaked with purple; and the various crops that made rows of green lace-work on the ground. The trees were full of silver-white sunlight and the meanest of them sparkled. (CS p.119).

All of these images are patently beautiful: the mountain, the granite, the red clay, the crops, the trees, the sunlight, and in the combination that O'Connor places them, they are poetic and constitute a potential vortex, a radiant node or cluster into which the meaning of the story eventually enters. Only five of the twenty-one pages of the story do not contain cognate imagery. Even though we do not perceive it as beauty as it casually occurs, this imagery represents the macrocosm of the story and permits the reader to come into the open thematically on what O'Connor calls elsewhere "the true country." (MM p.27) The fleeting signs of the reality of that country are in this story the woods filled with light, beginning with the grandmother's paean and moving through the chinaberry tree at Red Sammy Butts', the "blue tops of trees for miles around," trees that look down on the family car, "woods, tall and dark and deep," "woods [that] gaped like a dark open mouth," and the woods that relentlessly devour the family before the awestruck grandmother: "Alone with The Misfit, the grandmother found that she had lost her voice. There was not a cloud in the sky nor any sun. There was nothing around her but woods." (CS p.131). At this point the story has moved from the circumstantial beauty of the affective world to the ideal and permanent beauty of the action of grace that paradoxically informs the irrational gesture in which the grandmother reaches out to touch The Misfit, anagogically accepting him as her own, as Christ accepted sinners.

This remarkable conclusion to the story has been explained by O'Connor herself in terms of grace and its focus on the grandmother (MM pp.108-114), but her explanation is not easy for many readers who see in the foreground a homicidal maniac carrying out a mass murder. However, if the reader examines the structure of the story, the affirmation of this reading is more available, even to the reader who may be unfamiliar with O'Connor's explanation. The pattern already described is enhanced by its contrapuntal movement with reference to the imagery of enclosure. The grim, threatening quality of the story begins before the appearance of The Misfit and is associated with the microcosm of the family, specifically as they are presented enclosed and entrapped, so confined and relentlessly bound to each other's presence that, except for the grandmother, they are unable to look out to the larger world or to conceive of the possibility that they may come into the open, enter a larger, freer, more beautiful world.

The first of these enclosures is the home itself. Only one and one-half pages long, it is a tightly blocked stage setting which conveys the maddening intimacy of family life. Bailey, the father, is unsuccessfully trying to escape by immersing himself in the sports section of the *Journal*. The garrulous grandmother is invading everyone's space by fatuously claiming a role as wise elder, warning the family of The Misfit and trying to change the plans for the trip to Florida; that she is expressing her desperate lack of belonging, of being an unwanted outsider is borne out by the cruel remarks of the children, who are lying on the floor reading the funny papers: "...why dontcha stay at home?" one of them asks. The mother, "whose face was as broad and innocent as a cabbage," (CS p.117) sits on the sofa in quiet desperation, feeding apricots to the baby. The terrible proximity of them all creates an atmosphere of hysteria, and the reader's inclination is to scream and flee. This first instance of enclosure is brief and quite intense.

The enclosure in the automobile is similarly cloying because of the quite raw conflicts between the generations: a lonely and silly old woman trying to be cheerful and agreeable, children who are by turns ill-mannered or sullenly oblivious, and parents who are almost stupefied and overtaxed by their role as the responsible adults. They are caged and baffled in a rolling domestic zoo, objectified with satire and irony by the grandmother's stories, the children's cloud game, the baby being passed to the back seat, and occasional glimpses of the quickly passing stable world outside the car, one of which, the Negro child, the grandmother would like to bring into stasis: "If I could paint, I'd paint that picture," she says. (CS p.119). The overwhelming irony of the boredom and tension is that the end of it in the affective world is not reconciliation or a coming into love and harmony but sudden death.

The same ironic pathos informs the details of the third objectification of the existential enclosure of life in the countryside or the fallen world. Red Sammy Butts' restaurant, "The Tower was a long dark room with a counter at one end and tables at the other and dancing space in the middle." (CS p.121). The discontent and hostility continue: Bailey glares at his mother when she asks him to dance, June Star insults Red Sammy's wife, he tells his wife "to quit lounging on the counter and hurry up with these people's order." (CS p.121). The conversation is premonitory and pessimistic in its concern with The Misfit and the degeneration of mankind in general. It is a relief when "The children ran outside into the white sunlight and looked at the monkey in the lacy chinaberry tree." (CS p.122).

The next narrative block returns to the enclosure of the automobile. It is at this time that the grandmother awakens "outside of Toombsboro" (note the extension of the irony and the imagery) with her plan to visit an old plantation, the venture that leads them to their encounter with The Misfit. The children are eager to get out of the car. The imagery of the secret panel and hidden silver and the sudden emergence of the cat from its basket foreshadow the sudden and catastrophic opening up of the narrative and of the six lives.

With the grandmother, the reader is awed by the ten-page conclusion to the story, more than one-third of its length. O'Connor protracts this event. She has prepared us for it carefully, so that when we see the hearselike car on the hill and look down upon the family spilled out from their banal entrapment into the big world, we know the terrible outcome at once. Thus we must participate in the moment of dying, with horror, outrage, and finally with wonder. This narration is somewhat like the medieval drama *Everyman* in which the protagonist's moment of death is expanded artistically and dramatically to include his realization, his pleading, his acceptance, and his receiving the sacraments and God's grace. A similar effect is achieved by Tolstoy in "The Death of Ivan Ilyich" and by William Faulkner in his treatment of the death of Joe Christmas in *Light in August*. To stand for so long before the mystery of death enables the reader to realize the irrelevance of the banalilty, the tension, the petty egotism and pride which constitute the ordinary life in physical and metaphysical confinement. This we are made aware of by the events at large and by passages of humbly apocalyptic beauty: "There was a pistol shot from the woods, followed closely by another. Then silence. The old lady's head jerked around. She could hear the wind move through the tree tops like a long satisfied insuck of breath. 'Bailey Boy!' she called." (CS p.129). That the grandmother's action of reaching out to The Misfit signifies the moment when grace is manifest is a received truth about the story. It is not, however, a surprise ending. Her identity with grace occurs early and at several points before this conclusion. Coming into the open is clearly part of the story's structure and imagery, and part of the grandmother's character. We see this, for example, after the others have been taken away; she is alone with The Misfit and O'Connor confirms in this penultimate moment her having come into the open: "There was not a cloud in the sky nor any sun. There was nothing around her but woods. She wanted to tell him that he must pray. She opened and closed her mouth several times before anything came out. Finally she found herself saying, 'Jesus, Jesus,' meaning Jesus will help you...." (CS p.131). Again the imagery of clouds, sky, sun, and trees objectifies beauty, spare and stark though it be; the end thus returns to the beginning image of the meanest trees filled with light.

Finally, I want to examine O'Connor's most carefully worked out use of beauty in *The Violent Bear It Away*. Like "A Good Man Is Hard to Find," its pattern may be understood in terms of Heidegger's phrase: coming into the open. In its simplest structural form, the novel represents the protagonist's resistance to beauty and baptism, the acceptance and administration of baptism of the child Bishop by water and drowning, and the acceptance of his own baptism by violation and fire and the consequent mission of prophecy in the city. This is a suspenseful action, the outcome of which is beautiful. In fact, beauty is an important feature of the narrative anticipation and informs the story frequently and in terms of an understandable and well enunciated aesthetic.

The first significant passage (and the most important one) which enables us to enter into this aesthetic occurs just after old Mason Tarwater's death, when F.M. Tarwater is going to get the shovel to dig the grave. This actually precedes the moment in time specified by the novel's opening sentence. Here is the key passage:

It was as if he were afraid that if he let his eye rest for an instant longer than was needed to place something - a spade, a hoe, the mule's hind quarters before his plow, the red furrow under him - that the thing would suddenly stand before him, strange and terrifying, demanding that he name it and name it justly and be judged for the name he gave it. He did all he could to avoid this threatened intimacy of creation. When the Lord's call came, he wished it to be a voice from out of a clear and empty sky, the trumpet of the Lord God Almighty, untouched by any fleshly hand or breath. He expected to see wheels of fire in the eyes of unearthly beasts. He had expected this to happen as soon as his great-uncle died. He turned his mind off this quickly and went to get the shovel. (VBIA pp.21-22).

It is important to understand from this passage that young Tarwater, immediately following his great-uncle's death, feels like Adam in Paradise, contemplating the beauty of the created world. Old Mason's teachings have indeed permitted him to see how the world is put together. He knows at first hand the intimacy of creation, but he fears it, is threatened by it, is unwilling to admit and accept its beauty. He knows that to accept this is to accept the sacramental view, the sacramental bond that by linking man to God's creation inevitably links man to God and his injunctions. This Tarwater is unwilling to do, and it is his

155

resistance that constitutes the action of this book. As the *Iliad* is about the wrath of Achilles, *The Violent Bear It Away* is about the resistance of Tarwater to God's will.

Beautiful imagery from the natural world occurs regularly, often with considerable irony and from unusual perspectives, but the next significant passage is a keystone for the meaning of the novel. It is Lucette Carmody's sermon, the child evangelist visited by Tarwater when he is being followed by Rayber. "'I want to tell you people the story of the world,' she shouts. 'I want to tell you to be ready so that on the last day you'll rise in the glory of the Lord.'" (VBIA pp.129-130). Her sermon is indeed about glory, beauty, and love. It is beautiful in its rhythms and its delivery (like the Rev. Shegog's sermon in Section IV of *The Sound and The Fury)*. The sermon is placed in the specific context of the red furrow imagery from the "intimacy of creation" passage quoted above. As Rayber first looks upon Lucette, he recalls his own childhood when he was taken to the country by old Mason Tarwater and when his father came to take him back to the city: "Rayber had a clear vision of plowed ground, of the shaded red ridges that separated him from the lean figure [of his father] approaching." (VBIA pp.125-126). Rayber as adult atheist remembers his affection and need for the beauty that his uncle bequeathed him: the furrows, the woods, the "waxy pine needles" underfoot, the bamboo thicket, and the stream of water where he had been baptized. As he listens to the child's sermon on love, the old images and meanings become beautiful to him, even as he twists them to his own pagan corruptions: he sees himself "fleeing with the child to some enclosed garden where he would teach her the truth...." (VBIA, p.133).

The specific beauties of this sermon about love and the way the world is put together occur in two passages, each of which contains apocalyptic imagery that brings to mind the "Book of Revelation" and the etchings of William Blake: "God told the world He was going to send it a king and the world waited. The world thought, a golden fleece will do for His bed. Silver and gold and peacock tails, a thousand suns in a peacock's tail will do for His sash. His mother will ride on a four-horned white beast and use the sunset for a cape." (VBIA p.131).The second passage is also apocalyptic, but its imagery is beautiful in a more homely and rural manner:

Listen world...Jesus is coming again! The mountains are going to lie down like hounds at His feet, the stars are going to perch on His shoulder and when He calls it, the sun is going to fall like a goose for His feast. Will you know the Lord Jesus then? The mountains will know Him and bound forward, the stars will light on His head, the sun will drop down at His feet, but will you know the Lord Jesus then? (VBIA p.133).

Like the Reverend Shegog in *The Sound and the Fury*, Lucette Carmody is an unlikely exponent of the basic affirmation of the novel, but this sermon is the keystone of the narrative pattern of beauty. Rayber must turn off his hearing aid and hide from it, while young Tarwater, who claims he went only "to spit on it," begins his movement toward the inevitable acceptance of his role as prophet. Following the sermon, "His fury seemed to be stirring from buried depths that had lain quiet for years and to be working upward, closer and closer, toward the slender roots of his peace." (VBIA p.137).

The almost immediate result is Tarwater's "terrible compelling vision" (VBIA p.145) of baptism when he sees the idiot child Bishop Rayber run toward and leap into the water at the park fountain, where the sun shines brightly on him, making him a single, brilliant spot of light. The beauties of the water, the light the innocent child, and the incipient baptism are repeated two chapters later in a more elaborate description of the same event, this time from the point of view of young Tarwater after he has arrived at the Cherokee Lodge. At this recapitulation the boy "began to feel again the approach of mystery." The beautiful images are all here but enhanced: "The sun, which had been tacking from cloud to cloud, emerged above the fountain. A blinding brightness fell on the lion's tangled marble head and gilded the stream of water rushing from his mouth. Then the light, falling more gently, rested like a hand on the child's white head. His face might have been a mirror where the sun had stopped to watch its reflection." (VBIA p.164). This extraordinary repetition is O'Connor's way of objectifying the benediction that she wishes to convey about baptism in general and about Bishop's baptism specifically. The concrete reflecting pool at the park fuses in Tarwater's imagination with the lake at the Cherokee Lodge; both are to him baptismal fonts and are presented to him as God's inescapable imperative. The lake, to his eyes, is beautiful as God's creation and as God's sign presented specifically to him: "It lay there, glass-like, still, reflecting a crown of trees and an infinite overarching sky. It looked so unused that it might only the moment before have been set down by four strapping angels for him to baptize the child in." (VBIA p. 167). Tarwater is feeling what he did when he went for the shovel to bury his great-uncle: the intimacy of creation. At this point he has almost moved from escaping to accepting and celebrating in the manner of Hopkins' "Spring":

A strain of the earth's sweet being in the beginning
In Eden garden. - Have, get, before it cloy,
Before it cloud, Christ, lord, and sour with sinning,
Innocent mind and Mayday in girl and boy. (ll.10-14).

The baptism/drowning occurs, as it were, off-stage in Rayber's mind as he realizes what has happened. While we see the beauty surrounding the event we are not shown the specific death. Subsequent to this baptism by water and the child's dying to this world, O'Connor moves to "Book Three" and its exclusive concern with Tarwater's baptism by violation and by fire. The entire section, three chapters, pp.207-243, is like the long suspiration of someone surfacing after a deep and terrifying dive into destructive waters. It is the realization of Heidegger's aesthetic concept of coming into the open. The three chapters are filled with the beautiful imagery of sun, sky, moon, earth, and woods. The purgatorial and apocalyptic fires come together in a single vision with the felicities of the landscape and the beauties of the heavens above:

The sky, the woods on either side, the ground beneath him, came to a halt and the road assumed direction. It swung down between high red embankments and then mounted a flat field plowed to its edges on either side. Off in the distance a shack, sunk a little on one side, seemed to be afloat on the red folds. Down the hill the wooden bridge lay like the skeleton of some prehistoric beast across the stream bed. It was the road home....(VBIA p.233).

This vivid landscape is the one O'Connor has used throughout the novel; gradually it has been transformed as the boy's vision has been, so that it is no longer the countryside but is instead the true country, the road home. Such landscapes occur in many of her stories. Though they are direct, spare, and simple, they are not finally subtle or elusive. Though they are found within the context of pain, suffering, death, and violence, their essential affirmation is not thereby compromised. And though they are the sights she saw outside her door in rural Georgia, they are the universal, archetypal landscapes of eternity in which the beauty of this world converges and becomes one with the beauty of God.

Notes

1 T.S.Eliot, "The Waste Land," *Complete Poems & Plays* (New York, 1952), p.38.
2 Robert Fitzgerald, "Introduction." *Everything That Rises Must Converge* (New York, 1965) p.xi.
3 Fitzgerald, p.xxxii.
4 Fitzgerald, p.xii.
5 Fitzgerald, p.xi.
6 Ezra Pound, "Vorticism," *American Literature: Tradition and Innovation*, ed. Harrison T. Meserole, Walter Sutton, and Brom Weber (Lexington, Mass., 1969), II, 2931. This essay was originally published in *Fortnightly Review*, 96 (September 1, 1914), 461-471.

7 *Philosophies of Beauty From Socrates To Robert Bridges*, ed. E.F. Carrit (New York, 1931), p.236.

8 Martin Heidegger, *Being and Time*, trans. John Macquarrie and Edward Robinson (New York, 1962), p.193.

9 Martin Heidegger, *Poetry, Language, Thought,* trans. and with Introduction by Albert Hofstaądter (New York, 1971), p.174.

10 Heidegger, *Poetry, Language, Thought,* p.93.

11 Heidegger, *Poetry, Language, Thought,* p.94.

12 Heidegger, *Poetry, Language, Thought,* p.140.

Inescapable Lucidity: Flannery O'Connor's Gift and Most Terrible Affliction

Matej Mužina

It would be hard to find a sharper contrast in the work of Flannery O'Connor than the one she has drawn between ordinary people and her demonic, violent, destructive or self-destructive freaks. It can be seen in their use of language. The ordinary person will in any situation most predictably resort to the collective, conventional wisdom of proverbial commonplaces in his fumbling attempts to explain life to himself. The demonic restless character will express his quintessential truth from the depths of his experience of those extreme situations in life which the German existentialist philosopher Karl Jaspers called *Grenzsituationen* . In fact, Jaspers' "concern with himself," his attempts at "radical sincerity," and his interest in "the human condition and its inescapable extremities of death, suffering, chance, guilt, and struggle"[1] seem to me to describe fairly accurately Flannery O'Connor's demonic doubters.

Let me illustrate this assertion with a few examples. Having guessed wrongly that Hazel Motes is going home, Mrs. Wally Bee Hitchcock, at the beginning of *Wise Blood*, is quick with the ready-made comment, "...there's no place like home." (WB p.11). It is a polite remark anyone could have made in a train to an unknown fellow passenger, but the depth of inattention to the mental state of another person and of unthinking self-satisfaction expressed by this platitude become clear when Hazel Motes, out of the depths of his own experience of the extremities of life, gives his verdict, "You might as well go one place as another,... That's all I know." (WB p.14). This is not simply a matter-of-fact realization of Hazel's own situation. It is true, he himself has nowhere to go; he has come back home from his four years of service in the army to find not only that the members of his family, brothers and parents, are all dead, but that his native home is a ruin and that his birthplace Eastrod is practically abandoned. Yet, this is certainly not the essence of his remark, and one can barely detect a personal note of self-pity in it. His generalization transcends the trite platitudes of Mrs. Hitchcock's assertion that there is no place like home. What he is trying to communicate by these words is an insight into the essence of not only his own but of everybody's condition. This is made quite clear in "Chapter Ten" of *Wise Blood* where Haze, the self-appointed preacher, presents his existentialist nihilism to two women and a boy in front of the Odeon Theater in Taulkinham, trying to answer the age-old questions of philosophy: where do we come from, where are we going, and what is man? "Where you come from is gone, where you thought you were going to never was there, and where you are is no good unless you can get away from it. Where is there a place for you to be? No place!" (WB p.165). Haze is responding to what is for him the tormenting metaphysical question of man's place in the universe. Mrs. Hitchcock on the other hand, is not responding to any vital, basic need of her own while mouthing, "there's no place like home." She has spoken not from her own experience but from an urge to engulf Haze in a feeling of fellowship and community by offering to share with him one of the almost universally accepted social banalities of our everyday contact - there is no place like home. This is not her opinion, this is no opinion at all. Instead, it is a statement concocted by an irresponsible, collective social entity, by the "mass 'I'" or the "social 'I'" as José Ortega y Gasset defined it.[2] When one subscribes to it by repeating it ever so often, one is showing one's credentials, and is accepted by society.

The contrast between the two groups of characters in O'Connor is between two totally different ways of experiencing and observing life. The ordinary human being remains shut inside this inauthentic world and lives a false life, he is perfectly well adjusted to it and has no sense of transcendence. The ordinary character is, without being aware of it, very much like Leora Watts who "was so well-adjusted that she didn't have to think any more." (WB p.60). Similarly, he is like the girl Sabbath who asked for advice from a psychologist employed by a newspaper to answer questions from the sexually perplexed. "Dear Mary, I am a bastard and a bastard shall not enter the Kingdom of Heaven as we all know, but I have this personality that makes boys follow me. Do you think I should neck or not? I shall not enter the Kingdom of Heaven anyway so I don't see what difference it makes!" (WB p.119). A grotesquely confused answer appeared in the paper. "Dear Sabbath, Light necking is acceptable, but I think your real problem is one of adjustment to the modern world. Perhaps you ought to re-examine your religious values to see if they meet your needs in Life. A religious experience can be a beautiful addition to living if you put it in the proper perspective and do not let it warf you. Read some books on Ethical Culture." (WB p.119). Sabbath answered that confused advice with disquieting collectedness and shocking ease, "Dear Mary, What I really want to know is should I go the whole hog or not?

That's my real problem. I'm adjusted okay to the modern world." (WB pp. 119-120).

Sabbath is *aware* of her nihilism, takes pleasure in it, and consequently she does not belong to that vast category of ordinary mindless people to which I have provisionally and imprudently assigned her. Her assertion that she is adjusted okay to the modern world is cited here for the sole purpose of pointing out that what she has said is a *reductio ad absurdum* of the modern age, its inmates, their nihilism and their mindlessness. Of course, there is no lack of examples of collective, conventional commonplaces in Flannery O'Connor's work, and of characters that voice them. They sound a note so different from Sabbath's radical sincerity that there is surely no need for sophisticated discrimination. To Red Sammy's complaint in "A Good Man Is Hard to Find," that "These days you don't know who to trust," the grandmother gives a politely compassionate answer, "People are certainly not nice like they used to be," which triggers off Red Sam's response, "A good man is hard to find.... Everything is getting terrible. I remember the day you could go off and leave your screen door unlatched. Not no more." This prompts the old lady, in discussing better times, to air her opinion that "... Europe was entirely to blame for the way things were now." (CS p.122). In "The Life You Save May Be Your Own" similar "absolute truths" are voiced, "'Nothing is like it used to be, lady,' he said. 'The world is almost rotten.'" (CS p.146). Such examples could be multiplied by dozens.

This repetitive babble, false conversation, or *Ersatz* communication omnipresent in Flannery O'Connor's fiction stands in contrast to the experience and the language of her demonic characters. Although they move and act in the same physical universe as the mentally inert ordinary people, theirs is another world, the world of last things, of sin and death and the horror of existence. Some of O'Connor's most innocent though devilishly subtle ironies lie in her descriptions of situations in which an ordinary person totally misunderstands a demonic character on account of the discrepancy between their two worlds. A good example of this kind of subtle irony is the description of the encounter between Mrs. Hopewell and the Bible selling crook in "Good Country People." He introduces himself to her with the words, "'Lady, I've come to speak of serious things.'" (CS p.278). This can superficially be understood as a self-advertisement of a traveling salesman accomplished at selling Bibles and is, most likely, taken to mean just that by Mrs. Hopewell. She is brimful with commonplaces such as, "'...good country people are the salt of the earth!'" (CS p.279) or, "'It takes all kinds to make the world.'" (CS p.273). Such commonplace popular wisdom prevents clear observation of fact simply because it does not allow a person to detach himself or herself from the limited utilitarian world of daily pragmatism. Mrs. Hopewell's vision and thought are dulled by it so she mistakes Manley Pointer for a young, honest, simple country boy, a cardinal mistake reinforced in her mind by his admission that he is "real simple" and that he does not "'...know how to say a thing but to say it.'" (CS p.278). And that he is "'...from out in the country around Willohobie, not even from a place, just from near a place.'" (CS p.279). This, most certainly, has a double meaning: one for Mrs. Hopewell - that he is a poor, good, simple country boy to be invited to dinner and fed properly - and the other, intended by Flannery O'Connor - that he is a specimen of what C.G. Jung has called modern man, the man who is "aware of the immediate present," unhistorical and solitary. That is to say he is separated both from unity with other men and unity with God and therefore sinful and burdened with guilt.[3] I am tempted to think that O'Connor relished this situation almost as a private joke, describing it tongue in cheek, because it is hard to believe that she was capable of the illusion that her ordinary reader was radically different from the characters of her stories; her disappointment with her readers and reviewers was notorious.

What Manley Pointer is quite simply saying or prefiguring by his words, is that he is a demonic preacher whose preaching is done by means of shock and that his words are not meaningless babble but metaphysical truth. What he says about himself reminds us of Hazel Motes, The Misfit, Mr. Shiftlet. His last words to Hulga, the Ph.D. in philosophy who embraces nihilism, "'...you ain't so smart. I been believing in nothing ever since I was born!'" (CS p.291) could have been but were not predicted by Hulga when she was asked the unusual question, "'You ever ate a chicken that was two days old?'" (CS p.283). Eating such a "mighty small" chicken would obviously be a sign of nihilistic blasphemy and a sin against utilitarianism since such a morsel would not satisfy hunger at all. Moreover, the eating and wasting of it would raise the question of what other need it would satisfy. Probably the need to show that one did not have illusions and that one belonged to the people who "'see through to nothing,'" (CS p. 287) to whom Hulga believed that she belonged and was forced to realize that she did not. She thought that her bookish nihilism had given her freedom, whereas she was like everybody else, enclosed in and exposed to the small grotesque world of her mother and Mrs. Freeman, whose name ironically suggests what she is not capable of being. And this is true despite Mrs. Hopewell's fear that her daughter every year "grew less like other people and more like herself - bloated, rude, and squint-eyed."(CS p.276). It is hard to resist the temptation of quoting George Santayana on the subject of the philosophy of the common man, not because Santayana was one of the authors whom O'Connor read, but simply because what he says is so pertinent here: "The philosophy of the common man is an old wife that gives him no pleasure, yet he cannot live without her, and resents any aspersions that strangers may cast on her character."[4] The common man does not want to leave the prison of his customary assumptions and collective superstitions. However narrow, dull and vague they may be he clings to them jealously for fear of what he might encounter beyond them.

Hulga in "Good Country People," and Calhoun in "The Partridge Festival," who would like to imagine himself as "the rebel-artist-mystic," and not as what he unmistakably is by talent and heredity, a master salesman of "air-conditioners, boats and refrigerators," best represent the characters in O'Connor's fiction who want to be different from others but who cannot manage. Faced with O'Connor's devilish characters they fall back into the safety of their ordinary routines. Flannery O'Connor could be justly accused of innocently malevolent pleasure in the failure of such characters to live up to their own expectations. She often seems to overdo the naiveté of such persons by making them either attempt to seduce the devil, as Hulga does, or by making them proffer "a box of candy, a carton of cigarettes and three books - a Modern Library *Thus Spake Zarathustra*, a paperback *Revolt of the Masses*, and a thin decorated volume of Housman," (CS p.441) as an offering in sign of kinship to the devil incarnate, as Mary Elizabeth does in "The Partridge Festival." Whatsoever the devil does to them, it seems to be O'Connor's opinion that it serves them right. They have to pay for their inattentiveness and for their obsession with their own selves. Sympathy and compassion would be of no use here as authorial stylistic attitude; only the cold light of the author's intellect seeing through them is appropriate.

The order of lucidity now begins to appear before our eyes as one of the most important things in O'Connor's fiction. The creatures that have no lucidity whatsoever, the vulgar or *profanum vulgus*, are first in order of appearance. They are characterized by unthinking acceptance and ritualistic repetition in conversation of what has been called the collective popular or conventional wisdom of proverbial commonplaces. They are given an appearance made to match their words. Since their words result from lack of thought and are a confusion of everything, a gallimaufry of sorts, the descriptions become studies in grotesque art. The description of Mrs. Hitchcock at the beginning of *Wise Blood* may suffice here as an example: "She was a fat woman with pink collars and cuffs and pear-shaped legs that slanted off the train seat and didn't reach the floor." (WB

p. 9). Not only is it difficult to distinguish between the child in her (pink collars and cuffs and legs so short that they could not reach the floor of a railway carriage) and the adult woman somewhat advanced in age (a fat woman), but a further confusion between a rational human individual and a plant is suggested by the pear-shaped legs. All this suggests a mixture of insensitive plantlike life and the mindlessness of babyhood which has encroached upon an adult, who should show intelligence and discrimination. And this is, according to Wolfgang Kayser, a hallmark of the grotesque style in both art and literature.

So, the common man is a grotesque mixture both in mind and body lacking even elementary lucidity. O'Connor has expressed her distaste for this type of human being many times and on different occasions. One instance which seems to be very telling is this, "I believe and the Church teaches that God is as present in the idiot boy as in the genius." (HB p.99). Characteristically, Flannery O'Connor emphasizes here the extremes of humanity in which God is present, leaving out the ordinary human being, the statistically average man. The genius, by reason of his mind or his intuition, and the idiot, by reason of his purity, are aware of the fact of God's presence, whereas the ordinary man has severed himself from God by his lack of awareness. Degree of consciousness, of awareness, of lucidity is, without much doubt, the criterion of the author's evaluation of each individual human being. Defective though it may be and always is the higher degree of awareness of her extraordinary characters is what distinguishes them from the mob. There is another characteristic slighting of the ordinary man: In giving an account in a letter to "A" of her reading of Simone Weil's books, O'Connor skips from the works of that author to her life in order to say:

The life of this remarkable woman still intrigues me while much of what she writes, naturally, is ridiculous to me. Her life is almost a perfect blending of the Comic and the Terrible, which two things may be opposite sides of the same coin. In my own experience, everything funny I have written is more terrible than it is funny, or only funny because it is terrible, or only terrible because it is funny. Well Simone Weil's life is the most comical life I have ever read about and the most truly tragic and terrible. (HB p.105).

This was said in a letter written on 24 September 1955. Six days later, in a letter to the same person, we learn that this account of Simone Weil's life was meant to be a praise.

By saying Simone Weil's life was both comic and terrible, I am not trying to reduce it, but mean to be paying her the highest tribute I can, short of calling her a saint, which I don't believe she was. Possibly I have a higher opinion of the comic and terrible than you do. To my way of thinking it includes her great courage and to call her anything less would be to see her as merely ordinary. She was certainly not ordinary. (HB p. 106).

A perfect blending of the comic and the terrible seems an appropriate definition of O'Connor's demonic characters. Such a blend involves knowledge and awareness of the grotesqueness of the world and excludes an ordinary, irresponsible confusion of ideas, a kind of muddledom which results in compassion, pity, and sentimentality and which is best expressed by a smug tolerance of everything. "It takes all kinds to make the world go 'round" (CS p. 279) is not, in essence, different from, *homo sum, humani nihil a me alienum puto*. It is an admission of weakness which, no matter whether made by a half literate or an educated person, O'Connor best dis-owned by expressing her admiration for St. Thomas's intolerance of sin: "In any case, I feel I can personally guarantee that St. Thomas loved God because for the life of me I cannot help loving St. Thomas." His brothers didn't want him to waste himself being a Dominican and so locked him up in a tower and introduced a prostitute into his apartment; her he ran out with a red-hot poker. It would be fashionable today to be in sympathy with the woman, but I am in sympathy with St. Thomas. (HB p.94). In other words tolerance of sin is nothing but the irresponsibility of man without God. You are either in sympathy with St. Thomas or with that woman and there is nothing else to it in O'Connor's way of thinking. She seeks simplicity, not subtlety of thought, as it is so wonderfully expressed in a piece of advice given by her to a close friend, "Subtlety is the curse of man. It is not found in the deity." (HB p. 452). In another letter to the same correspondent O'Connor has clarified her view of St. Thomas' act and of the principle that guided her in her art of writing.

Both St. Thomas and St. John of the Cross, dissimilar as they were, were entirely united by the same belief. The more I read St Thomas the more flexible he appears to me. Incidentally, St. John would have been able to sit down with the prostitute and said, "Daughter, let us consider this," but St. Thomas doubtless knew his own nature and knew that he had to get rid of her with a poker or she would overcome him. I am not only for St.Thomas here but am in accord with his use of the poker. I call this being tolerantly realistic,...(HB p. 97).

An explanation concerning O'Connor's dislike of the intellectuals is appropriate here. Unlike St. Thomas, a social worker like Sheppard in "The Lame Shall Enter First" would be in sympathy with the prostitute and would try to "save" her and so would any other type of modern intellectual, social scientist, culture monger, psychoanalyst and psychologist with their interest in personality development. But it is not only the members of these intellectual professions that have taken over from the Church the task of illuminating people's minds, consoling and directing them. In an altogether confused fashion they are doing so pretending to be in possession of the knowledge about what is good and bad, what true and false although they are demonstrably in possession of no truth at all; but it is not only these pseudo-intellectuals whose profession makes fakes of them that O'Connor disowns, it is the whole category, and this, of course, deserves an additional explanation. It can be said that intellectuals came into being with the modern age. It is the mind of modern twentieth century man that can most easily be fitted into the mould of a sceptical intellectual. Scepticism is both his virtue and his vice. Although her surface meaning is different and very limited, Mrs. Hopewell in "Good Country People" hits the mark well by making her mental remark, "You could not say, 'My daughter is a philosopher.' That was something that had ended with the Greeks and Romans." (CS p.276). A present day intellectual with a doctorate in philosophy is quite a different breed of man from, let us say, Heraclitus or Plato. What characterizes an intellectual nowadays is what Aldous Huxley in *Point Counter Point* so aptly called his amoeboid quality:

There was something amoeboid about Philip Quarles's mind. It was like a sea of spiritual protoplasm, capable of flowing in all directions, of engulfing every object in its path, of trickling into every crevice, of filling every mould and, having engulfed, having filled, of flowing on towards other obstacles, other receptacles, leaving the first empty and dry. At different times in his life and even at the same moment he had filled the most various moulds.... The choice of moulds depended at any given moment on the books he was reading, the people he was associating with.... Where was the self to which he could be loyal?[5]

The mind of the modern intellectual is digestive and when his ego is "learned and omnivorous," as is suggested by George Santayana, then he is adrift with no firm criterion by which to judge things, an empty shell that can be filled with any content.

If we take the order of lucidity as our criterion here, which I would like to argue O'Connor was always taking as hers, then the modern intellctuals would form an intermediary step between the mass of uncritical people who take everything for granted, and those who are "a different breed of dog," like The Misfit. The grandmother in "A Good Man Is Hard to Find" in fact immediately recognized The Misfit as not belonging to the category of common man. "'You're not a bit common!'" (CS p.128) she said to him in despair and horror of death. To quote Santayana once again, "People are not naturally sceptics, wondering if a single one of their intellectual habits can be reasonably preserved," and the ultimate scepticism of the modern intellectual therefore has some merits, but quite certainly not the merit of a firm criterion of values, particularly because ultimate scepticism cannot be sustained for long and this or that narrow-mindedness is quickly and unconsciously, or at best with a guilty conscience, embraced by the former sceptic.

What O'Connor has to say about the Catholic novelist in the Protestant South may well be true of her preferences. "I think he will feel a good deal more kinship with backwoods prophets and shouting fundamentalists than he will with those politer elements for whom the supernatural is an embarrassment and for whom religion has become a department of sociology or culture or personality development." (MM p.207). About her Christian orthodoxy she said:

Let me make no bones about it: I write from the standpoint of Christian orthodoxy. Nothing is more repulsive to me than the idea of myself setting up a little universe of my own choosing and propounding a little immoralistic message. I write with a solid belief in *all* the Christian dogmas. I find that this in no way limits my freedom as a writer and that it increases rather than decreases my vision. It is popular to believe that in order to see clearly one must believe nothing. This may work well enough if you are observing cells under a microscope. It will not work if you are writing fiction. For the fiction writer, to believe nothing is to see nothing. I don't write to bring anybody a message, as you know yourself that this is not the purpose of the novelist; but the message I find in the life I see is a moral message. (HB p.147).

Parenthetically, one might add that Erich Fromm would have taught O'Connor that "rational faith," not the "irrational faith" like the most drastic contemporary phenomenon of faith in dictatorial leaders, is indispensable for scientific discovery too.[6] O'Connor is a writer painfully aware of the disintegration of the world and of the ensuing dissolution or anarchy of values. A firm footing is desirable in such hard times, yet she is not a person who would, in a time of crisis, rush to find shelter from an earthquake into, as M. Scheler wrote,

the house which, in Europe, had long resisted the ravages of time and which had demonstrated the greatest immunity to the movements of the ground. Everyone rushes and runs in that direction, not in order to cultivate his soul, not to seek *the* culture which corresponds to his own individual nature and destiny and to an objective, serious knowledge of contemporary culture, but in order to look for something quite different - a master who will direct how we are to think, act and live.[7]

Lucidity and the smugness of the Catholic Church do not, as O'Connor knew, go hand in hand. Her simple assertion is that in order to see clearly one has to believe something. When she claims Christian orthodoxy by saying, "I take the Dogmas of the Church literally," I take her to mean that she is concerned with ultimate questions asked in the extreme situations of life which Jaspers called *Grenzsituationen*. I feel confirmed in this view (that the light of sceptical reason has its say with her) by what O'Connor says about herself as a Catholic writer: "However, I am a Catholic peculiarly possessed of the modern consciousness, that thing Jung describes as unhistorical, solitary, and guilty." (HB p.90). This reference to Jung explains the central position of O'Connor's demonic characters in her fiction. First, for Jung, "the man we call modern, the man who is aware of the immediate present, is by no means the average man."[8] Then, he is a solitary individual and there are not many of them around. "There are few who live up to the name, for they must be conscious to a superlative degree."[9] Modern intellectuals "appear suddenly by the side of the truly modern man as uprooted human beings, blood-sucking ghosts,"[10] says Jung and he calls them "Pseudo-moderns." Modern man is conscious to the superlative degree and almost invisible, "hidden from the undiscerning eyes of mass-men by those clouds of ghosts, the pseudo-moderns.[11] The pseudo-modern is intelligent, quick and omnipresent, but lacks substance.

So it is this quality of modern man that he is conscious to the superlative degree and characterized by incessant awareness that is present in The Misfit, in Hazel Motes and in Flannery O'Connor herself, and this is why I see her in the company of her demonic figures rather than in any other company. Unceasing awareness and lucidity are a curse from the point of view of the common man, an abnormality in fact, and it is hence from his point of view that O'Connor's misfits appear as demonic figures. Clear vision and firm belief may (for all I know) not be a contradiction. What O'Connor used to say to her mother seems to me to be true of her own position or of the position of any martyr of lucidity: When asked by her mother late at night to stop reading, turn off the light, and go to sleep, her answer, modified by a preliminary humorous remark, was invariably, "I with lifted finger and broad bland beatific expression, would reply, 'on the contrary, I answer that the light, being eternal and limitless, cannot be turned off. Shut your eyes...'" (HB pp.93-94). Flannery O'Connor couldn't shut hers.

Notes

1 K.Jaspers, "Philosophical Memoir," *Philosophy and the World*, Chicago, 1936, p.221.
2 This remark is in part based on an illucidation of the "mass I" or the "social I" given by José Ortega y Gasset *Man and Crisis*, London, 1959, pp.92-93.
3 C.G. Jung, "The Spiritual Problem of Modern Man," *Modern Man in Search of a Soul*, New York, 1933.
4 George Santayana, *Scepticism and Animal Faith*, New York, 1955, p.11.
5 *Collected Works*, London, 1963, pp 268-269.
6 E.Fromm, *Man For Himself*, Greenwich, Conn., 1947, pp.206-207.
7 "The Forms of Knowledge and Culture," *Philosophical Perspectives* , Boston, 1958, pp.15-16.
8 C.G. Jung, *op.cit. p.196.*
9 *Ibid.*, p.197.
10 *Ibid.*, p.198.
11 *Ibid.*

From the State to the Strait of Georgia: Aspects of the Response by Some of Flannery O'Connor's Creative Readers

Waldemar Zacharasiewicz

Studying the roots of Flannery O'Connor's fiction and, secondly, relating her handling of character portrayal, of themes and her use of literary traditions have been standard fields of research during the last twenty years. Our knowledge of her art of fiction has certainly been enriched by several fruits of this worthwhile and illuminating line of inquiry. Many articles and various chapters in the score of monographs that have appeared so far have shed light on O'Connor's relationship with writers of the 19th and 20th centuries and some go as far back as Dante and other classics.[1] Critics have explored the profound influence of various philosophers, theologians and sociologists on the writer from Georgia. Facts about her library and reading and her own book-reviews, which mirror her interests, are now available.[2] But the complexities of the question of influence, which involves much more than perfectly legitimate source-hunting and cannot be handled in a positivistic manner alone, are obvious in the debate, e.g. of O'Connor's attitude towards, and use of, Teilhard de Chardin's ideas.

Very few critics have confronted the question of how contemporary writers and authors of a younger generation have responded to O'Connor's consummate narrative skill and her presentation of a haunting fictional world. I admit that Melvin J. Friedman has commented on the reception she has met with in France,[3] yet the remarkable echo she has found among her peers, especially outside her region and her country, and among authors who did not share her religious convictions and world-view - John Hawkes is the most obvious example - is a phenomenon that deserves to be investigated as it might shed light on her achievement as a writer and also on the way in which literary tradition functions today.

There are, of course, numerous authors in O'Connor's region of the United States who bear witness to her impact on fellow writers. But there are also members of her craft from outside her region who at various times expressed their deep respect and admiration for her artistry. Some of them, no doubt, consciously or unconsciously, drew on the energy that a confrontation with the powerful texts by the Southern author could release. It would seem worthwhile to examine her influence on this specific group of "creative readers" (in Ralph Waldo Emerson's sense), who responded intensely to her fiction, and to speculate on the impact it had on the genesis of texts for which it functioned as a model or at least as a catalyst. While Melvin J. Friedman's exploration of the relationship between O'Connor and John Hawkes - their reciprocal admiration is a well-known fact[4] - might possibly be further documented by a study of some unpublished private letters written by Hawkes to various correspondents, a case might be made for an even closer connection between O'Connor's art and that of Joyce Carol Oates than has been assumed. It is bound up with the fact that the younger author, born in 1938, viewed and experienced O'Connor's work not only as a critical, but also as a creative reader.[5] A consideration of Oates' dismissive remarks about originality after her apprenticeship and her strees on traditions to which she is indebted and her temporary espousal of the cause of 'postmodernist' writers and contemporary critics who regard literature basically as "palimpsestic" (Gérard Genette) surely would not weaken the claim made here.

It would be rewarding to speculate on the factors which caused the delay and the, at first, fairly modest success of the British editions of O'Connor's books, Evelyn Waugh's praise notwithstanding.[6] But this and an analysis of the surge in interest since the publication of O'Connor's correspondence is beyond the scope of this essay.[7] One might also ponder why her art has been more readily appreciated in France than in Britain, where there is no or hardly any language barrier. M.J. Friedman in his survey of her reception in France touches upon various factors which may have helped the reception of her fiction. One is tempted to claim a certain affinity between French literature and fiction from the American South, and we may regard the presence of a lively Catholic literary tradition intensely preoccupied with religious and philosophical problems, a literature to which O'Connor herself was indebted, as a major element which facilitated her reception in France. The case of William Faulkner also reminds us that the recognition of an author abroad (in his case long before his appreciation at home) has often been due to the efforts of individuals who became successful mediators. It would be proper in this context to acknowledge fully the contribution of another important category of creative readers: the translators, who, in offering adequate and congenial versions of foreign texts, provide the basis for a wider response. It is obvious that O'Connor has fared well in France as she attracted the attention of a leading practitioner in this field, Maurice-Edgar Coindreau, the famous translator of Faulkner's works into French. He devoted his attention to both her novels.[8]

The reaction to O'Connor's work in German-speaking countries has, by comparison, been fairly limited, though the first German version of O'Connor's *A Good Man Is Hard to Find* was provided by Elisabeth Schnack, who had also shown her skill in the translation of Faulkner's stories, and received very friendly reviews.[9] The limitation of the reception is apparent in the fact that neither *Wise Blood* nor the bulk of the stories in O'Connor's posthumous collection have been rendered into German. At the moment only tentative explanations can be supplied for this comparative lack of enthusiasm among German-speaking readers. As a provisional examination of the translations reveals no glaring weaknesses, there must be other reasons for the only moderate success of Schnack's version of *A Good Man Is Hard to Find*.[10] One reason may be that by the time O'Connor's stories and one novel became accessible to the German reading public the heyday of literature catering to the needs of readers in search of spiritual values after the cataclysmic changes and disasters of WW II was beginning to wane. The relative lack of familiarity with the social world in which O'Connor's fiction is rooted was presumably another factor which hampered its appreciation outside academic circles in Germany and prevented success for which the popularity of Graham Greene's classic conflicts of sin and grace might have prepared the readership. References by creative readers are correspondingly rare. It seems, in addition, as if the interest in the grotesque and Gothic fiction by other Southern writers like Truman Capote and Carson McCullers had detracted from the potential response to O'Connor.

My primary objective here is to focus on the reception and impact of Flannery O'Connor in anglophone Canada. This choice may seem less arbitrary if I draw attention to the fact - ignored so far - that remarkably many contemporary Canadian authors have directly or indirectly shown their deep respect for the technical brilliance of her work. I propose to examine to what extent their admiration for her narrative skill and their grappling with O'Connor's idiosyncratic blend of grim humor and the disturbing religious message found expression in their own fictional works. I shall also try to demonstrate how, and to adumbrate why, in a time when writers speak of a "literature of exhaustion" and deconstructionist critics provocatively refer to the writing process as a "playing with used-up literary texts,"[11] O'Connor's stories were able to inspire and encourage the rendering of authentic fictional worlds. That such an attempt in talented writers also implied and involved a departure and a deliberate deviation from the model goes without saying after Harold Bloom's controversial analyses of literary influence as a kind of psychopathology of authors or Claus Uhlig's learned exposition of a theory of literary history and several more pragmatic studies under the aspect of "intertextuality," to use Julia Kristeva's term.[12] Several Canadian critics have, over the last decade, commented on a certain affinity between authors outside the mainstream of American literature and Canadian writers and have not failed to notice that in Canada women writers play a central role as women writers do in the American South. The strong inclination to tell real stories is something Anglo-Canadian writers in particular share with their colleagues from the American South, with whom the narrative impetus is stronger than with postmodernist writers and authors of self-conscious fiction. Yet there are further points of connection. Margot Northey has traced the presence of Gothic and grotesque elements in a dozen books of Canadian fiction from what she claims to have been the beginning of a genuine Canadian tradition in the early 19th century. [13] She has argued that such features are not idiosyncratic outcroppings but reflect a persistent interest of Canadian authors in the dark sides of life. She has closely linked the predilection for elements like deformity, disorder, incongruity to certain spiritual needs and preoccupations characteristic of her fellow countrymen. In the course of her argument, which stresses the function of horrifying or fearful aspects also in books by Quebecois writers like Anne Hebert or Marie-Claire Blais (e.g. *Mad Shadows*), she underlines the resemblance between Sheila Watson's novel *The Double Hook* (1959) and O'Connor's fiction as the writer from British Columbia offers "a story about redemption written from a Christian vantage point." The fact that Watson (born 1909) renders a bleak picture of existence through scenes of violence, cruelty and victimization and employs several figures who are reminiscent of types used in allegories or old morality plays with a satanic agent among them, clearly relates her book to O'Connor's parabolic fiction. Yet while Watson may have been aware of the early achievement of O'Connor, there is no evidence that *The Double Hook* with its biblical rhythms and its peculiar fusion of dialogues and flat statements on the one hand and precise imagistic phrases rendering thoughts of characters on the other was directly influenced by the writer from Georgia. Instead, one is strongly reminded of certain patterns and devices in Faulkner's *As I Lay Dying*, with which this book shares the central position of a strong-willed and negative mother figure. The fractured, multi-faceted sequence of sub-chapters more or less attributed to individual characters also suggests Faulkner's short novel. More important is the general debt this book owes to Faulkner, whose pervasive influence among contemporary Canadian authors must be taken into account when examining the impact of any other Southern writer on the Canadian literary scene. Faulkner's towering status in a country where the vastness of the land and the inclemency of the environment and climate are so much in evidence is of course partly due to the absence of a genuine tradition in short fiction and the scarcity of convincing native, national models in the longer form. Especially in the field of short fiction Canada lacked masters equalling Sherwood Anderson, Hemingway, or Faulkner, a fact that Desmond Pacey acknowledged in his pioneer survey *Creative Writing in Canada*.[14] When a new generation of authors began to write stories, they naturally turned to the writer from Mississippi, who had preceded them in prizing and eternalizing the "little postage stamp of native soil"[15] he knew so well. They were - in their respective regions - eager to emulate his art though some of them experienced the veracity of O'Connor's warning that this could be a hazardous undertaking: "Nobody wants his mule and wagon stalled on the same track the Dixie Limited is roaring down." (MM p.45). One of these writers was a young author from Vancouver Island who began writing while looking across the Strait of Georgia to the mainland of British Columbia: Jack Hodgins. He was later to admit that he had difficulties in finding his own authentic voice because of his fascination with Faulkner's unique art. I submit here that he was similarly inspired by O'Connor's fiction. Yet before evaluating his indebtedness to the author from Georgia it seems proper to deal briefly with another Canadian writer who has paid tribute to the master from Mississippi but who has indirectly admitted that he was under O'Connor's spell too: Rudy Wiebe.[16]

Few Canadian writers were better qualified by heritage and inclination to assimilate the radical world-view contained in O'Connor's fiction than Wiebe was. The reader of his books cannot but be conscious of the affinity when he is confronted with the early examples of Wiebe's probing and profound inquiries into the nature of human responsibility and with the violence which lurks beneath the surface of strict religious communities. Wiebe, himself the descendant of Mennonites, has offered a revisionist version of Canadian history in complex historical novels, which may owe a great deal to Faulkner in their successful transmutation of history into fiction.[17] But he has also shown a keen awareness of central moral and religious issues, of the "mystery of evil" and original sin, and has repeatedly juxtaposed religious belief with violence in a way which is suggestive of O'Connor's major concerns. The semblance is, perhaps, nowhere as striking as in a haunting story which originally appeared in 1970 and since then has been reprinted in several collections: "Did Jesus Ever Laugh?"[18] Though perceptive and knowledgeable critics like Bill Keith have noted that this story seems to exist in a contextual vacuum,[19] one cannot but be aware of the central parallel that exists between the unnamed first-person narrator and O'Connor's "The Misfit," though Wiebe admittedly uses different narrative devices. He reproduces the thought-processes of the psychotic murderer and places this gruesome story of the demonic figure, who preaches to the ladylike woman after killing her mother-in-law, before shooting her and later, presumably, her little daughter, in a highrise building somewhere in Edmonton. While further evidence needs to be carefully sifted the weird fusion of religious obsession with violence and sexual perversity seems to be indebted to O'Connor's classic rendering of diabolic rebel-prophets.

That Canadian writers did not only profit from O'Connor's mastery in inventing weird Gothic stories of sinfulness and obsession, but also derived considerable benefit from her example in the handling of narrative tools emerges from an analysis of Jack Hodgins' early career. This has so far remained unknown, though John Metcalf, an able editor and skillful author of fiction in his own right, has recently unequivocally praised O'Connor's model role for Canadian writers[20] and has emphasized the extent to which Canadian fiction writers are indebted both to Flannery O'Connor and Eudora Welty. Welty's crucial contribution to the training of Canadian authors in their craft has been established by Tim Struthers, who also recognized various factors which facilitated the process through which these Southern authors could become models for young writers from various Canadian provinces.[21] The resemblance in the socio-cultural setting between the rural or small-town South and areas in Ontario or Manitoba rendered an assimilation fairly easy and helps to account for the striking parallels between e.g. Alice Munro's cycles of short stories and E. Welty's books. The way in which patterns of behavior were affected and changed by social and technological developments - how extended families were gradually broken up and society and its values generally reshaped - was also a familiar phenomenon. Similarly O'Connor's detailed, quasi-realistic rendering of rural areas in the Piedmont area with backwoodsmen and fundamentalist Christians came close enough to the experience of young writers from the Canadian regions to be a kind of revelation for them, particularly as they felt that although it was ostensibly concerned with the specific, local and regional, it clearly had universal implications. O'Connor's "realism of distances" must have struck a responsive chord in

Jack Hodgins (born in 1938) who is now an established writer and a winner of the Governor General's Award for 1979. If one surveys his early work, one realizes that at least three of the ten stories contained in his first collection, published in 1976 under the title *Spit Delaney's Island*, and one uncollected story show remarkable parallels with the fictional work of O'Connor. Such a resemblance is apparent in the first story Hodgins ever published, "Every Day of His Life," (1968), which in its plot, the constellation of characters and some motifs reminds one of "The Life You Save May Be Your Own." The depiction of the arrival of the potential bridegroom Mr. Swingler at the isolated home of Miss Big Glad Littlestone in the early evening and his wooing of the somewhat grotesque bride are reminiscent of O'Connor's tale. The detailed description of the appearance and physiognomy of the visitor, who later takes an interest in the neighboring mountain and the setting sun and afterwards in the car the prospective bride possesses, similarly parallels elements of O'Connor's story.[22] It is true that in contrast to O'Connor's story Hodgins' tale does not dramatize an act of unscrupulous desertion by a self-centered, materialistic individual, though the small man approaching Miss Littlestone's garden and finally entering her house and her life surely has his eye on his advantage. He can play up to the eagerness of the unmarried mother with a child to win a husband. Yet instead of the tragicomic tone which is engendered in O'Connor's story by the revelation of the strange succession of inhuman callousness and sentimentality in Mr. Shiftlet there is an aura of unmitigated humor connected with the successful handling of the affair by the corpulent young woman. A major difference, however, lies in the fact that the focus of sympathy rests on her throughout, and that the reader is in fact invited to sympathize with her. When she feels some palpitation of the heart and has to admit to a degree of anxiety after this far-too-brief period of wooing, one is tempted to take this as a weak echo of the anxieties Mrs. Lucynell Crater may have endured during and after her crafty arrangement and agreement with Mr. Shiftlet. The bridegroom's reference to the strange ritual of drinking his first wife's ashes and his earlier description of her death in an accident introduce an uncanny, weird undertone. Though Hodgins placed the action in a former logging camp and gave it a personal touch with the description of the relish which Big Glad Littlestone derives from the provision of food and other nourishment, the parallels seem to be too close to be coincidental.

A similar claim could be made for the exceptional story "At the Foot of the Hill, Birdie's School," (1974), which approaches the genre of allegory. Here Hodgins dramatizes the painful initiation of a seventeen-year-old lad after his descent from the seclusion of a deserted utopian community in the hills presided over by the Old Man who taught him the tenets of his sectarian creed. While Webster Treherne has been instructed to believe not in a God of Wrath but a God of Love, and though he has not remained a semi-literate only trained to become a preacher and to follow in the footsteps of his great-uncle, but has instead been exposed to reading material about Western outlaws and their reckless adventures, the trials he undergoes evince at least a vague resemblance to the crucial period in Francis Marion Tarwater's life. In the town to which he has descended Webster Treherne encounters several bizarre figures, among them the proprietress of a strange free school, where he falls into new bondage and is physically abused while he is trying quickly to satisfy his desire to be corrupted. The way in which this problematic progress is rendered gives a Kafkaesque touch to the story, which rapidly leads on to illness and presumably ends with the death of Webster. It also aligns it with O'Connor's work, for more than any other story by Hodgins "At the Foot of the Hill..." is preoccupied with questions of good and evil and teems with unexplained acts of violence. It also contains numerous references to graves and other signs of death, though not to the ritual of baptism. The story presents painful encounters with freakish or demonic figures who are eager to teach Webster their "counter-lore," to make him unlearn what he has known and in particular to make him reject love. The fact that the sick boy finally refuses to believe in the patently absurd and nihilistic views of his grotesque instuctors and anticipates his escape from the weird and suspiciously maternal Ms. Birdie into the freedom of his earlier home may represent a modern, though bizarre version of the perennial story of the country boy seduced by evil urban influences who is finally yearning for the purity of his original environment. It may also reflect, I should like to argue, Hodgins' response to O'Connor's novel.

Among the uncollected stories by Hodgins the "Promise of Peace" (1969)[23] is also evocative of O'Connor's mode of fiction in the range of characters depicted and particularly in the conclusion with a violent death, which ironically exhibits the illusory hope of the protagonist, Mr. Raymond Fleming, a retired logger. This domestic tragicomedy dramatizes estrangement in a rural setting and reveals abysses of vindictiveness which finally prompt the disastrous action of Mr. Fleming's alienated spouse. It terminates his return to his home after an abortive attempt to leave it for a world trip in the wake of the wedding of his old, ugly daughter. The way in which humor and violence are combined is redolent of O'Connor's tales of corruption and of the exposure of unfathomable evil in the individual heart and of the shock tactics she aptly employs when closing her stories.

O'Connor's critics unanimously ascribe to her the special skill of rendering female gossip and conveying in this way paradoxical and often frightening dimensions of experience. It is in "Three Women of the Country," (1972), a longer story commonly regarded as Hodgins' most substantial early contribution to the genre, that his receptivity to O'Connor's influence can be most strikingly demonstrated. We are reminded of her stories by the title, the grouping of characters, the graphic description of the rural setting and the incidental use of drastic similes as early as on the first page of this haunting novelette. Its effect also hinges on the consistent application of the multiple point of view, the consecutive illumination of the private dilemmas of three female characters in the three chapters of the text. This arrangement of material, it is true, deviates from O'Connor's practice in short stories, which often involves an oscillation between various characters. Yet the other obvious parallels suggest that Hodgins moulded the fictional world largely on O'Connor's fiction when rendering a composite and in itself persuasive picture of dilemmas in a rural community, here pointedly named Cut Off. The narrative technique chosen is apt to underline the problems faced by the isolated female characters, two of whom remain completely unaware of the crucial factors determining the crisis in the life of Mrs. Edna Starbuck, a middle-aged woman with a retarded child. The delay in the provision of expositional material is clearly prompted by the author's interest in creating suspense and irony. The device chosen allows him to open his story with a particularly limited and impercipient view of Mr. Starbuck's position and seeming incompetence by the self-satisfied Mrs. Wright. The distanced view of this busybody, who completely trusts her rational judgement and thus resembles several female characters in O'Connor's fiction, gradually merges into a more intimate perspective, verging on what Dorrit Cohn has termed "narrated monologue,"[24] only to be followed by strikingly idiomatic dialogues and some graphic authorial surveys, which resemble O'Connor's habitual narrative technique.

One encounters a more perplexed observer character similarly reminiscent of O'Connor's figures, in Charlene Porter, the teenage daughter of a neighbor to whom Mrs. Starbuck has been a mother substitute for the last year. Mrs. Starbuck's unexpected killing of her Hereford calf, which has fallen into an abandoned well, aggravates Charlene's latent discomfort. It has arisen from the conflict between her docile adherence to her father's religious sect with its blandly optimistic negation of evil forces in man and her own experience, including her

179

recent discovery of Mrs. Starbuck's retarded boy. While the depiction of this adolescent perplexity with its explicit spiritual dimension echoes comparable anxieties and dilemmas in O'Connor's fiction, it is in the third and final part of the story that we observe some striking instances of Hodgins' response to O'Connor. Charlene's attempt to take the sick boy from his hiding place in the attic of Mr. Starbuck's house precipitates Mrs. Starbuck's action in the evening of this critical day. After her solitary nightly search for a solution, which is movingly portrayed, and after abortive attempts to end the nightmarish concealment of the boy demanded many years before by Mrs. Starbuck, her activity culminates in a desperate attempt to save the boy from being hit by Mrs. Wright's car. The boy has run away during her preparations for a new beginning and Mrs. Wright has finally thought it worth her while to visit her apparently unsettled neighbor. Mrs. Starbuck is killed by her own car, crushed to death in the ditch. That it is her car that causes the violent end - possibly as a quasi-sacrificial act, an expiation for sins committed against the boy over many years - strengthens the impression that Hodgins has here taken advantage of a formula creatively employed by O'Connor. He further allows himself the liberty of borrowing one of O'Connor's devices when depicting the dead human being with glassy eyes, seemingly suggesting a message of general importance: "One of Mrs. Starbuck's eyes was under water; the other, a dull plastic ball, stared swollen and incredulous up at Mrs. Wright as if Mrs. Starbuck in the last failing moment had seen something she badly needed to tell about. But from her open mouth only dark fluid bubbled out and was carried away by the moving water."[25] One is clearly reminded of several comparable situations in O'Connor's novels and stories.[26] This impression is further strengthened by Hodgins' adoption of the hallmark of her narrative style since her revision of "The Train," as Frederick Asals has demonstrated in his penetrating study.[27] Here, as with increasing frequency on the last pages of the story - at least fifteen times on the last six pages - Hodgins uses one of various conjectural and hypothetical phrases so dear to O'Connor since the first sentence of *Wise Blood*. While describing the outward appearance, the bearing, gait or mode of action of a character with seeming detachment these phrases frequently suggest inner truth, underlining and visualizing the grotesqueness of a situation: "...as if." Yet Hodgins' novelette itself is concluded with a different scene showing the shock of the two female survivors now aware of the narrow limits of their knowledge and their isolation. We are given what critics have called a "mirror-look," a device popular among short story writers. This coda to the story illustrates among other things that as Jack Hodgins' concern is predominantly secular and not with anagogical meaning he can dispense with the more prominent signposts pointing to the "true country" in O'Connor's religious territory. He can basically restrict himself to the exposure of a major flaw in his isolated characters, in this case especially the shattering of Mrs. Wright's self-confidence, but he can also explode blandly optimistic theories, which blink at signs of evil, corruption and suffering in the world.

This demonstration of Hodgins' debt to O'Connor is not intended to create the erroneous impression that he is a mere imitator copying successful narrative devices, nor is it designed to present him as belonging to the now common species Raymond Federman has called "pla[y]giarists." I was merely eager to establish O'Connor's impact on Hodgins during his formative years as a writer and a creative reader. His original gift of observation soon enabled Hodgins to project persuasive and unique pictures of the socio-cultural reality in which he is rooted. His models from the American South helped him to discover and render mysteries beneath the surface of life along the Strait of Georgia. His talent, however, imposed strict limits on his discipleship. As he has himself admitted in various interviews to an inclination "to be supersensitive to the way other people might feel,"[28] he was particularly reluctant to abandon the predominant modernist technique of employing a central consciousness and replacing it by a distanced, objective narrator. Even in "Three Women of the Country" he had not given up this modernist achievement, and his further development shows that he was confirmed and assisted in using this mode by his appreciation of other Southern writers like William Faulkner and Eudora Welty. Even in the bulk of his early texts his emphasis had been on human isolation rather than on corruption or on acts of violence committed by agents of destruction, who expose intense metaphysical dilemmas. Later he seems to have developed an instinctive tendency towards the expression of a joie-de-vivre which at least balances the manifestation of evil forces and negative figures, who appear in the settlements on Vancouver Island, e.g. in *The Invention of the World* (1977). His second novel, *The Resurrection of Joseph Bourne* (1979), which has been aligned with the form of the sacred parable and credited with profound religious meaning,[29] also introduces negative characters who are eager to destroy and abandon traditional values.[30] Yet they are kept under control by eminently positive figures, like the externally unprepossessing or even grotesque eponymous figure who approaches the status of a savior in *The Resurrection of Joseph Bourne*. O'Connor's grim humor has also been replaced by a preference for burlesque effects and a lighter mood so that the book projects a world-view radically different from that of O'Connor. One may perhaps deplore such a development as bordering on trivialization, but the literary historian will only note the factors which originally facilitated Hodgins' training in the art of fiction under the spell of O'Connor and later precluded the continuation of such a relation to the major writer from the state of Georgia. This relationship is also one facet of the complex mosaic of O'Connor scholarship.

Notes

1 These studies have illuminated the connection between her fiction and various traditions in the arts like the grotesque and have elucidated O'Connor's affinity with painters such as Hieronymus Bosch. Her debt to the tradition of the romance, to Nathaniel Hawthorne in particular, and to a native American tradition of humor has been established beyond doubt. Frederick Asals' significant study on *The Imagination of Extremity* has once more stressed the links between O'Connor's work and Nathanael West's *Miss Lonelyhearts*, and has also drawn attention to O'Connor's response to Edgar Allan Poe. J.O. Tate has plausibly argued in "The Force of Example: Flannery O'Connor and Stephen Crane," *The Flannery O'Connor Bulletin*, XI, 1982, 10-24, that Crane should be included in the long gallery of writers whose achievement stimulated O'Connor's work.

2 *The Presence of Grace and Other Book Reviews by Flannery O'Connor* compiled by Leo J. Zuber (Athens, Georgia, 1983) and Lorine M. Getz, *Flannery O'Connor: Her Life, Library and Book Reviews* (New York, 1980). [Cp. Arthur Kinney, *Flannery O'Connor's Library: Resources of Being* (Athens, Georgia, 1985).]

3 Melvin J. Friedman, "Flannery O'Connor in France: An Interim Report," *Revue des langues vivantes* 43 (1977), 435-42.

4 "John Hawkes and Flannery O'Connor: The French Background," *Boston University Journal* 21, 3 (1973), 34 - 44, and O'Connor's letters to Hawkes over a period of six years in *Flannery O'Connor: The Habit of Being*, ed. Sally Fitzgerald (New York, 1979) passim (1958-64). The basic differences of opinion are reflected in Hawkes' well-known argument in "Flannery O'Connor's Devil," *Sewanee Review* 70 (Summer 1962), 395-407.

5 In spite of the denial in *Commonweal* 91 (5 Dec. 1969), 307-310, Joyce Carol Oates seems to have initially been inspired by O'Connor. While her scholarly articles reflect her critical interest in O'Connor, several early stories published in 1963 seem to hark back to the fiction of O'Connor.

6 "If this [*Wise Blood*] is really the unaided work of a young lady, it is a remarkable product." Cp. O'Connor's appreciation of this remark in her correspondence. (HB p.35).

7 A reviewer of a reissue of *Wise Blood* in 1968 (*Guardian* , Feb. 8) spoke of O'Connor's "subterranean" reputation mainly among writers. Meanwhile Faber & Faber has provided paperback editions, a fact that seems to reflect a gradually growing audience. The new editions have elicited a strong response from reviewers (Cp. *TLS*, Nov. 21, 1980, *London Review of Books*, Sept. 3-16,

1981, *New Statesman*, Nov. 7,1980 and BBC program Radio 4, Monday, Oct. 6, 1980).

8 Cp. the reflection of this contact and mediation in *Delta* 2 (Mars 1976) with O'Connor's letters to M.-E. Coindreau and an interview with the translator conducted by Michel Gresset, who with Claude Richard has rendered the stories into French which had not been included in the two separate collections translated by Henry Morisset.

9 This translation published under the title *Ein Kreis im Feuer* by Claassen Verlag (Hamburg, 1961) contains only eight of the original ten stories. O'Connor's correspondence contains a brief reference to this publication. (HB p.425).

10 In spite of favorable reviews the book sold only 3000 to 4000 copies. Details provided by the publishing house of Claassen.

11 Cp. Roland Barthes, who defines the writer as "quelqu'un qui joue avec le corps de sa mère."

12 Cp. especially Harold Bloom, *The Anxiety of Influence* (1973) and *A Map of Misreading* (1975) and C. Uhlig, *Theorie der Literarhistorie: Prinzipien und Paradigmen* (Heidelberg, 1982).

13 *The Haunted Wilderness: The Gothic and Grotesque in Canadian Fiction* (Toronto, 1976).

14 *Creative Writing in Canada* (Toronto, 1952), 2nd rev.ed. 1961. p.252.

15 Faulkner's statement, interview with Jean Stein. *Writers at Work. Paris Review Interviews*, 1st series, ed. Malcolm Cowley (New York, 1959), p.141.

16 Canadian writer and contributor to the present volume, Sheldon Currie admits to have been influenced by O'Connor's art. Cp. his collection of stories *The Glace Bay Miner's Museum* (1979).

17 *The Temptations of Big Bear* (1973) and *The Scorched-Wood People* (1977).

18 *Fiddlehead* 84 (March-April 1970) and later R. Wiebe, *Where Is the Voice Coming From?* (Toronto, 1974).

19 *Epic Fiction* : The Art of Rudy Wiebe (Edmonton, 1981), p.109.

20 John Metcalf, "The Curate's Egg," *Zeitschrift der Gesellschaft für Kanada-Studien* 5, 1 = Vol.8 (1985), 43-59,

21 Cp. "Alice Munro and the American South," (1974), rev. version in John Moss, *The Canadian Novel: Here and Now* (Toronto, 1978), pp. 121-133.

22 Hodgins comments on his own apprenticeship in several interviews, e.g. with Geoff Hancock, *Canadian Fiction Magazine* 32/33 (1979/80), 33-63. On various aspects of Hodgins' debt to Southern fiction writers (Faulkner, Welty and O'Connor) and the development of his narrative art in general cp. my article in F.K. Stanzel and W. Zacharasiewicz, *Encounters and Explorations: Canadian Writers and European Critics* (Würzburg, 1986), pp.94-109.

23 Cp. *The North American Review* NS 6, No. 4 (Winter 1969). For information about Hodgins' uncollected stories I am indebted to Tim Struthers' provisional version of his bibliography of J. Hodgins' work.

24 D. Cohn, *Transparent Minds* (Princeton, 1978).

25 *Spit Delaney's Island* p.68.

26 Mason Tarwater's death on the first pages of *The Violent Bear It Away*, or Mrs. Flood's scrutiny of Haze Motes' "deep burned eye sockets," and the closure of the first part of " The Displaced Person," when Mrs. Shortley's husband and

children are confronted with "her eyes like blue-painted glass [which] seemed to contemplate for the first time the tremendous frontiers of her true country."

27 Asals p.19.
28 Interview with Alan Twigg, "Western Horizon: Jack Hodgins," *For Openers. Conversations with 24 Canadian Writers* (Madiera Park, British Columbia, 1981), pp.185-195, esp.p.188f.
29 Cp. J.R. (Tim) Struthers, "Thinking About Eternity," *Essays on Canadian Writing* 20 (Winter 1980/81), 126-133.
30 Cp. the demonic figure of the fake savior and law giver Donald Keneally in *The Intervention* and the more restricted impact of Jeremy Fell in *The Resurrection*, an associate of materialistic real estate agents and promoters of progress, who have increasingly come to represent evil in Hodgins' more recent fictional worlds.

Thinker and Believer

The Sacred and the Profane: Redefining Flannery O'Connor's Vision

Patrick J. Ireland

Few writers have achieved the astute level of critical self-awareness that marks the essays and letters of Flannery O'Connor. The intentional fallacy notwithstanding, we sometimes might do better as critics to trust the instincts of the writer herself. In her now famous defense of Southern Realism against charges that it read more like the mythical "School of Southern Degeneracy," O'Connor comically dismissed the widespread use of the term 'grotesque' in mainstream American responses to Southern literature. She said, "I have found that anything that comes out of the South is going to be called grotesque by the Northern reader, unless it is grotesque, in which case it is going to be called realistic." (MM p. 40). Implicitly, her observation about the relativity of human perception not only discounts the grotesque as a peculiar Southern literary aesthetic but also refuses to countenance Northern social assumptions about the South as some kind of exclusive, cultural hotbed of freaks. More importantly, as I have argued elsewhere, O'Connor's comments in "Some Aspects of the Grotesque in Southern Fiction" make it patently clear that Southern Realism is nonetheless "at its root a romantic aesthetic."[1] By that I mean Southern Realism offers a romantically "relative view of reality" in which, to the Southern writer, reality itself is sometimes grotesque by nature. In that effectively universal assertion about human nature O'Connor's voice anticipates Joyce Carol Oates' own when the latter subsequently argued that reality "must be fiction" because it is grotesque and that therefore the grotesque is "the only kind of fiction that is real."[2]

Certainly, in the years since O'Connor's death serious contemporary American fiction, especially the more experimental fiction, has steadily become less conventionally realistic, evolving greater sympathies, if not kinship, with Southern fiction. Non-southern writers like Joyce Carol Oates, John Irving, Larry Woiwode, Donald Barthelme, and scores of others have come to envision the world and its reality in terms as bizarre as anything in O'Connor, such that the term 'grotesque' is no longer practical or functional for distinguishing Southern literature from mainstream American fiction. Some, like myself, who perhaps eccentrically fail to find anything grotesque about O'Connor's misfits, much less Faulkner's alleged miscreants, find the term a generic conundrum and prefer it would just go away altogether, for even in the hands of O'Connor's apologists the term requires a defensive posture which focusses the critic's attention on justifications of the grotesque, thereby narrowing the critic's perceptual horizons as to what the writer is actually about. To be sure, the writers who gave life to the Southern Renaissance remain different, if no longer distinct, from these later mainstream writers, in ways we all know, but the difference in their use of the grotesque is a difference in culture rather than in sympathies. The Southerner and these mainstream writers both perceive reality as grotesque, but they differ usually in their focus, in their cultural identification of its causes and manifestations, and hence, in the way they fictionally represent the grotesqueness of reality.

For O'Connor, obviously, evil is the root of all things grotesque. But as a term, 'grotesque' obscures the larger issue at work in her fiction, for it is neither the central conflict of the two jarring worlds she beholds, nor that conflict's cause; the grotesque is merely the conflict's phenomenological effect on reality. In O'Connor, evil cuts a broad swath, beyond the narrow scope of moral sinfulness; for her, evil encompasses even the practical errors which complicate and sometimes undo our everyday living. In her fiction various manifestations of evil find their greatest comic and tragic expression in the conflict between the polar extremes of belief and unbelief. As O'Connor herself explained to John Hawkes, "I don't think you should write something as long as a novel around anything that is not of the gravest concern to you and everybody else and for me this is always the conflict between an attraction for the Holy and the disbelief in it that we breathe in with the air of the times." (HB p. 349). The hazards that await both this "attraction for the Holy and disbelief in it" constitute, then, the substance of her grotesque plots. In the same letter to Hawkes, O'Connor more neatly defines both her sympathies and revulsion for the believer, at the same time she pinpoints the evil that makes him grotesque:

The religion of the South is a do-it-yourself religion, something which I as a Catholic find painful and touching and grimly comic. It's full of unconscious pride that lands them in all sorts of ridiculous religious predicaments. They have nothing to correct their practical heresies and so they work them out dramatically. If this were merely comic to me, it would be no good, but I accept the same fundamental doctrines of sin and redemption and judgment that they do. (HB p. 350).

These "practical heresies" of which she speaks, what Robert Coles defines as "natural hazards that get in the way of would-be believers,"[3] make for a grotesque reality because in practice they are inconsistent with nature, with practical reality, or with a genuinely Christian spirit - from the proud social and racial sense of superiority of a Mrs. Turpin to the banal vanities of the grandmother in "A Good Man Is Hard to Find" to the xenophobic fear of displacement which grips several believers (and one unbeliever) on the McIntyre farm, leading them all to complicity in the death of the Polish Mr. Guizac.

If O'Connor makes short-shrift of the mistakes of the true believer on the road to redemption, she, likewise, does not spare the unbeliever, the misguided and supercilious secular thinker, his practical heresies either. As is the case with Joy Hulga Hopewell, who *believed* in nothing, unbelief to O'Connor is a kind of religion that also has its practical hazards, its tragicomic stumbling blocks. As Jefferson Humphries has described them, "Her fictions can be read as a catalog of the unbeliever in his many incarnations."[4] The practical heresy of the unbeliever is that his thinking accounts for only those things of the world that can be intellectualized or reasoned and his thinking is often foiled by those things in experience mysteriously irreducible to reason.

Why in O'Connor does the reality of these practical heresies make the believer and unbeliever alike appear so grotesque? To answer that question, we must look to the Gnostic roots of Southern literature and to O'Connor's particular understanding of the tension between belief and unbelief in the human sphere. A few years ago Robert Coles eloquently delineated the Gnostic impulse inherent in the Southern evangelicals of O'Connor's fiction, and almost concurrently the research of Jefferson Humphries undertook to demonstrate the same in her unbelievers.[5] What their work ultimately makes clear, from my vantage point, is that whichever the choice in the human dimension, belief or unbelief, an exclusive choice between sacred and profane is a quest for transcendence of the human situation that is fraught with impossible difficulties, because, unquestionably in O'Connor's orthodox theology, the human world is not one-dimensional or exclusively sacred or profane but a place where sacred and profane interact in mysterious ways.

Now, in the mythical cosmography of Gnosticism, as Coles and Humphries have so ably delineated it, the Godhead is originally male and represents Light, or the Spirit, but ultimately the Godhead becomes androgynous by self-absorption, the Light allowing the female principle of Darkness (and ultimately, Corporeality) to arise within him. That androgynous act of self-love by self-union creates or incarnates the universe, and with it, humankind. All creation thus mirrors the duality of the Godhead - Light and Darkness, Male and Female, Spirit and Body, Good and Evil, and so on. Accordingly, the separate sexes of mankind are an imperfect expression of the Godhead's unity or totality - the contamination of Light by Darkness. Equally important, mankind multiples and thereby divides God. As a consequence of that contamination and self-division, which the universe mirrors by its dualism, man's creation is itself a fall, a corruption of the original Light or Spirit. Forgetful of his dependence on the Godhead, man mimics the self-absorption of the Light, as though by his own imperfect self-love he, too, can obtain self-sufficient unity. Seeking to discover and liberate within himself that small portion of divinity or Spirit imprisoned by the limitations of his body, the Gnostic must necessarily turn inwardly. Gnostic salvation is thus indistinguishable from narcissistic self-absorption and requires the rejection of the world, especially of the body. The Gnostic's redemptive goal, then, is a sacred self-transcendent unity, like the Godhead's, but one that does not admit of the dualistic divisiveness or contamination signified by the natural world. Its inherent contradiction as a quest is that such a redemption is sought *in* the profane world *from* which the Gnostic seeks escape.

The quest for such knowledge of the Godhead, or gnosis, is what truly makes the Gnostic tragic in Christian terms, because the quest requires an exaggerated Manichaean consciousness of the finite world's dualism and at the same time it seeks to deny and thereby escape from that duality as a corruption of the Light. Characteristically, the Gnostic is subversive of outside authority and antipathetic toward the world, preoccupied as he is with his own self-love; he is also marked by a narcissistic confusion of himself with others and by a confusion of his ideas of the world with the world's reality; and he is condescendingly superior toward some higher world of light, purity, and goodness. The Gnostic's proud self-love is his practical undoing, because in his blindness he ignores or denies the finite limitations of his own bodily incarnation, which pathetic act forever denies him the redemptive way back to what Humphries calls the "lostness of the Light within him."[6]

The classic example of such a Gnostic manifestation in Southern literature is, of course, Thomas Sutpen in Faulkner's masterpiece, *Absalom, Absalom!* His innocence compromised at age fourteen by an awareness of his own finite limitations, Sutpen thereafter sets out, in contradiction to both the past and experience, to re-create corporeally his own pure and inviolate idea of himself through his dynastic "grand design" of Sutpen's Hundred. Despite its social and material accoutrements, the design's intent, like Sutpen's own anti-social behavior thereafter, is to erase all knowledge, all memory of that youthful rejection and fall, by creating and retreating into a transcendent, self-conceived world that is virginally innocent, white, male, and immortal. The ultimate failure of the design is that though women and slaves pragmatically figure as emblems of the design's social, material, and dynastic success and are, in fact, the essential means to its execution, the design also requires ultimately the effective exclusion of both women and blacks. Struggling to the last to preserve the design in the face of such a practical inconsistency, the still "virginal" but rapacious Sutpen perishes along with his design, cut down by the scythe of Father Time, Wash Jones.

The quest for an Edenic recovery so characteristic of Gnosticism, as highlighted here in the Sutpen example, is seldom so visibly central or directly showcased in O'Connor's fiction, but the Gnostic impulse of her characters, believer and unbeliever alike, is just as strong and compelling. Because she usually eschews the dramatization of consciousness and because the context of prevailing Southern social mores is so important in her stories, we often know her Gnostics by their social and behavioral eccentricities. In O'Connor's fiction belief is not defined in wholly theological or religious terms, though she does have her strictly evangelical Gnostics, like Hazel Motes, Enoch Emery, Mrs. Shortley, and O.E. Parker's wife, some of whom work at it only part-time, admittedly. Others, however, like Mrs. Turpin, the grandmother in "A Good Man Is Hard to Find," Julian's mother in "Everything That Rises Must Converge," and a virtual passel of Mrs. Freemans and Mrs. Hopewells, all possess a vague belief in some kind of moral goodness they confuse with their hankerings after a lost social order in the traditions of the antebellum South. Secure in the moral righteousness of their belief in that world, they do not recognize how out of step their practical heresy is with present reality or with religious faith. Misguided as they are, they at least have made a choice for belief in something, their do-it-yourself religion, which, for them, approximates the Holy. Neither evil nor innocent, they, as O'Connor said of the grandmother, merely "lacked comprehension." (MM p.110). "She would of been a good woman...if it had been somebody there to shoot her every minute of her life." (CS p.133).

In such a context, matters of race, social superiority, polite manners, banal but all-consuming human vanities - the same practical heresies noted earlier - are the social masques of her Gnostic believers and function as the means of their exclusionary escape into a pre-lapsarian world of the Elect. Such a Gnostic calculates his virtues and then numbers among the

Elect only those whose appearances mirror the spirit he perceives within himself. Of the rest of the world, he is contemptuous. The practical heresy and irony of such a self-conceived and self-deceiving world of light, purity, and goodness is that it requires a rather large dose of pride, hypocrisy, meanness, blindness, or any one of a number of good, old-fashioned vices O'Connor finds fictively delicious. The exclusionary tendencies of Mrs. Turpin, for example, are so blinding, her human development so stunted and piggish, that in her final jumbled fantasy of the procession of the saved into heaven, where she and husband Claud march last but are least on key, she still cannot grasp her own error or flaw - the very point of Mary Grace's revelation when she threw the book *Human Development* at Mrs. Turpin. Mrs. Turpin's self-image simply does not admit to the corruptions of the body reflected by her mean spirit, and hence she cannot see herself in the wart-hog; indeed, for her, Mary Grace must be lunatic. So, too, the willful grandmother of June Star and John Wesley finds goodness a thing lost in the remote past but kept alive in a few chosen individuals, true ladies like herself and the fatuously insincere Red Sammy, with whom she babbles nonsense at The Tower Restaurant. So single-minded is her conception of the world that more than once she confuses reality for her own willful ideas of it. And wholly absorbed by selfish concerns for her own safety as her family is slaughtered one by one, she will hypocritically say anything to The Misfit to save herself, even if it is inconsistent: "You've got good blood! I know you wouldn't shoot a lady! ...I'll give you all the money I've got!" (CS pp.131-132).

O'Connor's unbelievers are, similarly, a mixed bag of Gnostic intellectuals, simple and complex, all lost in the life of the mind. Some, like Mrs. McIntyre of "The Displaced Person,"parallel the believers who identify their private social foibles with goodness and belief. However, Mrs. McIntyre, who is indifferent to her peacock and who rejects Mr. Guizac, both of whom are patent symbols of Christ, seeks a "salvation" postulated on her equivalent of unbelief - the wholly practical economics and utilitarian racial order of her farm. Another, the simple atheist like Joy Hulga Hopewell, is the type who, to borrow O'Connor's words, "recognizes spirit in himself but fails to recognize a being outside himself" he can call God. (MM p.159). Another type, like The Misfit, is a Gnostic convert by experience who "recognizes a divine being not himself, but who does not believe that this being can be known. ...Spirit and matter are separated for him." (MM p.159). He "wanders about, caught in a maze of guilt he can't identify, trying to reach a God he can't approach...." (MM p.159). Still another type, like Julian, is an indefinable apostate "who can neither believe nor contain himself in unbelief and who searches desperately, feeling about in all experience for the lost God." (MM p.159). He is the most Gnostic of all.

As Gnostics, O'Connor's unbelievers live by profane reason exclusively but dwell in neither the profane nor the sacred worlds. To them, only their reasoning is sacred and, like Julian, they seek to rise in a "mental bubble" above the world they hold in such contempt. But for O'Connor, the world is itself an expression of the Holy because it was created by God, and so the Gnostic unbeliever, who is trapped by the unholy limitations of his own mind, must effectively deny the world, his natural habit, because he is blind to that in it which is genuinely sacred. Logically, the objects of his greatest scorn are usually the poor, misguided believers already catalogued. Nonetheless, O'Connor's Gnostic unbelievers - and this is their practical heresy, their Achilles heel - seek outside confirmation of the spirit whose depths they plumb within themselves. The unloving Hulga abuses all the "good country people" about her for their cretinous platitudes and yet looks for love from Manley Pointer, ostensibly their foremost representative, if only to prove that she who loves no one and believes in nothing is neither unlovable nor insubstantial. And so it is with The Misfit. Because he feels the punishment he has endured for some forgotten Original Sin is excessive and unjustified spiritually, The Misfit kills the grandmother in order to confirm the pointlessness of punishment and redemption by affirming the pleasure of meanness in a wholly profane life. And Julian abuses his mother for her condescending racism and looks futilely to the blacks on the bus for confirmation of his own superior mind. It is fittingly ironic, vulnerable as they are in their dependency on the physical world of the community of man, that O'Connor's unbelievers are often themselves marked by physical limitations, social ineffectiveness, alienating personality quirks, and the like, all of which prevent their successful interaction with the world when they need it most. So much do they live inside themselves, so alien is the outside world to them, that they can find no worldly verification for their unbelief.

It is easy to see the Gnostic roots of O'Connor's true believers in the fundamentalist heritage of evangelism. To the evangelical, baptism is an all or nothing proposition that requires the rejection of the world and a steadfast faith in the spirit within that saves. As The Misfit himself says of Jesus, "If He did what He said, then it's nothing for you to do but throw away everything and follow Him...." (CS p.132). It is more difficult to unravel the kinship O'Connor perceives between the believer and the unbeliever. An orthodox Catholic, whose shared sympathies are with her evangelical believers, at least in certain basic tenets of faith - the reality of sin, the need for redemption, judgment in Christ - O'Connor wishes to make the point that unbelief, as she characterizes it, is also an all or nothing proposition that requires the rejection of the world, precisely because the world is an expression of the Holy by the fact of God's creating it. Her ultimate revulsion for both the believer and the unbeliever arises at this point of their kinship, in the practical heresies of their mutual rejection of the world by their exclusionary escape into a life of either the spirit or the mind.

To O'Connor, the world is not one-dimensional; it is not exclusively profane, and it is certainly not wholly sacred. Her Gnostic believer may pretend to escape into the sacred and her Gnostic unbeliever may contradictorily sacralize his profane intellect, such that he affects a quasi-transcendence of both the sacred and the profane, but the temporal world remains, and remains a place where sacred and profane interact in mysterious ways. As O'Connor explains her position:

Since the eighteenth century, the popular spirit of each succeeding age has tended more and more to the view that the ills and mysteries of life will eventually fall before the scientific advances of man, a belief that is still going strong.... On the other hand, if the writer believes that our life is and will remain essentially mysterious then what he sees on the surface will be of interest to him only as he can go through it into an experience of mystery itself.... His way will much more obviously be the way of distortion.... He's looking for one image that will connect or combine or embody two points; one is a point in the concrete, and the other is a point not visible to the naked eye, but believed in by him firmly, just as real to him, really, as the one that everybody sees.... (MM pp.41-42).

Whenever I'm asked why Southern writers particularly have a penchant for writing about freaks, I say it is because we are still able to recognize one. To be able to recognize a freak, you have to have some conception of the whole man, and in the South the general conception of man is still, in the main, theological. (MM p.44).

Consummate anti-intellectual though she is, O'Connor's point here, nonetheless, is an intellectual, not a Catholic, one - that it is naive to envision the profane world in reducible, intellectual terms exclusively, because the world remains too mysterious and therefore irrational, to be comprehended by reason alone. Her view of the profane world places her, at least initially, in the odd company of her opposite, the nihilist. O'Connor's effective equation between the sacred and the profane worlds - that religious mystery is no more mysterious than the commonplace everyday mysteries of the profane world - sympathizes with the nihilistic axiom that the universe is ultimately irrational and unknowable by nature because it is not comprehensible by reason alone. Hence, her fiction's relative or romantic focus exclusively on the profane world's irrational and incomprehensibly mysterious - dare we say "grotesque" - moments is, perhaps, the only fairly rational view of the world, for in that light we see the world as grotesque by its finite nature. It is also perhaps the best secular defense of her work as Southern Realism - a relative view of reality that proceeds from the strength of its intellectual certainty and clarity.However, if O'Connor concurs with the nihilists that the profane world, considered alone, is meaningless, she parts company with them, in Catholic fashion, by refusing to divorce the profane and sacred worlds, for with Mircea Eliade[7] she believes the profane world's ultimate mysteriousness makes possible faith in sacred mystery, or rather, necessitates it as the only answer to an otherwise incomprehensible universe. Accordingly, her stories of revelation thus seem secular analogues for religious mystery.

In the desacralized modern world we customarily presume the mutual opposition of the sacred and the profane, but O'Connor sees their interaction and its end in humanism as the only legitimate translation of religious belief possible. It is no coincidence that so often when her Gnostic believers and unbelievers get their come-uppance, the believers are introduced to some mysteriously humanizing revelation about the profane world they hold at arm's length and her unbelievers discover some redeeming sacred truth in profane experience that brings them to a closer identity with the world they deny. In the noumenal moment her head clears, when just before death the grandmother sees the evil in herself mirrored in The Misfit, she murmurs, "Why you're one of my babies. You're one of my own children!" (CS p. 132). Her Gnosticism vanishes in that moment and the good woman is spiritually, if not physically, saved. To The Misfit, her revelatory identification with him is as effectively disconcerting as it is initially repulsive, for its truth deprives him of his reason for being what he is, The Misfit, and takes from him the pleasure-in-meanness principle for all his actions as a misfit. As he concludes to Bobby Lee afterwards, "It's no real pleasure in life." (CS p. 133). Though The Misfit is a long way from being saved, Gnostic unbelief is no longer a possible avenue of escape for him.

In their compelling need to sacralize their profane human endeavors, O'Connor's Gnostics express a sacred and human need to elevate man's nature above its profane and finite limitations, which admittedly is the whole point of Christian redemption. However, without a genuine grasp of the sacred, they have only profane and sadly inadequate means to that sacred end, and that is the pathetic irony of their human predicament. Eliade, however, views that irony also from its opposite vantage point, explaining that the sacred's *hierophany*, or revelatory *act of manifestation* is wholly dependent on the profane realities.[8] That is a view which O'Connor certainly seems to share, and one that underscores her notion that the sacred manifests itself most intensely and mysteriously in those objects that are most shockingly profane. Such is the stunning, almost enigmatic manifestation in the "artificial nigger" of the story by the same name. Initially, the reader almost fails to grasp the extent of the manifestation's transformational effect on Nelson and Mr. Head, because mysterious and seemingly illogical, it is not immediately reducible to reason.

As the manifestation of a wholly different order than our own, the sacred can confront sensate man only by means of natural objects that are an integral part of our profane world. Thus, even a supreme hierophany, like the incarnation of God in Christianity, is dependent on mortal human form. The importance of every hierophany is that the profane becomes a means to the sacred, the fundamental paradox being that while an object becomes something else (the sacred), it remains itself (the profane): "In other words,for those who have a religious experience all nature is capable of revealing itself as cosmic sacrality."[9] Above all, O'Connor is asking us as readers to learn to see with different eyes. At our best, she would have us see with her characters beyond the mere concrete reality to the sacred mysteries revealed by their profane experiences. At the least, she expects us to see beyond the concrete naturalistic object to the lesser, secular mysteries of profane experience, if only to teach us, as whole human beings, to recognize a true freak when we see one.

All of which brings us full circle, to the matter of the grotesque. As a writer, O'Connor admits to a certain amount in "the way of distortion," if only to teach us what we have long since forgotten in the desacralized modern world, to see with the eyes of whole beings beyond the reducible object to its irreducible deeper reality. In that, she would save us from becoming freaks ourselves. But her repeated confessions to purposeful distortion in her fiction does not compromise in the least her belief that reality is sometimes grotesque and that the world is populated by freaks. For O'Connor, even on its basest level, the profane directs man spiritually toward the sacred. But when opposed or divorced from each other, as her Gnostics and modern man would have them, both the sacred and the profane are obscene, because they fail to maintain even elemental respect for human dignity. In stories where believer and unbeliever are often paired, the two regard each other with as much contempt and enmity as puzzled lack of recognition. Alone, the sacred and the profane are both useless, producing merely suffering in the human order. The human condition is an obscenity when it is so dispossessed of love and compassion. That is the point in her stories where O'Connor allows her revelations of the world's mysteries to manifest themselves with such shocking violence, when her Gnostic believers and unbelievers are at their most obscene depths of estrangement from the world. Then do her sacred and profane worlds collide.

Notes

1 Patrick J. Ireland, "The Place of Flannery O'Connor in Our Two Literatures: The Southern and National Literary Tradition," *The Flannery O'Connor Bulletin*, 7 (Autumn 1978), 47.
2 From the "Author's Note," *them* (New York, 1969), p.11.
3 Robert Coles, *Flannery O'Connor's South* (Baton Rouge, Louisiana, 1980), p.72.
4 Jefferson Humphries, *The Otherness Within* (Baton Rouge, Louisiana, 1983), p. 100.
5 For a more detailed examination of Gnosticism and O'Connor, see Chapter 2 in Coles and Chapters 1, 6, and 7 in Humphries, from which this essay draws extensively.
6 Humphries, p. 6.
7 Mircea Eliade, *The Sacred and the Profane*, trans. Willard R. Trask, New York, 1961.
8 Eliade, p. 11.
9 Eliade, p. 12.

The Side of the Road: Flannery O'Connor's Social Sensibility

Jan Nordby Gretlund

St. Cyril of Jerusalem, in instructing catechumens, wrote: "The dragon sits by the side of the road, watching those who pass. Beware lest he devour you. We go to the Father of Souls, but it is necessary to pass by the dragon." No matter what form the dragon may take, it is of this mysterious passage past him, or into his jaws, that stories of any depth will always be concerned to tell.... (MM p.35).

When Flannery O'Connor first published "The Displaced Person," the first sentence read: "Mrs. Shortley stood on a small prominence to the left of the pump house."[1] In the final version of the story the pump house was dropped, and understandably so. Yet, the pump house and all the rest that make up "the side of the road" are not without interest. The side of the road is likely to be forgotten once the dragon appears, and so is the pump house when the peacock is in sight. This is perhaps the way it should be, but for the critic the side of the road is interesting in itself.

For a writer whose social concern is not supposed to have been notably pronounced,[2] O'Connor displays a remarkable social sensibility. She takes into account the social problems of her day and comments in much of her fiction on the social order of her native society. Several stories reflect the racial situation in much of the South during the 50s and 60s. Even if her concern is not to improve the material situation of poor whites and blacks, her fiction reveals her sympathies. Her characters, who often live in the country and mostly in Georgia, become concrete illustrations of social behavior through unsentimental characterizations. It was no accident that she majored in sociology, though many critics do not like to hear this.[3] From the beginning of her career she had a highly developed social sensibility, and it served her well in her writing. It is a question whether it is possible to understand her work fully if we see it as sermonizing. Not to consider the social experience that she presents, is to simplify and underestimate both her and her fiction. The purpose in stressing her social sensibility is to call attention to a neglected side of her genius. The purpose is not to try to obscure her Catholic faith, which manifests itself in all her work. For her the social realism is her access to the mystery of life, she writes: ...if the novelist "doesn't make these natural things believable in themselves, he can't make them believable in any of their spiritual extensions." (MM p.176). There is no conflict between the social and the Christian concerns; on the contrary it is her Christian faith that makes O'Connor, who obviously loves her neighbor, observe and describe social problems and conflicts.

Flannery O'Connor's writing career can be seen as a development from an early stereotyping tendency to the allegorizing skill of her final years. This career structure has often been recognized by critics, but it has been less readily accepted that she also had a creative middle period when she wrote fiction of obvious social concern. The characters in her fiction of this period are not just economic and social exemplars, but they are obviously also that. The middle period may be said to begin during the fall of 1949 with "A Stroke of Good Fortune," and it seems largely to end with "The Artificial Nigger" in the spring of 1955. The social concern was not sudden or new in 1949, it is obvious already in O'Connor's first stories. In "The Crop," from before February 1946, Miss Willerton encounters intruding reality in the shape of a poor white couple that she passes downtown, and she gives up her idea of writing "arty" fiction about poor white sharecroppers, at least for the moment. "The Barber" from the following year is a comment on the racial issues of the time and the frustration experienced by Southern liberals. By June 1955, when "Good Country People" was published, O'Connor's social concern had become less obvious, while the religious symbolism tended to be increasingly heavy-handed. It should perhaps be pointed out that it is impossible to overlook the social sensibility in several of her stories from after 1955. In "A View of the Woods" (1957) she records the rape of the land in the creation of a site for the new fishing club. Finally, the site is deserted except for the presence of Mr. Fortune and "one huge yellow monster which sat to the side, as stationary as he was, gorging itself on clay." (CS p. 356). With "Everything That Rises Must Converge" (1961) she has given us one of the best fictional accounts of the breakdown in the late 50s of the old order of the South. In this story Julian is forced to realize that you cannot take off your Southern heritage as easily as you take off a tie. The social stratification of Southern society and the end of it are also the subject of Mrs. Turpin's vision in "Revelation," the last story O'Connor saw in print. Mrs. Turpin had not expected "whole companies of white-trash" and "bands of black niggers" to precede her own tribe of middle-class respectability in the vast horde of souls "rumbling toward heaven." (CS p. 508). The most astringent social comment from her final period is probably the glimpse of starvation in "Parker's Back," the last story she completed. Sarah Ruth has skin that is "thin and drawn as tight as the skin on an onion;" (CS p. 510) and when she is offered an apple, she takes it quickly, "as if the basket might disappear if she didn't make haste. Hungry people made Parker nervous. He had always had plenty to eat himself. He grew very uncomfortable." (CS p.515). As most of us do at the thought of hunger in our own backyard.

In 1953 the social concern was often central to O'Connor's fiction. Several of the short stories from that year had their origin in newspaper articles.[4] The inspiration for her most famous story "A Good Man Is Hard to Find" was a newspaper headline that read: "'The Misfit' Robs Office, Escapes With $150." O'Connor's story is about a criminal called The Misfit and also about why he is a misfit. A second story from 1953 "A Late Encounter with the Enemy" is about our Hollywood version of the past, and what it does to our concept of everyday life. It originated in a newspaper headline that reads: "Confederate Vet to See Wife Get Degree at GSCW." A third story from 1953 is "The Life You Save May Be Your Own," whose main character called Mr. Shiftlet is clearly a have-not, who is out to have something. "The Shiftlet Fragment"[5] shows how he became so materialistic. And Lucynell Crater, mother, does not go about without teeth because she enjoys being toothless; and she would probably not refuse help for her idiot daughter, if it were offered. But it is not. The social criticism is obvious here and in the harsh contrast between poor and rich in "The River" (also from 1953), in which the city is seen as "a cluster of warts on the side of the mountain." (CS p.165). The city vs. country opposition is also essential in "A Circle in the Fire" from the following year, in which the boy named Powell clearly feels displaced in Atlanta. One of the boys tells Mrs. Cope that Powell's mother "works at a factory and leaves him to mind the rest of them only he don't mind them much" and that "one time he locked his little brother in a box and set it on fire." (CS p.184). Just how bad it is in Atlanta's urban wasteland is obvious in "The Artificial Nigger" from 1955. For Mr. Head and Nelson it seems to be a fate worse than death to be lost in the labyrinth of the city. The social sensibility and the true concern are unmistakable in all the stories from this period. O'Connor follows her own precepts for the novelist and descends "to the concrete where fiction operates" (MM p.92) and draws "large and startling figures" (MM p.34) of "what-is." (MM p.146). There is no excuse for a novelist who fails to notice the situation of his immediate surroundings, as far as she is concerned: "The novelist is required to open his eyes on the world around him and look. If what he sees is not highly edifying, he is still required to look." (MM p.177).

The novels follow the pattern of the short stories. There is more social concern in *Wise Blood* (1952) than in *The Violent Bear It Away* from her final years. In the first novel there is no doubt of Leora Watts' function in Taulkinham. She is one of the ugly and sad products of the city, like shallow lives and loneliness. Enoch Emory's background is sad, Hazel Motes' background is sad and so is their social situation. And the same is true of everybody they meet in Taulkinham. The city is just as frightening and sad in her novels as in her stories, and O'Connor can only write of life in the metropolis full of concern. In her second novel the Tarwaters live almost completely cut off from the community and their relatives. Social concerns are remote from the Tarwaters' universe and in general from this novel; even if we choose to consider the rejection of Rayber's Freudian psychology as a social statement. The novel is full of obvious Christian symbolism and the social concern expressed is insignificant in comparison. The side of the road is simply not described in most of "The Violent Bear It Away."

It would be fairly easy to demonstrate the presence of O'Connor's social sensibility in stories such as "Everything That Rises Must Converge," "An Exile in the East"[6] and in "The Artificial Nigger." Instead "The Displaced Person" (1954), also from her middle period, will be considered here, as it is a typical O'Connor story in several ways: the setting is rural Georgia, the theme is clearly Catholic and it deals with a universal problem. In this story she is right at the crossroads where time and place meet eternity. (Cp. MM p.59). The religious concern in this story is obvious as always and so is the social criticism. Not to see the latter is to underestimate O'Connor. She portrays reality as it manifests itself in the concrete sensual lives of everybody on the farm. It is important that a sense of place is established in order for the tale of spiritual displacement to work. To avoid over-emphasis on the abstract and the risk of impoverishing the imagination and the capacity for prophetic insight, the farm and its social hierarchy must first be made concrete. (Cp. MM p.203). This is done through the observation of the farm and its inhabitants by Mrs. Shortley and later by Mrs. McIntyre. The final version of the story is twice as long as the first version, which stopped already at Mrs. Shortley's death. The story as it now stands consists of two confrontations, first between Mrs. Shortley and the displaced person, and then between him and Mrs. McIntyre, the owner of the farm. And throughout the story there is Father Flynn, who drops in. Both women experience failure and death, but O'Connor does not permit these events to become sentimental. She does not want our sentiments to obscure the absurdity of the lives she describes, so she makes sure that we cannot identify wholly with her characters. She hopes, of course, that we will recognize the absurdity as a part of our own lives. Mrs. Shortley dies at the moment of her final vision, whereas Mrs. McIntyre lingers on after her revelation. At the end of the story all the survivors are thoroughly displaced both spiritually and socially.

On July 21 in 1949 the *Union Recorder*, the local Milledgeville paper, carried the story: "Displaced Family Arrives On Farm From Poland" on the front page. And a week later the same paper featured a photo of the displaced family also on the front page.[7] The newspaper was probably a source of inspiration for O'Connor. The main difference between the newspaper article and O'Connor's plot is the death of the displaced person in the fictional account; the Poles mentioned in the newspaper left the area quite unharmed. From O'Connor's letters we can see that there was also a displaced Polish family on Andalusia, the O'Connor farm. On March 3, 1957, she wrote Mrs. Rumsey Haynes: "Our [Polish displaced][8] family has got a better job and they are moving next week and so my mother is busy getting in another family. This is always a trying time because you never know what you are getting until you get them. This will provide her [Mrs. O'Connor] with an additional headache and me with an additional story probably." (HB p.205). The social milieu and characters of "The Displaced Person" are close to the milieu on Andalusia and the people there; this is confirmed by a letter to a friend known as "A". On May 19, 1956, O'Connor wrote: "The two colored people in "The Displaced Person" are on this place now. The old man is 84 but vertical or more or less so. He doesn't see too good and the other day he fertilized some of my mother's bulbs with worm medicine for the calves. I can only see them from the outside. I wouldn't have the courage of Miss Shirley Ann Grau to go inside their heads." (HB p.159). In spite of the disclaimer in the last sentence, it is her intimate knowledge of the local people and their ways that make O'Connor's stories such excellent material for the social observer and the film maker. She is a master of convincing dialogue, sensitive as she is to the speech of her native area. And she is aware of its importance for her fiction: "A distinctive idiom," she maintains in one of her talks, "is a powerful instrument for keeping fiction social. When one Southern character speaks, regardless of his station in life, an echo of all Southern life is heard. This helps to keep Southern fiction from being a fiction of purely private experience." (MM p.199). In her fiction she demonstrates that she can render the speech of any Southern character regardless of station in life. Here is a conversation between a poor white, Mrs. Shortley, and a black man, old Astor, upon the arrival of the displaced family on the farm:

The old man, Astor raised himself. "We been watching," he said as if this would be news to her. "Who they now?" "They come from over the water," Mrs. Shortley said with a wave of her arm. "They're what is called Displaced Persons." "Displaced Persons," he said. "Well now. I declare. What do that mean?" "It means they ain't where they were born at and there's nowhere for them to go - like if you was run out of here and wouldn't nobody have you." "It seem like they here, though," the old man said in a reflective voice. "If they here, they somewhere." "Sho is," the other agreed. "They here." The illogic of Negro-thinking always irked Mrs. Shortley. "They ain't where they belong to be at," she said. (CS p.199).

O'Connor demonstrates a remarkable ability in creating dramatic scenes out of the concrete details of life on a Georgia farm. Her characters not only sound right, they also look right. There is never any doubt that the characters, who are actors in the great tragi-comedy of man, are also real Georgia people.

Mrs. Shortley dominates the first half of the story. She seems to be indifferent to the beauty of nature and blind to its spiritual value. She ignores the peacock and calls it "Nothing but a peachicken," (CS p. 198) and she ignores "the white afternoon sun." (CS p. 194). But when the Poles try to become members of the social system, she takes up religion and dwells much on vengeance and destruction. But she still ignores the clouds that look like rows and rows of "white fish" (CS p. 210) and perhaps suggest Christian mercy. O'Connor's social concern in this story becomes obvious if we consider Mrs. Shortley as a representative of her class. She represents the malnutrition and marginal economic existence of the poor white South. Anni Maude, one of Mrs. Shortley's daughters, "had never got her growth," and Sarah Mae, the other daughter, "had a cast in her eye." (CS p. 197). These are medical problems that nothing seems to have been done about, although the girls are fifteen and seventeen years old. Mrs. Shortley herself is in bad health. Her distorted visions are made plausible by her ignorance and her bad physical condition. When she drives home the cows, she climbs a hill and probably suffers a minor heart attack. She knows she has heart trouble, but receives no medical treatment. She does prophesy the manner of her own death, whereas her Sunday afternoon revelation originates, it seems, in war newsreels, her distrust of foreigners, and her highly selective Bible reading. The entangled limbs of the Shortleys during her last moments recall the tangle of bodies in the newsreels. In this way Mrs. Shortley is united with the dead concentration camp victims through her own death. (CS pp. 213-214).

In the second part of the story Mrs. McIntyre takes over from Mrs.

Shortley as "the giant wife of the countryside." (CS p. 194). As her language reveals Mrs. McIntyre is of another class. Her ultimate concern is and has always been the finances of the farm. And it is through Mrs. McIntyre's materialism that O'Connor voices her most direct social criticism in this story. Mrs. McIntyre's worst worry is her tenants. Over the years she has had the Ringfields, Collins, Jarrells, Perkins, Pinkins, Herrins, and now the Shortleys. It is obvious that Mrs. McIntyre thinks of them as so much cattle, as human beings she considers her tenants completely "worthless." She behaves and sounds like Mrs. Hopewell in "Good Country People," who "had averaged one tenant family a year." (CS p. 273). Mrs. McIntyre feels that she has been fooling with "sorry people" for years. And she cannot understand why the people she hires always leave her. But it is no wonder, for while she works tirelessly for material success, she thinks of the hired help as just means to her end. To be a tenant on the McIntyre farm is not an enviable life. When the Guizacs arrive, they receive "things that Mrs. McIntyre couldn't use any more herself." (CS p. 196). They are allowed to move into a tenant's shack, and they are told that "they should be grateful for anything they could get." (CS p. 196). For their labor the four Poles will receive seventy dollars a month. Mrs. McIntyre's self-seeking callousness towards the Guizacs illustrates the cruelty of the system. Tenants are only valued in proportion to the money they earn for the farmers. Mrs. McIntyre claims that "people are selfish," (CS p. 216) but she herself wages a regular war on mankind: "...she had survived. She had survived a succession of tenant farmers and dairymen that the old man himself would have found hard to outdo, and she had been able to meet the constant drain of a tribe of moody unpredictable Negroes, and she had even managed to hold her own against the incidental bloodsuckers, the cattle dealers and lumber men and the buyers and sellers of anything...." (CS p. 218). In short every human being she gets into contact with is a menace to her, or at least superfluous in her eyes: "All of you are extra. Each and every one of you are extra!" she screams at her black and white help. (CS p.232). She feels that she alone is essential, for the farm is "her place." The criticism leveled at her pride, egotism and materialism constitutes O'Connor's violent denunciation of the whole social system that breeds these characteristics. There are times, however, when Mrs. McIntyre suspects her own insufficiency. She then seeks her tabernacle, which is a room with a safe surrounded by old ledgers and bank-books. It is the room where her first husband had conducted his business. It is here, facing the safe that she tries to understand why "there was nobody poorer in the world than she was." (CS p. 221). She never suspects her own shortcomings or those of the social order. Father Flynn understands her nature very well, and he uses the introduction of the displaced family on the farm to try to save Mrs. McIntyre from her own materialism and her all-devouring self-interest. She becomes a benefactress, even if her motive is greed. The old priest is well aware of this and lets out "a great ugly bellow" when Mrs. McIntyre asks him "if he thought she was made of money." (CS p. 230).

When Mr. Guizac threatens to upset the social and the racial balance on the farm by working too much and by planning to let Sulk marry a Polish girl, Mrs. McIntyre's reaction reveals no uncertainty: "Mr. Guizac! You would bring this poor innocent child over here and try to marry her to a half-witted thieving black stinking nigger! What kind of a monster are you!" (CS p. 222). Clearly, it is Mrs. McIntyre who is the monster. She feels no obligation to other human beings, but she does feel that " *her* moral obligation" is to "her own people." (CS p. 228). "He's upset the balance around here," she says about Mr. Guizac. And for her this is more important than some girl's suffering in distant Europe. It is significant that it is Astor, the old black man on the farm, who helps remind her of the traditional order on the place. Their relationship reflects the social order which is the gauge for everything they do. (Astor's presence is a flaw in the story in one respect. It is hard to believe that he would not have put a quick end to Sulk's plans, it is impossible to imagine that Astor did not know, and given the time and place it is difficult to imagine that Sulk would ever get the notion to marry a white girl, even when encouraged by Mr. Guizac. O'Connor sees the weakness and indicates that Sulk is half-witted.)

It is only at the murder of Mr. Guizac that Mrs. McIntyre begins to suspect that she may not be in full control even on her place. She watches the figures bending over Mr. Guizac's body. Among them is Father Flynn (who has gotten there unbelievably fast), he is administering the last rites to the Pole when Mrs. McIntyre wakes up after she had lost consciousness. She now experiences the sense of displacement that supposedly also characterized Mrs. Shortley's last moments. Though it all takes place on her own farm, Mrs. McIntyre feels that she is "in some foreign country." (CS p. 235). The irony is, of course, that the class conscious Mrs. McIntyre would never have expected to share an experience with one of her sorry tenants. Her punishment is that she is not allowed to die right away as Mrs. Shortley did. All of her life Mrs. McIntyre has hated discussions about religion, they embarrassed her, and now she has to accept the weekly visits of Father Flynn, who comes to explain the doctrines of the Church to her. Ironically, the proud, practical and materialistic Mrs. McIntyre is condemned to suffer religious instruction she has not asked for.

The difficulties between the displaced person and the two women represent a confrontation of value systems. One system derives from the social stratification of Southern society, the other is the product of a frightening European experience. Mr. Guizac's foreign social behavior brings the value systems into violent opposition. He poses a threat to a society that has always dealt with class, race and sex in its own ways. The Pole's willingness to work hard and his ability to improve his financial position together with his willingness to accept blacks as equals are potentially lethal to the established social order. It is when Mrs. McIntyre realizes this that she complains: "He's extra and he's upset the balance around here." (CS p. 231). The daily life on the farm depends on everyone's tacit acceptance of the social stratification. Everybody on the farm knows that Astor and Sulk steal, but in doing so they confirm the stereotype image of blacks, so nobody thinks much of it. Mrs. McIntyre knows that Mr. Shortley smokes in the milking barn, but that is what can be expected of poor white help, so she only hints at it. Both the blacks and the poor whites run stills on Mrs. McIntyre's property. It seems that everybody knows it, but it does not constitute a transgression against the accepted behavior patterns for blacks and poor whites, so nobody even considers interfering. This is the system that the Guizacs threaten to disrupt by their mere presence. Mr. Guizac is finally sacrificed, because the accepted social order is considered more important than any moral consideration could possibly be. It could be argued that the Polish immigrant must die because he undermines social patterns whose existence he does not even know about. "The balance" that is upset is finally not so much based on divine justice as on social convention. What threatens is the dissolution of all social distinctions through the planned marriage between a young black man and a blond Polish girl. Surely the social satire is too obvious to be overlooked.

The social context is always clear in "The Displaced Person," as O'Connor feels it should be in all fiction: "The larger social context is simply left out of much current fiction, but it cannot be left out by the Southern writer," she said in one of her talks. (MM p.198). It is, after all, the portrait of the class-divided society that makes the story about the displaced person so convincing. This is always the case O'Connor maintains in her advice on writing: "You can't cut characters off from their society and say much about them as individuals. You can't say anything meaningful about the mystery of a personality unless you put that personality in a believable and significant social context." (MM p.104). The social situation of the Shortleys is only too plain when they load their boxes and "old battered suitcases from under the bed," two iron beds with the mattresses rolled up between some rocking chairs, and "a crate of chickens" on top of their old car. (CS p.212). They prepare to leave the farm in their "overfreighted leaking ark" before they are asked to leave. The only ones worse off than the Shortleys are the blacks; and they will be next to go, according to Mrs. Shortley, now that nobody has mules any more. (CS p.205). The only comfort for the blacks is that their social position is too low for anybody to dispute with them for it. It is her "moral obligation" to this social order that makes it impossible for Mrs. McIntyre to prevent the killing of Mr. Guizac. She becomes the accomplice of the poor whites and blacks in "collusion forever." (CS p.234). Bound as she is by her particular past and by the institutions and traditions that this past has left to her.

Flannery O'Connor's social and moral ideas invoke the milieu of her region and the society of which she was a product. In this sense large social issues were always the stuff of her work. [9] A true appreciation of O'Connor as a fiction writer must also take into account her rendition of her time and place and the people there. Her style in "The Displaced Person" is that of the social satirist. In her story of what the social order and the accepted system can do to us, she demonstrates her social awareness. There is no reason to exaggerate the importance of her social sensibility, but it should not be overlooked. Whenever she plunges us into the lives of good or bad country people, we do not have to read far to understand that their situation often is less than enviable. She obviously enjoys showing that we are human and made of dust, but it is also obvious in her fiction that Flannery O'Connor had great love for the people who try to pass the dragon at "the side of the road."

Notes

1 *Sewanee Review*, 62/4 (Autumn 1954) 634.
2 See Sally Fitzgerald, "Introduction," *Three by Flannery O'Connor*," New Jersey, 1985, p.xxiv. Fitzgerald claims that O'Connor did not treat "a current social issue" in her fiction until "Everything That Rises Must Converge."
3 See e.g., Sally Fitzgerald, p.viii: "...she had majored - for the last time ever - in Sociology."
4 Harvey Klevar, "Image and Imagination: Flannery O'Connor's Front Page Fiction," *Journal of Modern Literature* 4/1 (September 1974) 121-132.
5 *The Flannery O'Connor Bulletin*, 10 (1981) 78-86.
6 *South Carolina Review*, 11/1(Spring 1978) 12-21.
7 Harvey Klevar, pp. 126-127.

8 The brackets contain the actual wording of the letter on deposit with Georgia College, Milledgeville, Ga.
9 Cp. Sally Fitzgerald, p.xxv: "Large social issues as such were never the stuff of Flannery O'Connor's work,... "

"The Length, Breadth, and Depth of the World in Movement": The Evolutionary Vision of Flannery O'Connor and Teilhard de Chardin

Ann Ebrecht

In the introductory chapter of *The Divine Milieu,* Teilhard de Chardin discusses the religious ferment "caused by the revelation of the immensity and unity of the world all around us and within us." He says the discoveries of the physical sciences cause a "collective awakening" to which the individual may respond in one of two ways:

To some the world has disclosed itself as too vast: within such immensity man is lost and no longer counts; and there is nothing left for him to do but shut his eyes and disappear. To others, the world is too beautiful; and it, and it alone, must be adored.[1]

The protagonists in Flannery O'Connor's "A View of the Woods" and "Everything That Rises Must Converge" adopt these approaches to their experience of the material world. Mr. Fortune takes the second approach. He adores his property. He sees his future solely in terms of material progress. He sells off his property because he wants gas stations, motels, and drive-ins within easy distance of his house. When he hears talk that a new town will spring up in his area, he thinks that this town "should be called Fortune, Georgia" because he "was a man of advanced vision, even if he was seventy-nine years old." (CS p. 338). Mr. Fortune is future-directed. Julian, in "Everything That Rises Must Converge," takes the first approach. He comes to the conclusion that there is "of course no future ahead of him" and withdraws "into the inner compartment of his mind" because he cannot cope with the world. (CS p. 411). When Julian hesitates to think of how much he owes his mother, he thereby tacitly admits his own inadequacies. In most of Julian's reflections, he is saying, I count for nothing, and I may as well disappear.

In this essay it is not my purpose to show the direct influence of Teilhard de Chardin's theories on "A View of the Woods." Obviously it would be impossible to do so since the story antedates the first English translation of *The Phenomenon of Man.*[2] Rather my purpose in examining this story is to show why O'Connor found Teilhard's theories so attractive, and to show how closely akin they are to her own beliefs. Then I will examine "Everything That Rises Must Converge" considering how O'Connor clearly uses some of Teilhard's thought and his multi-dimensional imagery in the story.But before I begin my discussion, I must note the differences between Teilhard de Chardin's theories and O'Connor's beliefs. I agree with Marion Montgomery who clearly explains the inconsistencies between Teilhard de Chardin's and O'Connor's ideas about evil in "O'Connor and Teilhard de Chardin: The Problem of Evil" (Renascence , 1969), and more recently in Why Flannery O'Connor Stayed Home . (La Salle, Illinois, 1981). Like Montgomery, I see contrasts between O'Connor's orthodoxy and Teilhard de Chardin's somewhat heretical view concerning the nature of evil.

I believe O'Connor found Teilhard de Chardin's theories important not because she literally believed them but because she admired the breadth of his imagination. She might have described him in the same way that she did Baron Frederick von Hügel, whom she called "an antidote to much of the vulgarity and rawness of American Catholics." (HB p. 331). Teilhard de Chardin, like the Baron and O'Connor, saw man's spiritual-physical life as a rich and complex experience. O'Connor says that she was much taken with Teilhard de Chardin because "he was alive to everything there is to be alive to and in the right way." (HB p. 449). She admires Teilhard's effort to face a scientific age toward Christ, and she finds in him a way of controlling the nihilism a scientific age produces. In a letter to Alfred Corn, a young poet who feels he is losing his faith, she says:

I might suggest that you look into some of the works of Pierre Teilhard de Chardin.... I don't suggest you go to him for answers but for different questions, for that stretching of the imagination that you need to make you a sceptic in the face of much that you are learning, much of which is new and shocking but which when boiled down becomes less so and takes its place in the general scheme of things. (HB p. 477).

Despite her great admiration for Teilhard, O'Connor knew that his beliefs were heretical. In her book review of his Letters from a Traveller, O'Connor says:

The picture these letters give is one of exile, suffering, and absolute loyalty to the Church on the part of a scientist whose life's effort was an attempt to fit his knowledge of evolution into the pattern of his faith in Christ. To do such a thing is the work of neither scientist nor theologian, but of poet and mystic. That Teilhard was to some degree these is also evident and that his failure was the failure of a great and saintly man is not to be questioned.... These letters are further evidence that his life of faith and work can be emulated even though his books remain incomplete and dangerous.[3]

The common ground that O'Connor and Teilhard de Chardin share is their strong belief in the interpenetration of man's physical and spiritual natures. To put this concept in Teilhard's terms, "Omega-Christ is in existence and operative at the very core of the thinking mass."[4] O'Connor abhorred science's effort to categorize experience and to explain it solely in material terms. Like Teilhard, she would describe human experience, if man lives rightly, as incarnational. For them the Incarnation means that Christ did not simply become man but that he is still man and a part of all that exists. The Incarnation is both eternal mystery and timeless presence. In *The Divine Milieu* Teilhard describes the richness of the physical and spiritual interpenetrating and the responsibilities it implies for man.

Let us look around us: the waves come from all sides and from the farthest horizon. Through every cleft, the sensible world inundates us with its riches - food for the body, nourishment for the eyes, harmony of sounds and fullness of heart, unknown phenomena and new thruths, all these treasures, all these urges, all these calls, coming from the four quarters of the world, pass through our consciousness at every moment. What is their role within us?... They will merge into the most intimate life of our soul and either develop it or poison it.[5]

Clearly Mr. Fortune has been poisoned by his possessions. By examining O'Connor's satire of Fortune's blind materialism, I found several bases for O'Connor's attraction to Teilhard de Chardin's ideas. First, this story is a critique of "motorization," as Teilhard calls it in *The Phenomenon of Man*, and of the commercialism which accompanies it. Second, it satirizes Fortune's tendency "to confuse individuality with personality" - to use another of Teilhard's expressions. And last, it explores the world's motion in and through Christ in the final imagery of the story. In "A View of the Woods," O'Connor expresses this motion through linear imagery, but in "Everything That Rises Must Converge," she shifts to Teilhard's spiral or wave imagery while the earth-bound imaginations of Julian and his mother appear in linear terms.

First I will discuss O'Connor's critique of mechanization. Mr. Fortune and Mary Fortune are fascinated by machines. They go out almost every day to watch a backhoe prepare the site for a fishing club beside an artificial lake.

...they watched, sometimes for hours, while the machine systematically ate a square red hole in what had once been a cow pasture.... "Any fool that would let a cow pasture interfere with progress is not on my books," he had said to Mary Fortune several times,... But the child did not have eyes for anything but the machine. She sat on the hood, looking down into the red pit, watching the big disembodied gullet gorge itself on the clay, then, with the sound of a deep sustained nausea and a slow mechanical revulsion, turn and spit it up. (CS p. 335).

Clearly Mr. Fortune, as his name would suggest, is interested in the future, but he conceives of the future in terms of matter alone. His kind of progress comes through the production of goods and money, through factories and mechanization. Teilhard's comment on this idea of progress is that "the great human machine is designed to work and *must* work by producing a super abundance of mind. If it does not work or rather if it produces only matter, this means that it has gone into reverse."[6] I doubt that O'Connor literally accepted Teilhard's theory that evolution is moving us toward a psycho-genetic state, but she certainly would have found his criticism of mechanization as well as of commercialism sympathetic. Along with the disease imagery of the backhoe's mechanical nausea, we see the death-dealing of commercialism in O'Connor's description of Tilman's business. Tilman is the man to whom Fortune plans to sell the lawn and thereby block the Pitts' view of the woods.

Tilman operated a combination country store, filling station, scrap-metal dump, used-car lot and dance hall...he was an up-and-coming man - the kind, Mr. Fortune thought, who was never just in line with progress but always a little ahead of it....
Tilman's was bordered on either side by a field of old used-car bodies, a kind of ward for incurable automobiles. He also sold outdoor ornaments, such as stone cranes and chickens, urns, jardinieres, whirligigs, and farther back from the road, so as not to depress his dance-hall customers, a line of tombstones and monuments. (CS p. 345).

Another of Fortune's errors is his vanity in idolizing Mary Fortune. O'Connor's critique of this self-fascination shows why she found Teilhard's notions of individuality and personality attractive. Interestingly enough, O'Connor describes Mary Fortune as a "throwback," an evolutionary aberration, because she looks so much like the old man. However, to Fortune, she is the loveliest of creations. "No one was particularly glad that Mary Fortune looked like her grandfather except the old man himself. He thought it added greatly to her attractiveness, he thought she was the smartest and the prettiest child he had ever seen." (CS p. 336). He always thinks of her as a Fortune and not as who she really is - a Pitts. To Fortune he and she are a different breed from the Pittses, who are nevertheless their family. According to Teilhard this fascination with individuality is a fatal mistake. The personality "in trying to separate itself as much as possible from others...individualizes itself; but in doing so it becomes retrograde and seeks to drag the world backwards toward plurality and into matter.... According to the evolutionary structure of the world we can only find our person by uniting with others.[7] Teilhard's idea of the unity of human experience would also be attractive to O'Connor.

O'Connor suggests that Fortune never realizes either of his errors. In her letters she says the old man is damned; still, in the story she does show that he has the capacity for grace, limited though his abilities may be. Fortune can hardly begin to understand why Mary Fortune is angry with him for selling the lawn to make way for a filling station. After a particularly nasty spat with her over the matter, Fortune goes upstairs to take a nap.

Several times during the afternoon, he got up from his bed and looked out the window across the 'lawn' to the line of woods she said they wouldn't be able to see any more. Every time he saw the same thing: woods - not a mountain, not a waterfall, not any kind of planted bush or flower, just woods.... A pine trunk is a pine trunk, he said to himself, and anybody that wants to see one don't have to go far in this neighborhood. (CS p. 348).

The third time that the old man gets up, his perception is slightly different. He stares "for some time, as if for a prolonged instant he were caught up out of the rattle of everything that led to the future and were held there in the midst of an uncomfortable mystery that he had not apprehended before." (CS p. 348). His conception of the future, even as he glimpses the mystery, is a mechanical one. Man *rattles* toward it, yet for a moment he senses the mystery of the Incarnation and Crucifixion, for in his vision it is "as if someone were wounded behind the woods and the trees were bathed in blood." (CS p. 348). This larger vision does not last long. Fortune next thinks:

All men were created free and equal. When this phrase sounded in his head, his patriotic sense triumphed and he realized that it was his duty to sell the lot, that he must insure the future. He looked out the window at the moon shining over the woods across the road and listened for a while to the hum of crickets and treefrogs, and beneath their racket, he could hear the throb of the future town of Fortune. (CS p. 349).

In effect Fortune is transforming the natural, which is invested with

212

mystery, into the purely mechanical and commercial. For a moment when he saw the woods bathed in the light of the setting sun, he saw what Teilhard calls "the within of things," the mystery at the heart of existence, but he reverts to seeing only the without.

The vision he has during his heart attack indicates the limitations of those who fail to see "the within of things." The trees, which O'Connor says are the Christ symbol in the story, are moving forward. O'Connor points out that "in the end [they] escape the old man's vision and march off over the hills." (HB p. 190).

...[Fortune] saw that the giant trees had thickened into mysterious dark files that were marching across the water and away into the distance. He looked around desperately for someone to help him but the place was deserted except for one huge yellow monster which sat to the side, as stationary as he was, gorging itself on clay. (CS p. 356).

Fortune has not moved forward toward the future; he has remained stationary. The trees escape Fortune's narrow materialistic vision through their march, a linear movement.

In "Everything That Rises Must Converge" O'Connor treats the world's movement in and through Christ in a more complex fashion by pointing out the limitations of linear movement through her imagery. In addition her plot seems to affirm Teilhard's theories concerning chance's and free will's interplay in shaping human destiny. She also repeats one of the messages of "A View of the Woods": one must not separate himself from others.

First I will explore Julian's desire to isolate himself from others. Julian's attempt at individuality is slightly different from Mr. Fortune's. Julian enters the past, not the future, in his illusions. In his "mental bubble" he usually retreats to the decaying Godhigh mansion. Julian lives in this illusion because he cannot wed thought and experience. According to Teilhard, this failing is characteristic of twentieth-century man. "We are continually inclined to isolate ourselves from the things and events which surround us, as though we were looking at them from the outside."[8] Julian isolates himself from the most dominating reality of his world, his mother. In consequence of his self-imposed isolation, he knows neither himself nor her.

In fact both Julian and his mother, in their pride and prejudice, attempt to separate themselves from others, to escape what Teilhard describes as the "ever-ascending curve" the "constantly rising tide below the rhythmic tide of the ages." Julian's description of his mother's views indicates a linear movement, not Teilhard's spiraling curve or rising tide. She rolls into the topic of racial integration "every few days like a train on an open track. He knew every stop, every junction, every swamp along the way, and knew the exact point at which her conclusion would roll majestically into the station: 'It's ridiculous. It's simply not realistic. They should rise, yes but on their own side of the fence'." (CS p. 408). Earlier in the story, she says to Julian of her reducing class "Most of them in it are not our kind of people...but I can be gracious to anybody. I know who I am." (CS p. 407). Julian's mother summarizes the social changes she has seen in linear terms as well. She says, "I tell you, the bottom rail is on the top." (CS p. 407). Through O'Connor's incisive use of point of view, she criticizes both Julian's view of his mother's opinions and the opinions themselves; she shows their earthbound imaginations. Through this critique, she is making two points. First there is no rising on opposite sides of the fence because all men are moving together through time toward God. Second, Julian's mother cannot know precisely who she is because we are all in flux - moving, changing, converging. Thus Julian's remark to his mother that "Knowing who you are is good for one generation only. You haven't the foggiest idea where you stand now or who you are," (CS p. 407) bears some truth. But then so does her retort to him, in another argument that true culture is "in the heart...and in how you do things and how you do things is because of who you *are*. (CS p. 410).

The events at the end of the story show that neither Julian nor his mother know themselves. Each attempts to control his or her world and fails. The violent events occur partly because of chance - the coincidence of the black woman and child exiting the bus at the same stop as Julian and his mother. But both Julian's and his mother's condescending attitudes generate the violent convergences. The forces which combine to cause the black woman's attack and its results for Julian parallel the forces Teilhard describes controlling the evolutionary spiral. In *The Phenomenon of Man*, he says, "It is only through strokes of chance that life proceeds,but strokes of chance which are recognized and grasped - that is to say psychically selected." In another explanation of this process he says, "Not only do we read in our slightest acts the secret of evolution's proceedings; but for an elementary part *we hold it in our hands* responsible for its past and to its future."[9]

Julian's mother's giving the shiny penny to the black child is a conscious act. The black woman's exploding "like a piece of machinery that had been given one ounce of pressure too much" (CS p. 418) is a conscious act. (In this act of hate, the black woman becomes less than human and throws "the great human machine into reverse.") And Julian's attack on his mother is also a conscious act. The convergence of these acts moves Julian forward into the future which he seeks to escape. As John Burke points out in his article "Convergence of Flannery O'Connor and Teilhard de Chardin," Julian gains the ability to reflect upon himself. He enters Teilhard's noosphere for this first time. This ability advances him toward his mother whom he perceives throughout much of the story as "the other."[10] Julian clearly underlines the connection between himself and his mother when, at the end of the story, he addresses her as, "Darling, sweetheart" and finally, "Mamma, Mamma!" (CS p. 420). Thus Julian becomes the insecure little boy he has behaved as throughout the story, but he also becomes his mother's son.

The imagery O'Connor employs in this final scene, as I stated earlier, owes something to Teilhard de Chardin. It suggests a center of unity from which experience emanates and repeats itself in some measure. After the attack Julian's mother stands "swaying slightly as if the spots of light in darkness were circling around her." (CS p. 419). A "tide of darkness" seems to be sweeping Julian's mother from him, and then as he runs for help the "tide of darkness" seems "to sweep him back to her." (CS p. 420). In the first incident a kind of spiral encircles Julian's mother, one which she cannot perceive. Her eyes remain "shadowed and confused." The tide imagery, which is also typical of Teilhard's writing, is more difficult to explain. The first tide seems to sweep Julian away from his mother toward the world of guilt and sorrow mentioned at the story's end. But the second tide seems to sweep him back to her. Because of these opposing motions, I cannot say O'Connor is describing Teilhard's "rising tide" of consciousness. The second tide, in fact, seems to sweep Julian away from the guilt and sorrow which O'Connor believes will raise his consciousness. However O'Connor's using the tide imagery shows Teilhard's thought entering her art though O'Connor clearly uses his ideas in her own framework and for her own purposes. Here, in the ebb and flow, she is perhaps indicating the confused state of man, a creature pulled by God's grace in one direction and by his own limitations in another.

In discussing "A View of the Woods" I have shown why O'Connor found Teilhard de Chardin's theories attractive and how closely her sensibilities and beliefs lay to his. She, like Teilhard, abhorred mechanization for its own sake and saw the dangers of vanity. Both Teilhard and O'Connor also believed the world is moving toward God. In "A View of the Woods" O'Connor describes this movement linearly, in terms of one dimension only. "Everything That Rises Must Converge" is a positive response to Teilhard's theories not only in theme and plot, but in imagery as well. It repeats the earlier story's message concerning the delusions of vanity. It explores the roles of chance and free will in man's movement toward God. And its spiral and wave imagery, typical of Teilhard de Chardin's thought, suggests a multi-dimensional center, an organizing principle from which the energies of the world emanate and return - the Lord who exists in space-time, in the "length, breadth and depth of the world in movement."[11]

Notes

1 Pierre Teilhard de Chardin, *The Divine Milieu* (New York, 1960), pp. 13-14.
2 Pierre Teilhard de Chardin, *The Phenomenon of Man* (New York, 1959). The story was published in 1957.
3 Flannery O'Connor, *The Presence of Grace and Other Book Reviews* , ed. Leo J. Zuber and Carter Martin (Athens, Georgia, 1983), p. 161.
4 Chardin, *The Phenomenon of Man*, p. 291.
5 Chardin, *The Divine Milieu*, p. 28.
6 Chardin, *The Phenomenon of Man*, p. 257.
7 Chardin, *The Phenomenon of Man*, p. 263.
8 Chardin, *The Phenomenon of Man*, pp. 218-219.
9 Chardin, *The Phenomenon of Man*, p. 149, p. 253.
10 John J. Burke, Jr., "Convergence of Flannery O'Connor and Chardin," *Renascence*, 19 (1966), 44.
11 Chardin, *The Phenomenon of Man*, p. 297.

Flannery O'Connor's Unique Contribution to Christian Literary Naturalism

Sara Mott

Any attempt to plow new ground to uncover anything astoundingly different about Flannery O'Connor as a Southener and a Catholic seems both futile and unnecessary. But summarizing a few generalizations about these two identifications is necessary in order to show how these "givens" influence her treatment of what I choose to call Christian literary naturalism, an expression to be dealt with in detail later in the principal argument.

O'Connor was proud of her Southern heritage and of being a Southern writer, but she wanted to be certain that as a Southern writer, she was an American writer who did "express this great country," (MM p. 29) and not a regional writer whom she said "the woods are full of." She remarked that "Southern writers are stuck with the South and it's a very good thing to be stuck with."[1] Continuing in this vein, she complimented Marion Montgomery on his book, *The Wandering of Desire*, saying "The Southern writer can out-write anybody in the country because he has the Bible and a little history...." (HB p. 444).

Stereotypic Southerners abound in O'Connor's works. One that she handles deftly is the matriarchal Southern woman who was the paradox of the antebellum days and a strong force in the Reconstruction South. The earlier matriarch is paradoxical because she is the "moonlight and magnolia" flirt until she gets her husband; then she turns almost overnight into the manager of the plantation from the main house to the slave quarters. By the time O'Connor depicts them, these matriarchal figures have lost much that is admirable, but they are still dominating females such as Mrs. McIntyre in "The Displaced Person," Mrs. Hopewell in "Good Country People," the grandmother in "A Good Man Is Hard to Find," Mrs. Crater in "The Life You Save May Be Your Own," and Mrs. Turpin in "Revelation."

Another type, not purely Southern but certainly common to the backwoods South, is the itinerant who may be a jack-of-all-trades like Tom T. Shiftlet in "The Life You Save May Be Your Own," a traveling salesman like Manley Pointer in "Good Country People," a fugitive psychopathic killer like The Misfit in "A Good Man Is Hard to Find," or a fake blind preacher like Asa Hawks with his lecherous daughter, Sabbath Lily in *Wise Blood*. Other Southern types she depicts well are the migrant farm workers such as the Shortleys in "The Displaced Person," and the oftentimes shiftless, but faithful black farmhands such as Shot and Louise from the real world of Andalusia Farm and Sulk and Astor in "The Displaced Person."

Although Flannery O'Connor traveled rather extensively away from her South, she always came back, and she spent the greater part of her short life in and around Milledgeville, Georgia. Robert Coles says, "...she understood the southern scene...," and "...she did find in that scene her particular refuge - a spiritual home as well as a place where she lived and died."[2] Josephine Hendin summarizes O'Connor's Southernness to show how it is important in her work: "She would use the trappings of Southern life, but make them explode in new and unexpected directions."[3]

O'Connor's "double heritage as both Catholic and Southerner" has evoked interesting speculations and some provocative comments from the writer herself. Louis Rubin sees this double heritage - "the primitive fundamentalism of her region, the Roman Catholicism of her faith" working "sometimes with and sometimes against each other in a literary counterpoint that has enabled her to create some of the most distinguished and exciting fiction of her time."[4] But even with this evaluation Rubin quotes another critic [Walter Sullivan] as saying, "the marriage of Rome and South Georgia is odd to say the least."[5]

O'Connor herself is the best source for ideas about her Catholic orientation. At no point does she ever seem to feel that her Catholicism is a hindrance to her as a writer. Seeing her Catholic background as a great asset, she wrote to John Lynch in 1955, "I feel myself that being a Catholic has saved me a couple of thousand years in learning to write." (HB p. 114). She feels far more comfortable not writing about Catholics as a primary subject and not writing solely for a Catholic audience. To Father John McCown, she said in 1956 "... A Catholic has to have strong nerves to write about Catholics." (HB p. 130). In 1958 she wrote to "A" that not using Catholic settings or characters was her way of "trying to make it plain that personal loyalty to the person of Christ is imperative, is the structure of man's nature, his necessary direction, etc. The Church, as an institution, doesn't come into it one way or another." (HB p. 290). She told Elizabeth Bishop in 1960 that she did not wish to be labeled a Catholic writer "as it is then assumed that you have some religious axe to grind." (HB p. 391).

At one point in 1955, she expressed her feeling about the neglect by Catholics as being based on real misunderstandings of her as a person. She wrote to John Lynch:

...the ironical part of my silent reception by Catholics is the fact that I write the way I do because and only because I am a Catholic. I feel that if I were not a Catholic, I would have no reason to write, no reason to see, no reason ever to feel horrified or even to enjoy anything. I am a born Catholic, went to Catholic schools in my early years, and have never left or wanted to leave the Church. I have never had the sense that being a Catholic is a limit to the freedom of the writer, but just the reverse. (HB p.114).

A significant extension of her being Catholic is her being Catholic in the fundamental Bible Belt and choosing to write primarily about characters and situations rising out of the fundamental Protestant beliefs. Here is the point at which her own brand of literary naturalism manifests itself most clearly. Preston Browning has rightly termed this "convergence of Catholic dogma and fundamentalist Protestant belief...a peculiar mating," and he continues, "Miss O'Connor did not minimize the difficulties which this alliance entailed...."[6] She commented on the advantages of this convergence:

But the fact that the South is the Bible Belt increases rather than decreases his [The Catholic novelist's] sympathy for what he sees. His interest will in all likelihood go immediately to those aspects of Southern life where the religious feeling is most intense and where its outward forms are farthest from the Catholic....[7]

Focusing on the Catholic novelist who lives in the South, especially on herself as such, she says the novelist "will feel a good deal more kinship with backwoods prophets and shouting fundamentalists than he will with those politer elements for whom the supernatural is an embarrassment and for whom religion has become a department of sociology or culture or personality development."[8]

Moving to the primary focus of this discussion, I will continue by referring to an article by Jerold Savory in *Christian Scholar's Review* which introduces a definition of "literary naturalism broadened from its usual association with scientific determinism to include a form of naturalism that embraces certain religious perspectives, themes and archetypes that are clearly rooted in Christian thought and action."[9] Savory insists that naturalism, especially literary naturalism, should not emphasize man's animalistic behavior to the exclusion of man's human behavior that includes a spiritual level. His ideas are reinforced by those of Henry Weiman who has said:

Naturalism as theology results from an understanding of the religious problem. The religious problem is: What operates in human life to transform man as he cannot transform himself to save him from evil; to bring him to the greatest good, provided he gives himself to this transforming power with that wholeness of self which is called religious faith?[10]

Weiman's belief that "nothing can transform man unless it actually operates in human life"[11] is very close to O'Connor's ideas about the means of man's redemption, the instruments of man's salvation by grace. As Weiman says, "It [the instrument of transformation] may 'come from' beyond human life; but regardless of from where it 'comes,' it can do nothing for man unless it operates in the human personality and between persons in society and history...."[12] This redemptive power is revealed in Jesus Christ, and O'Connor reiterates the necessity of man coming to terms with Jesus Christ. Her letters are filled with these comments, and many of her stories in the two collections and the two novels are peopled with characters who are Christ-haunted in search of redemption. This redemptive process in instance after instance is brought about by a naturalistic detail that is transformed into "theological mystery."[13]

The writer has no tools and no sphere of activity to show that the supernatural is taking place except on a literal level. Thus he must make the details and events on this level believable. O'Connor's conviction is, says Preston Browning, that "mystery can only be adumbrated through the mundane, the natural, the 'what is'."[14] So saying, she does not align herself with the common concept of naturalism as anti-God, anti-religious determinism. But she surely sees man's destiny as "determined" when he does respond to natural forces, often "culminating in decisive, violent action, [which] gives way to a visionary conclusion."[15] In the same vein, Miles Orvell compares the Georgia writer to Hawthorne who "violates the decorum of realism in his fantastic symbolism" while "O'Connor stays within the limits of a realistic fiction, inducing in characters a dreamlike vision or, more characteristically leaving them on the brink of some insight into mystery through the impact of a naturalistic violent action."[16]

Dorothy Walters perhaps summarizes best the manner in which Weiman's ideas about the transforming power operating on a human level and O'Connor's ideas that naturalistic events at work in man's life can bring man to redemption. Walters' ideas are as follows:

God's detractors insist that the defective being is undeniable proof that ours is a godless universe, or it is one powered by forces indifferent or hostile to man's welfare. The opposition insists that these apparent deviations from the divine scheme are but mysterious fragments in an inscrutable design whose ultimate purpose will be accounted for once the scheme is revealed in its totality.[17]

Among O'Connor's natural events - some more violent than others - which bring about directly or indirectly a redemptive process is the accident, caused by a pet cat, which leads to the destruction of an entire family and also to the grandmother's moment of grace brought about ironically by an encounter with a psychopathic killer. Another of these natural events is the chance encounter between a little boy and the arch con-man Tom T. Shiftlet, who seems to have some change of heart, perhaps a moment of grace which could lead to his repentance and redemption. The natural detail of the hitching post in the shape of a little black boy, "the artificial nigger" as O'Connor calls him, brings about a reconciliation between Mr. Head and his grandson. O'Connor carries this detail even further to specify that what she had in mind: "...with the artificial nigger was the redemptive quality of the Negro's suffering for us all." (HB p. XVIII). Irving Malin catches O'Connor's drift when he queries, "Would it not be more ironic, and ultimately Christian, if Jesus were to use 'artificial niggers' - the trivial, the commonplace, and the unreal - to transform sinners?" Malin is not sure that O'Connor is committed to this task, but he thinks it is a possibility.[18]

Similar details and events with similar results are found in the bird sound Tarwater hears when he goes deep into the woods at Powderhead and also in his first drink of liquor; in Singleton's imprisonment in the privy and later in the state mental hospital; in the Byzantine Christ on Parker's back; in the greater displacement of persons brought about by Mr. Guizac's death and in the symbolic process of redemption begun with Mrs. McIntyre's suffering; and perhaps most graphically, first in the "New Jesus" mummy which Enoch brings to Haze, and second, in Enoch in the gorilla suit, "a symbolic 'new Jesus' in bestial form."[19]

Savory, whose article I referred to earlier, restates Weiman's idea in his own words as a key idea in his definition of literary naturalism. It is as follows:

The *power of operative reality* behind the natural order of things is not necessarily impersonal and indifferent to man's destiny; *eyes of faith* may see it as creative, *transforming*, and *saving* .[20]

Three other ideas of Savory's are the guidelines for discussion of "Revelation," a story in which Christian literary naturalism is abundantly evident. These guidelines are:

1. Man, though part of a fallen world, is, nonetheless, redeemable and capable of responding to forces that can transform and save him. Forces that damn and destroy him are not the only ones operating in nature.

2. There is not much evidence to claim that human destiny is fatalistically determined.

3. There is, in the natural order of things, an observable pattern of birth, death, and rebirth, a cycle of transformation that is at the heart of Christian belief in resurrection, affirmed in creed and celebrated in sacrament.[21]

O'Connor's "Revelation" exemplifies these particular tenets of Christian literary naturalism. The story selected may not qualify as a "Christian" story, but it is well suited for analysis in which the naturalism emphasizes the spirit rather than the animal in man. It shows man as part of the fallen world, yet redeemable and capable of responding to forces that transform him.

With her debilitating disease, O'Connor spent many hours in doctor's offices; in fact in a letter to "A" in the year of her death, she wrote "Yesterday we went to the doctor's office - same scene as in 'Revelation'...."(HB p. 571). The characters found there are part of her Southern scene. Gilbert Muller has termed this story:

...a fable of God's providence operating in a doctor's office and in a pig pen. A triumph of the comic grotesque, the story opens in a doctor's waiting room, where an extraordinary collection of patients who form a miniature society - a ship of fools - awaits examination. Assembled in this almost claustrophobic office are representative diseases of the body, the mind, and the spirit; the crippled bodies of the aged, the maimed intelligences of the poor and the neuroses of the intellectually gifted, and defective souls of the self-righteous. Their illnesses represent the maladies of society, and the traits of this society are progressively revealed to a point where the absurdity implicit in the character behavior must explode.[22]

In this setting, Mrs. Ruby Turpin, though totally unaware of her fallen state, is in great need of spiritual redemption. She is well satisfied with her self-image - the perfect situation in which the irony of grace can operate. She sees herself as a woman of propriety and good manners and as a woman of good looks with no wrinkles. And she is confident that her membership in the white middle-class society and her willingness to help anyone in need - regardless of color or condition - make her a good woman and put her in a high position among the redeemed. Any other possibility is just unthinkable to her, but she is brought to recognize the fact that her position is not so secure as she thinks it is.

The force that will ultimately put Mrs. Turpin into a different frame of mind is embodied in an ugly, acne-faced girl with the unlikely but well-chosen name of Mary Grace, the Virgin Mary being the refuge of sinners, and grace being the free gift of God, given so often in O'Connor's work through violent means. In Mrs. Turpin's mind, the girl has about her an otherworldly aura appearing first in her eyes which "seemed lit all of a sudden with a peculiar light, an unnatural light like night road signs give." (CS p. 492). As Mrs. Turpin and Mary Grace's mother try to converse, Mrs.Turpin "was aware that the ugly girl's peculiar eyes were still on her, and she had trouble bringing her attention back to the conversation." (CS p. 494). When Mary Grace makes "the ugliest face Mrs. Turpin had ever seen anyone make," Mrs. Turpin feels that the girl "had known and disliked her all of her life - all of Mrs. Turpin's life, it seemed too, not just all the girl's life." (CS p. 495). Again the girl grimaces, and "Her eyes fixed like two drills on Mrs. Turpin. This time there was no mistaking that there was something urgent behind them." (CS p. 497).

Even while all of this is going on, there are other patients waiting in the doctor's office where the greater part of the story takes place. Mrs. Turpin is not too distracted by Mary Grace to evaluate the persons around her and to cry aloud, "'Thank you, Jesus, for making everything the way it is!'" (CS p. 499) - *everything* for her being that she is not ugly or white trash or a "nigger." Because Mrs. Turpin has made this and other similar assertions before, Mary Grace can take it no longer and goes berserk, "eyes rolling and finally focusing on Mrs.Turpin." (CS p. 500). Mrs. Turpin is certain that "the girl did know her, knew her in some intense and personal way, beyond time and place and condition." (CS p. 500).

Only by being brought down can Mrs.Turpin be redeemed, and it takes a girl on the lunatic fringe to effect her downfall. After throwing a book at Mrs. Turpin, Mary Grace speaks in a low, clear voice, "'Go back to hell where you came from, you old wart hog.'" (CS p. 500). Mary Grace's words hit their target because, once back at her home, Mrs. Turpin cannot get the image of a razor-back wart hog out of her mind as she tries to deny the association. From this point on, her redemption process begins. In addition to showing redeemable man responding to transforming forces, naturalism provides as much evidence to claim that human destiny is divinely ordered as there is to claim that it is fatalistically determined.

O'Connor carefully selects the setting for "Revelation," a small-town doctor's office where a variety of social types can come together naturally. Since racial types would have been segregated at the time of the story, O'Connor lets a Negro delivery boy make an appearance in the office. Social types and racial types are of great importance in the main character's thinking. Mrs. Turpin often "occupied herself at night naming the classes of people," (CS p. 491) and she named them in ascending order from "most colored people," to "the white-trash," to "the home-owners," and above them to "the home-and-land owners" to which she and Claud belong. Another part of her stratification is not based on social class or race; rather it has to do with whether one is ugly or not. At one time Mrs. Turpin envisioned that the only two choices available were "nigger" and "white trash." If that choice had had to be made immediately, she would have chosen to be "a nigger" - "but that don't mean a trashy one." (CS p. 491). But when Mrs. Turpin is forced into close company with the very ugly, scowling Mary Grace, she realizes that being ugly is a third choice.

Mrs. Turpin seems to be able to speak out brashly about the white-trash present in the waiting room and about the "nigger," once the delivery boy has completed his task. But there seem to be no words with which she can fend off the visual assaults of Mary Grace. It is as if, after all these years of self-satisfaction and of her own verbal assaults whenever she felt like letting them go, Mrs. Turpin has come face to face with an ugly girl of seemingly supernatural force who has been put in that office to speak to her condition. She asks what the girl wants to say to her and waits "as for a revelation." (CS p. 500). Then come the condemning words. She doesn't even call her a fat old hog or just a hog, but an "old wart hog," an animal which would have had no place in the Turpin's fine pig parlor. After Mary Grace's physical attack of throwing the book at Mrs. Turpin and the verbal attack, Mrs. Turpin is sure that "She had been singled out for the message, though there was trash in the room to whom it might justly have been applied." (CS p. 502). But it is those words that jar Mrs. Turpin into some serious consideration of her real position in the order of things, especially of her position among the redeemed.

The idea of Christian literary naturalism presented most clearly in "Revelation" is that, in the natural order of things, there is an observable pattern of birth-death-rebirth, a cycle that is at the heart of the Christian belief in resurrection. Mrs. Turpin's physical birth into the fortunate position of being neither white-trash, "nigger," or ugly makes her feel vibrantly alive until she is brought into the land of psychological death by Mary Grace's hysterical pronouncement. Now as if possessed, Mrs. Turpin cannot stay away from "her and Claud's" pig parlor. She dismisses Claud from the job of "'scootin' down the hogs." There at the hog pen she speaks to Jesus in what O'Connor describes as "a low fierce voice, barely above a whisper but with the force of a shout in its concentrated fury." (CS p. 506). She rants on and on about being a hog or white-trash or a "nigger" - her usual spiel. In desperation she seems to be talking still to Jesus as if his voice has found its way to her through the disturbed Mary Grace. "A final surge of fury shook her and she roared, 'Who do you think you are?'" (CS p. 507). Mrs. Turpin's "death" is a spiritual journey to the underworld - a strange mixture of pagan Hades and Christian hell. Her loud question comes back in an echo just like an answer. The question is really *for her* : "Who do you think you are?"

The hogpen has become mysterious and supernatural, and "Mrs. Turpin remained there with her gaze bent to them as if she were absorbing some abysmal life-giving knowledge." (CS p. 508). O'Connor's choice of the word "life-giving" reinforces her intention that Mrs. Turpin will gain new life here and hereafter since Mrs. Turpin's vision reveals that she is assured of everlasting life in heaven. This final reward for Mrs. Turpin is not without a price. In the "vast horde of souls...rumbling toward heaven" are white-trash, niggers, freaks, and lunatics. And "bringing up the end of the procession was a tribe of people...who, like herself and Claud, had always had a little of everything and the God-given wit to use it right." (CS p. 508). Although her vision is somewhat reassuring, her final revelation is that this last group is shocked by the realization "that even their virtues were being burned away." (CS p. 508). Mrs. Turpin's return to the reality of the hog pen and the "cricket choruses" is still confused: "what she heard were the voices of the souls climbing upward into the starry field and shouting hallelujah." (CS p. 509).

Ruby Turpin is transformed by power, at least initially operative in human personality. Human destiny can be said to have been divinely ordered in Mrs. Turpin's life; the result is a return to life from psychological and spiritual death. O'Connor's fiction illustrates over and over that natural events, although sometimes violent, operate in human life to save man from evil and to bring him to the greatest good. For her, the redemptive process, grounded in Jesus Christ, is brought about by "naturalistic detail that is transformed into theological mystery."[23] Although O'Connor disavows scientific determinism, she sees man's destiny as "determined" when he does respond to naturalistic forces that often culminate in a moment of grace. Christian literary naturalism is a term descriptive of this divine ordering of human destiny; it provides a critical approach to a broader frame of interpretation of O'Connor's fiction.

Notes

1 Betsy Lockridge, "An Afternoon with Flannery O'Connor," *The Added Dimension, The Art and Mind of Flannery O'Connor* eds., Melvin Friedman and Lewis A. Lawson (New York, 1966), p.239.
2 Robert Coles, *Flannery O'Connor's South* (Baton Rouge, 1980), p.156.

3 Josephine Hendin, *The World of Flannery O'Connor* (Bloomington, 1970), p.131.

4 Louis Rubin, "Flannery O'Connor and the Bible Belt," *The Added Dimension*, pp.70-71.

5 Ibid., p.51.

6 Preston M. Browning, Jr., *Flannery O'Connor*, (Carbondale, 1974), p.8.

7 Frederick J. Hoffman, "The Search for Redemption," *The Added Dimension*, pp.32-33.

8 Coles, p.112.

9 Jerold J. Savory, "Toward a Definition of Christian Literary Naturalism." *Christian Scholar's Review*, Vol.VIII (1978), No.1,3.

10 Quoted by Savory, p.7.

11 Ibid.

12 Ibid.

13 Miles Orvell, *Invisible Parade, The Fiction of Flannery O'Connor* (Philadelphia, 1972), p.38.

14 Browning, p.69.

15 Orvell, p.36.

16 Ibid., p.34.

17 Dorothy Walters, *Flannery O'Connor* (Boston, 1973), p.95.

18 Irving Malin, "Flannery O'Connor and the Grotesque," *The Added Dimension*, p.116.

19 Leon V. Driskell and Joan T. Brittain, *The Eternal Crossroads: The Art of Flannery O'Connor* (Lexington, Ky., 1971), p.52.

20 Savory, p.8; my italics.

21 Savory, p.8.

22 Gilbert Muller, *Nightmares and Visions: Flannery O'Connor and the Catholic Grotesque* (Athens, Ga., 1972), pp.46-47.

23 Savory, p.9.

Flannery O'Connor: Realist of Distances

Marion Montgomery

It has been one of the most popular critical assumptions in our century that the realist's art is incompatible to a spiritual vision, an assumption endemic at the level of the academic intellectual. Especially, the assumption holds, an artist professing an orthodox Christian vision cannot adequately deal with the "real world." Just why our unreal modernist world should inherit and treasure this disease of the intellect has a long and intricate history in the Western mind, one which we must touch upon in considering why that poet of a Catholic vision, Flannery O'Connor, calls herself a "realist of distances." (I have explored the infection in its historical background in three long volumes, called collectively "The Prophetic Poet and the Popular Spirit.") We may note that Miss O'Connor is herself acutely aware of the disease. She attempts to remedy it, as prophetic artist, by recalling us to known but forgotten truths about our existence in the world. And the concern is a constant theme in her *Mystery and Manners*, as in the letters she so generously wrote to a spectrum of the popular mind, collected by Sally Fitzgerald in *The Habit of Being*. Flannery O'Connor is concerned with our world's deliberate exorcism of the spiritual from creation, a deconstruction of reality which she speaks of as modern Manicheanism.

The modernist version of that ancient heresy denies the spiritual dimension of creation in the interest of conquests of nature to please appetites, those appetites as various as the inordinate hunger for things and the more diabolical hunger for power over things. (*Things* here includes persons reduced from any spiritual dimension.) The ancient Manichean tended to a gnostic rejection of material being. Miss O'Connor finds evidence of a similar reduction of reality in our separating *reason* from *imagination*, *judgment* from *vision*, and (most particularly important to the sacramental question at hand) *nature* from *grace*. She affirms a complementary necessity in these pairs, urging our return to a larger reality through them; that is, she argues for a reassociation of sensibilities that goes much deeper than literary categories. To read her

227

well, then, requires that we understand carefully what she sees as a larger than literary dimension to such literary shibboleths as image or metaphor or allegory.

At the same time she insists that the artist's primary responsibility is to the thing he makes. This is to say that her understanding of the artist's role is delicately refined, most carefully precise. She is uncompromisingly committed to a vision; she would reflect that vision by her art, but only within the limits set by the nature of art itself. For her, reason and imagination are complementary aspects of a fundamental gift - namely, *being, existence* itself. They are not to be separated by the rational intellect as they generally are in our world, either in the interest of power (when reason becomes independent of and elevated over the imagination) or in the interest of feeling (when the imagination unbridled from reason becomes capable only of some form of sentimentality - pornography being the dominant mode of sentimentality at this juncture).

She is, preeminently among modern writers, a realist. In her own phrase, she is a realist of distances, though as one knows from having read her stories her sense perceptions of the immediate world is striking in itself. The epithet "realist of distances" is one she embraces directly out of her fundamental Thomism, about which a brief but necessary word. First of all, as we have said, she understands the artist's over-riding responsibility to be to his art, since his is an exercise of a peculiar gift, though one for which he may take no primary credit. (The artist is, of course, responsible for perfecting his gift.) She sets aside art defined as an imitation of nature, art as a mirror or as history. In its true definition, it is rather an imitation of the *creative activity* of nature. This is a crucial distinction which she finds explicated by Jacques Maritain in his *Art and Scholasticism*, the primary source this side of St. Thomas's own work for anyone exploring Miss O'Connor's aesthetic vision. As an artist imitating the creative activity of nature, she (like Maritain, and like St. Thomas before them) focuses upon reason's relation to imaginative vision. The consequences of these complementary faculties of the intellect in the artist is the made thing - the poem or story. The artist's necessary devotion is to the action of making, but always in the interest of the good of the thing made. The mutual accommodation of reason and imagination is what she is talking about when she says - again and again - that "art is reason in making."

The responsible artist, in her view, is obligated to what we in the academy recognize as fundamental Aristotelean aspects of artisanship. In reading *Mystery and Manners* carefully, we hear her deliberately echoing the *Poetics*. She is concerned with order, unity, clarity,

228

proportion, as those concerns apply to her fiction; she is particularly concerned with questions of the *possible* or *probable*. In short, she is aware of those abiding aesthetic categories that attach to questions of *craftsmanship*. But she is concerned at the most homely level of craftsmanship more than with theory's more intoxicating reaches; for those higher reaches of theory will take care of themselves if the artisan takes care of his peculiar homework. She speaks of the labor of finding the next word, remarking that "The Theories are worse than the Furies." Her reason pursues form at the level of *syntax* and *diction* and *image*, tuned to the immediate world, working from that level toward the complexities of metaphor. On occasion she will speak beyond this level - at a metaphysical level of metaphor. She will speak of good metaphors' resonances at that highest allegorical level, the *anagogical*, a word one encounters rather often in her essays and talks and letters. That word reminds us of the parallels she sees between her own concerns and Dante's. To a beleaguered graduate student, working on a thesis on her work under a director who allows no theological terms in relation to that fiction, she says:

The writer whose point of view is Catholic in the widest sense of the term reads nature the same way the medieval commentators read Scripture. They found three levels of meaning in the literal level of the sacred text - the allegorical, in which one thing stands for another; the moral, which has to do with what should be done; and the anagogical, which has to do with the Divine life and our participation in it, the level of grace.

Now if you use the word anagogical long enough, the idea of grace will become sufficiently disinfected for [those who reject the mystery of grace] to be able to take it. (HB pp. 468-469).

Put another way, because Dante has been thoroughly academized, his terms can be taken as part of a critical system by those for whom (as she says in another context), "Every story is a frog in a bottle...." (Cp. MM p.108). One recognizes in her fiction itself, that she eschews the moral and allegorical levels as here presented, but the anagogical, the level of grace in relation to nature, is the very center of her dramatic concern. Nevertheless, she always turns such discussions back to the homely level of the artist's labor. Before a wooden leg may be a symbol, she says, it must first be a wooden leg. (MM p.99). "Fiction," she says in *Mystery and Manners*, "is an art that calls for the strictest attention to the real." To the neophyte she advises, "Don't be subtle till the third page." Given the writer's attention at this level, the resonances of the anagogical will be

229

available to the good reader, not because the writer has built the anagogical into his story but because he has been true to the reality of existence immediately at hand. She reports with approval the response of a country neighbor who read her stories: "...she said, 'Well, them stories just gone and shown you how some folks *would* do....'" (MM p.90). Aristotle said it only a little better than this Georgia country woman when he speaks of the possible or probable.

If we recognize Aristotelean dimensions to her concerns, it is necessary to remind ourselves that hers is an Aristotle baptized by St. Thomas. When she speaks of the *possible* or *probable*, she is aware of the artist's temptation to assume a false prophetic power in moving from the possible to the probable, from what some folks *might* do to what they *will* do. It is a temptation which in itself may lead the artist to assume that his responsibility to the world requires him to be Moses, leading lost children out of whatever desert. We may recognize Milton's struggle with this temptation, I believe, in that most personal of his poems, *Lycidas*. Recognizing the danger, Miss O'Connor insists:

The Lord doesn't speak to the novelist as he did to his servant, Moses, mouth to mouth. He speaks to him as he did to those two complainers, Aaron and Aaron's sister, Mary [*sic*]: through dreams and visions, in fits and starts, and by all the lesser and limited ways of the imagination. (MM p.181).

This being so, it is reason that one must depend upon to clarify whatever fitful vision comes to the artist through the lesser and limited ways of the imagination. The artist has more than he can perfectly concern himself with in paying attention to the meticulous exercise of his gift, and he should leave Moses' labor to Moses, Cromwell's to Cromwell.

In speaking explicitly of the Catholic writer's responsibility, she cites the angelic doctor: "St. Thomas Aquinas says that art does not require rectitude of the appetite, that it is wholly concerned with the good of that which is made." (MM p.171). She knows all too well those artists who are dominated by a concern for "the rectitude of appetite," with a moral message. They range from Marxist ideologues, whose materialist god enflames appetite, to Sunday School tractarians, many of whom would not simply rectify appetite but abolish it altogether. Those artists advance programs disguised as fiction on occasion, practicing a species of sacrilege against art and nature, and inevitably thereby distorting reality. She complains, in one of her reviews, in her diocesan paper, of a novel which is evidence of "a depressing new category...light Catholic summer reading." And she advises that one might indeed buy a copy of Cardinal Spellman's novel *The Foundling*, since the proceeds go to charity, so long as one has the good sense to use it as a doorstop and not value it as a novel. (MM p.175).

There is for her a piety proper to her calling as artist, but it does not discover itself through tracts of whatever sort disguised as art. Nevertheless, she believes that what is good in itself glorifies God, whether that good thing be a person *becoming* or a poem or table or garden *made*. Man, because created in the image of God, is therefore inescapably a maker, and each of us is a maker according to our peculiar gifts. That principle, deduced by reason out of faith, returns us to our earlier definition of art. For in the action of imitating nature in its creative activity, rather than attempting merely to mirror nature on the one hand or to distort nature on the other through an art turned to some gnostic program for restructuring the world, the creative action realizes a potential within the thing - poem or story - even as that same action becomes a realization of the maker's own potential being.

When she speaks of good as something under construction, she understands her point to apply whether one is speaking about a person or the peculiar work that such a person does. The poem or story is an artifact projected by the imagination and brought through reason's labor into an existence of its own, more or less good. In either aspect of action's effect (and the effects are inextricable) - whether of a person's struggle to become or his struggle to make a thing beyond himself - a *given* is presupposed. It is first of all the gift of being itself that underlies all creation and binds all creation together. Existence is the common ground in creation. But all creation necessarily includes the person, the artist and gardener no less than poems or trees and shrubs and earth and stones. This aspect of the given is formally spoken of as *esse*. There is an additional gift beyond being, beyond *esse*, whereby a thing (*res*) exists and is the very thing it is. That additional given is particularity, which in individual men includes the special calling to act within the limiting gift of one's particularity. The point is summarized by Gilson in *The Spirit of Thomism* : "...actual existence, which [Thomas] calls *esse*, is that by virtue of which a thing, which he calls *res*, is a being, an *ens*."

The point is not so esoteric as it may sound in our taking recourse to St. Thomas through Gilson. And it is a point absolutely central to Flannery O'Connor's understanding of her own calling to be a realist of distances, as it is to our concern to understand her sacramental vision. What the scholastic point means by extension to the artist and his art is that man, in every instance of his action, is operating as a creative agent participating in his own existence, but at a secondary level. It is the refusal to accept our participation in our own being at a secondary level that is the well-spring of Sartrean existentialism, a philosophy as old as the fall from grace in the garden. Though man be given a freedom through which he may easily suppose himself the first, the sole or primary cause of his free actions of creation, reason will tell him at last that he is *himself* a given and that even his freedom is a given. In this view there can be no such thing as the self-made man, only the self-unmade man. For whatever the nature of his action as maker, man is always operating *upon* givens *with* givens *from* his own givenness.

Because Flannery O'Connor understands her own talents to be a gift, she is freer than most of us. She feels a joyful obligation to actions out of that gift, even as she supposes the same required of us all. She says in a letter, " You do not write the best you can for the sake of art but for the sake of returning your talent increased to the invisible God to use or not use as he sees fit." That is - as the Apostle Paul reminds us - we are called to imitate into being our own given natures, each according to his gifts. Thereby we discover ourselves members, one of another. Thus it is that we become a body, the Church, whose head is Christ. This is the vision of community Miss O'Connor never wavers from. And it is in the light of this vision that one sees her answering the endless seminar question, spawned by psychology - why do you write? "'Because I'm good at it,'" she says. (MM p.81). And does the burden of the disease she suffers (disseminated lupus, which increasingly made her invalid) affect her calling? Not particularly, she says, since she writes with her head and not with her feet. Her gift was not that of the bicycle rider.

If one understands the artist's gifts and powers as Flannery O'Connor does, he approaches the question of reality with a piety toward creation which will be reflected in his actions as artist. His address to existence does not presume the existential world, in which he is caught up, to be merely a reservoir of prime matter out of which to make whatever worlds he fancies. That world is a creation at a primary level. In this view, all creation must be seen as *creaturely*, depending in its being from the Prime Creator. Whatever *man* as *maker* manipulates requires of *man, the made,* a reverence for its being. From this creature - the created world - the artist borrows to build what J.R.R. Tolkien calls Secondary Creations, the poem or story. In doing so, the artist discovers a responsibility for a careful attention to the created world. And the degree to which he exercises this responsibility makes all the difference to that fullness, to the resonance, of any Secondary Creation he attaches his name to.

It is inevitable, Miss O'Connor believes, that even if the artist does not recognize and venerate the Cause of Primary Creation, his Secondary Creations will nevertheless carry larger resonances than he may suppose or intend. They will necessarily do so in so far as he makes his poem or story with a close eye upon the immediate world and with a careful respect for craftsmanship. As she puts the point in one of her essays: "...if [the novelist believes that actions are predetermined by psychic make-up or the economic situation or some other determinable factor, then he will be concerned above all with an accurate reproduction of the things that most immediately concern man, with the natural forces that he feels control his destiny. Such a writer may produce a great tragic naturalism, for by his responsibility to the things he sees, he may transcend the limitations of his narrow vision. (MM p.41).

By his responsibility to the things he sees. That is the necessity she keeps insistently before her, and it accounts for her realistic dimension. For as we have said, the artist has precisely this limit upon his power to create: his Secondary Creation is unavoidably dependent upon Primary Creation. Therefore, if he is attentive, what he makes must in some way echo the cause of Primary Creation. (Ironically, science fiction usually struggles to sever those bonds through imaginative extremes; the result is nevertheless a grotesque imaging of reality, any grotesque always reminding us of reality itself.) In so far as the artist is true to the Primary level of existence, including his own fallen nature and its particular gifts of becoming through making, his art will echo with anagogical resonances. The theologian or philosopher must concern himself with questions searching into the causes and ends of things; the artist need not worry about proving anything by his art. He must, however, be responsible to the thing he would give its certain existence - the made thing.

With eyes open, with the confidence of her faith that existence has meaning, however deep the mysteries of existence, she responds to the various world in imitation of its creative activity, under the guidance of reason. "I try to satisfy [she says] those necessities that make themselves felt in the work itself. When I write, I am a maker. I think about what I am making. St. Thomas called art reason in making. When I write I feel I am engaged in the reasonable use of the unreasonable. In art reason goes wherever the imagination goes. We have reduced the uses of reason terribly. You say a thing is reasonable and people think you mean it is safe. What's reasonable is seldom safe and always exciting." (Cp. MM p.82, p.109).

Reason reveals to her that, in engaging the particular, she is committed beyond the imagistic level, and in this respect her vision coincides with Gerard Manley Hopkins's. Again she says, "The longer you look at one object, the more of the world you see in it; and it's well to remember that the serious fiction writer always writes about the whole world, no matter how limited his particular scene." (MM p.77). The cause of creation must inevitably (for her) be reflected in art's inscape, in so far as the artist's eye is steady and his craft sure. The *instress* of Primary Creation will be caught by the *inscape* of the particular Secondary Creation, the poem or story, an additional effect of which is the deepening of the artist's *instress*, the realization of his own particular potential being. Catholic critics, she writes Sister Mariella Gable, should look in a work "...for its sort of 'inscape' as Hopkins would have it. Instead they look for some ideal intention, and criticize you for not having it." (HB p.517).

An artist who is troubled about the large questions - about whether the universe is random accident or a self-determined closed order or a caused creature - may well find himself engaging art as if it were an instrument of empirical value, directing him to conclusions beyond the reaches of the philosopher or theologian. It is a conspicuous inclination in the poet to assume the role of philosopher or theologian or scientist, most usually with bad effect upon his art. Indeed, such an untroubled writer as Miss O'Connor is a rarity, at least since the Renaissance - that childhood of our art during which there could be such free playfulness - an adolescent exuberance with metaphor, for instance, such as that we see in Donne's love poetry. I sometimes suspect that in Donne's love poetry we see a desperate last fling of high fancy before metaphor is to be denied its joyfulness, before poetry turns serious and solemn in Milton's great poems - after which point the poet is never again quite so free, never again quite so trusting of language itself. (The audacity of language in such extremes as surrealism is as much an action *against* as *with* language.)

What I see in Miss O'Connor is a rescue of the artist back to the fullness of reality. She appropriates metaphysical wit and some of its subsequent refinements, such as a Swiftean incisiveness, though she excludes the sardonic that so often threatens Swift. Because she accepts man for what he is, a creature fallen in his nature, within the mystery of pitiable, irritating man as he exists under the generous auspices of grace, she is able to complement wit with humor. She is very Chaucerean in this respect, it seems to me. Consequently, one may discover that her use of cliché, which is like Swift's and Joyce's in precision and incisiveness, is accompanied nevertheless by a tolerance of man's willful stupidities of mind and spirit. Hers is not a responsibility for the rectitude of appetites. Her tolerance is judgmental, for she says what she sees. But there is not in her the scorching acid of Swift nor the divine aloofness of Joyce. This difference in the effect of her wit as we encounter it in her art lies in her not having succumbed to the temptation to separate judgment from vision.

234

She does not, since she sees that man's fallen nature is not to be separated from the possibility of a rescuing grace. (Not *probability*, but *possibility*.) Firm of intellect, cautious of presumptuousness, she judges, but not without her own mercy toward that pitiable, even disgusting figure, man. The exercise of that mercy we discover in her stories and call it humor. The meanest of her characters is not, in her view, beyond rescue, and indeed she delights in protagonists who seem most nearly beyond the reaches of grace to the secular human eye, as she delights in the most ordinary mediums of grace to those agents of her fiction - a modern, clean pig parlor, a water stain on a bedroom ceiling. She is equally cautious, of course, about affirming that such characters are rescued. The Misfit, even Rayber, may or may not be damned. As artist, she does not feel called upon either to force the rescue of foolish or willful man or to deliver him over to an annihilation. The novelist or poet, she says, "feels no need to apologize for the ways of God to man or to avoid looking at the ways of man to God." (MM p.178).

She looks very closely at the ways of man to God, and comedy in both Dante's high sense of the term and in its more popular meaning is her inevitable mode of presenting the tragic dimension of man's struggle with grace. Having demurred from Milton's theme, she goes on with her point: "For [the artist] to 'tidy up reality' is certainly to succumb to the sin of pride. Open and free observation is founded on our ultimate faith that the universe is meaningful, as the Church teaches." (Cp. MM p.177). What she urges as the necessary responsibility of the artist may be summed up as follows: believe, and look where you will - so long as the actions of nature are not violated by the actions of art; so long as one sees clearly; so long as one does not distort his seeing by the arrogation of final judgment to the artist or by the presumption of rejecting the complexity of existence in which the mysteries of good and evil are in contention.

These, then, are the reasons - put in very abbreviated form - why Flannery O'Connor says with such confidence, "if a writer is any good, what he makes will have its source in a realm much larger than that which his conscious mind can encompass...." That larger world she accepts sacramentally, a gift of being, as she accepts her calling to be a writer with the old depths of the religious vow.

The Contributors

Jack Dillard Ashley has been Professor in the English Department at the University of South Carolina since 1963. His courses have included studies in the works of Shakespeare, Milton, Dickinson, and O'Connor.

Christiane Beck is Maître de Conférences at Université des Sciences Humaines de Strasbourg. She has also published a paper on "Flannery O'Connor ou la Persecution" in *RANAM* No.IX, 1976.

Mary V. Blasingham is Professor at Indiana-Purdue University, Indianapolis. She was educated at DePauw and Harvard Universities and the University of Illinois. She has given many professional lectures, including a number for national and international conferences.

Ashley Brown is Professor of English at the University of South Carolina. He has contributed essays, translations, and reviews to many journals, and he has also edited several books, most recently *The Poetry Reviews of Allen Tate, 1924-1944*.

Sheldon Currie is Chairman of the English Department, St Francis Xavier University, Antigonish, Nova Scotia, where he teaches modern American fiction. He has published a book of short stories, *The Glace Bay Miner's Museum*.

Robert Drake has been Professor at the University of Tennessee since 1965. He has taught at the University of Michigan, Northwestern University and the University of Texas at Austin. In addition to criticism of Southern literature and some nineteenth-century English authors, he has published three books of short stories, *Amazing Grace, The Single Heart*, and *The Burning Bush*.

Ann Ebrecht served as Assistant Professor at Tulane University in New Orleans. As Director of Exemplary Awards for Louisiana Endowment for the Humanities she has developed and implemented state-wide seminars in American, Southern and women's literature.

Kathleen Feeley , S.S.N.D., author of *Flannery O'Connor: Voice of the Peacock*, spends most of her time directing the College of Notre Dame of Maryland, a liberal arts college for women in Baltimore, where she has been President for several years. She finds relief from administrative activities by keeping current on Flannery O'Connor scholarship and occasionally contributing to that scholarship.

Sally Fitzgerald was Flannery O'Connor's friend and is her official biographer. She has edited O'Connor's letters in *The Habit of Being* and co-edited O'Connor's lectures in *Mystery and Manners*. She is at present preparing O'Connor's biography and the volume of O'Connor's work in the Library of America series.

Helen S. Garson is Professor of English and American Studies at George Mason University, Fairfax, Virginia. She holds degrees from George Washington University, the University of Georgia, and the University of Maryland. She teaches, lectures, and writes about twentieth century fiction. Among her publications is a book on Truman Capote.

Marshall Bruce Gentry is Assistant Professor at the University of Indianapolis where he teaches composition and modern American literature. He has taught at the University of Texas at Austin and Texas A&M. His essay is adapted from his *Flannery O'Connor's Religion of the Grotesque* (University Press of Mississippi, 1986).

Jan Nordby Gretlund is Associate Professor of American literature at Odense University, Denmark. He has published in various American periodicals on Barry Hannah, Madison Jones, Walker Percy, Katherine Anne Porter, Eudora Welty and Flannery O'Connor.

Patrick J. Ireland is Associate Professor of English at the College of the Holy Cross, Worcester, Massachusetts, where he teaches Southern literature, American realism and contemporary fiction.

Carter Martin is Professor of English and former Department Chairman at the University of Alabama, Huntsville. Among his publications are two O'Connor books, *The True Country* (Vanderbilt University Press, 1969) and *The Presence of Grace* (Co-ed., University of Georgia Press, 1983).

Marion Montgomery is Professor of English at the University of Georgia. He has published novels, poetry and criticism in fourteen books. His latest is a critical trilogy, *The Prophetic Poet and the Spirit of the Age:* Vol. I, *Why Flannery O'Connor Stayed Home.* Vol. II, *Why Poe Drank Liquor.* Vol. III, *Why Hawthorne Was Melancholy.* He gave the 1986 Lamar Lectures.

Sara Mott is Edens Professor of English at Columbia College, Columbia, South Carolina. She has several awards as outstanding faculty member at Columbia College. Her special areas of interest are Flannery O'Connor and Eudora Welty.

Matej Mužina is Associate Professor of English and American literature at the Department of English, The University of Zagreb, Yugoslavia. He holds degrees in English literature and philosophy from the Universities of Zagreb and Sussex.

Linda Schlafer is Assistant Professor and Assistant to the Chairman of the English Department, Marquette University, Milwaukee. She teaches American literature and creative writing and writes fiction.

Delores Washburn is Professor of English at Hardin-Simmons University, Abilene, Texas. She has written for *The Flannery O'Connor Bulletin, The Thomas Wolfe Review,* and *MOSAIC* and has presented papers at numerous professional conferences on Southern literature.

Karl-Heinz Westarp is Associate Professor of English and American literature and drama at the University of Aarhus, Denmark. He has published on British drama, Joyce and has written three essays for *The Flannery O'Connor Bulletin.*

Waldemar Zacharasiewicz is Professor of English and American literature at the University of Vienna. He has written two books on the impact of scientific thought on English literature in the 17th and 18th centuries, and he has co-edited a book on Anglo-Canadian literature.

Index

to the Fiction and Essays of Flannery O'Connor

References in this volume are to the following editions of Flannery O'Connor's work:

An Exile in the East (The South Carolina Review, 11(Nov. 78), 12-21)
46-49, *50, 54, 200.*

The Habit of Being (Farrar, Straus & Giroux, N.Y., 1979).Flannery
O'Connor's letters are not indexed.

Mystery and Manners (Farrar, Straus & Giroux, N.Y., 1969) *11, 13, 26,
44, 58-61, 67, 76-77, 79-80, 82, 149, 152, 168, 175, 186, 190-193, 197-201,
205, 217, 227, 229-235.*

The Presence of Grace and Other Book Reviews (Athens, Georgia,
1983), *9, 182, 216.*

The Violent Bear It Away (Farrar, Straus & Giroux, N.Y., 1960) *36, 39,
41, 58-59, 106,* ***110-111,*** *124,* ***131-133,*** *134,* ***140-146, 155-158,*** *178,
183, 200, 221.*

Wise Blood (Farrar, Straus & Giroux, N.Y., 1962) *18-19, 25, 33, 35, 62,* ***97-
101,*** *131, 139-142,* ***160-162,*** *164-165, 180, 182-183, 200, 221.*